ABOUT THE AUTHOR

Journalist Richard Shears is the author of more than twenty books, mainly non-fiction, covering such topics as the Azaria Chamberlain case; the life of Devi, the Indian Bandit Queen; and the sinking of Greenpeace boat, the *Rainbow Warrior*, by French commandos in Auckland harbour. He also co-authored a work on America's secret war games in the Middle East.

Richard Shears is the Australian and South East Asian correspondent for the London *Daily Mail*, and in 1995 won a major award as a Foreign Correspondent in the prestigious UK Press Awards.

HIGHWAY
— TO —
NOWHERE

RICHARD SHEARS

HarperCollins*Publishers*

HarperCollins*Publishers*

First published in Australia in 1996
by HarperCollins*Publishers* Pty Limited
ABN 36 009 913 517
A member of the HarperCollins*Publishers* (Australia) Pty Limited Group
www.harpercollins.com.au

HarperCollins*Publishers*
25 Ryde Road, Pymble, Sydney NSW 2073, Australia
31 View Road, Glenfield, Auckland 10, New Zealand
77–85 Fulham Palace Road, London W6 8JB, United Kingdom
2 Bloor Street East, 20th floor, Toronto, Ontario M4W 1A8, Canada
10 East 53rd Street, New York NY 10022, USA

National Library of Australia Cataloguing-in-Publication data:

Shears, Richard, 1944 – .
   Highway to nowhere.
   ISBN 0 7322 5105 2.
   1. Serial murders – New South Wales – Belanglo State Forest.
   2. Serial murderers – New South Wales. I. Title.
364.152309944

Cover design by Darian Causby, HarperCollins Design Studio
Cover photographs © Mirror Australian Telegraph Publications;
and The Photo Library of Australia
Text photographs reproduced with permission of John Fairfax Pty Ltd
and Mirror Australian Telegraph Publications
Typeset by HarperCollins Design Studio in 10.5/14 Baskerville
Printed and bound in Australia by Griffin Press on 80gsm UPM Fine Offset

9 8 7   08 09 10 11

On a Sunday afternoon in September 1992, deep in the Belanglo Forest, Father Gray conducted a memorial service for Caroline Clarke and Joanne Walters. He spoke:

'We have come here today, where something wicked happened, so that this place can be peaceful again and its memories put to rest. Where evil is very strong, and it has been in this place, it does not have the last word ... no-one is beyond the reach of God.'

In the clearing, with only a few members of the choir remaining, Father Gray closed his prayer book. The sun still shone through the gum trees. The cleansing, it seemed, had been completed. But neither the priest nor anyone else who had prayed there that afternoon could have known the horror that remained.

CHAPTER ONE

He'd trudged several hundred metres along the highway from the railway station — a solitary figure, his light-coloured hair flopping over his forehead, he moved slowly under the midsummer sun against a blurred backdrop of roaring trucks and family saloons. A depressing pattern was emerging — he could smile, stick out his finger or wiggle his thumb, but they weren't going to stop. No way. What was their problem? He wasn't going to hold them up or anything. He just wanted a damned lift!

Weighed down in the heat by his green ex-Army backpack, 24-year-old Englishman Paul Onions now understood why Australians headed for the beach at Christmas. It was now January and his home town of Willenhall was in the firm grip of the Northern Hemisphere winter, but the heat in New South Wales on this day in 1990 was unbearable. Although dressed in only a T-shirt, shorts and training shoes, he was sweltering, and desperate for a long cold drink.

It was the first time he'd tried hitch-hiking in Australia, and so far he wasn't too impressed with his prospects of an easy run to Melbourne. And he still had to get from there to the rural Victorian town of Mildura, where he planned to do some fruit-picking. It was a route taken by many other young travellers, so he'd heard, but he was beginning to wonder how they ever got there if lifts were this hard to come by. Until now, he'd had a lot of fun — hanging out in Sydney, having a few beers with other Europeans staying at the same youth hostel in the suburb of Glebe, and doing the tourist bit. He'd taken pictures of the Opera House and wandered around The Rocks, the historical part of the harbour foreshore where the first white settlers had landed 200 years earlier.

Determined to see the other side of the world that he'd heard and read so much about, Paul had set out from England on 8 December 1989. He first visited New Delhi, where he stayed for a little over a week, and then travelled on to Singapore for a few days. In his postcards to friends in England, he wrote about the contrast between India's poverty-stricken capital and the wealth and cleanliness of the island republic. Australia, he said, would probably fall somewhere in between — no miserable poverty and no bland, clinical streets. He'd arrived in Sydney on 22 December and hung around for a month, acclimatising himself, visiting the sights, and learning from other travellers about the best places to find part-time jobs. He was determined to experience as much of this vast, fascinating continent as his twelve-month tourist work visa would allow.

On 25 January he caught the train from Sydney to the satellite city of Liverpool, the last reaches of suburbia before the start of the Hume Highway that runs some 855 kilometres from Sydney to Melbourne, and made his way from the railway station to the main road that would take him to the highway. He'd thought about travelling to Melbourne by bus but, at the suggestion of other budget tourists, had decided to give hitch-hiking a try. With any luck, he hoped he'd be in Mildura within twenty-four hours, and be able to celebrate the Australia Day holiday there. It was now 1 pm, however, the hottest part of the day and, as the cars continued to speed by as if he wasn't there, the heat started to get to him. In the distance he saw, to his relief, a red hoarding — a Coca Cola sign.

'If it's a mirage,' he said to himself, 'I'll drop dead where I stand.'

But a newsagent's shop with a fridge full of ice-cold soft drinks brightened his spirits. As he was buying a can he became aware of someone standing beside him, looking him up and down. Casually attired in shorts and T-shirt, the stranger appeared to be a strong-looking fellow — much more burly than Paul's own slight build — and was about 178 centimetres (5 feet 10 inches) tall, with dark hair. But the most striking thing about him was his bushy moustache. Merv Hughes' older brother, Paul joked to himself, likening the man to the Australian fast bowler.

'Need a lift, mate?' the newcomer cheerfully offered.

Paul couldn't believe his luck.

'Do I ever!' he replied. 'I'm heading for Mildura, but anything along the way will do, Canberra even — that okay?'

'Same direction as me,' said the Good Samaritan.

As they headed out of the shop, Paul was directed towards a silver four-wheel-drive vehicle with large tyres. On the front he noticed a bull-bar — this was the first time he'd ever seen one; there was nothing like that back in the Midlands! He tossed his backpack over the back of the passenger's seat and settled into the comfortable sheepskin seat cover.

As they headed towards the freeway, he introduced himself. 'My name's Paul,' he said.

'Bill,' said the other man with a nod and a smile. 'Must be hot out there on foot.'

'You can say that again. I was beginning to wonder if I'd have to walk all the way.'

'Where're you from, mate?'

'It's not hard to pick that I'm from England, is it? I'm

actually from the Midlands. I'm a refrigeration engineer —
and I was wishing I could turn on some cool air back there
on the road. I'm hoping to stay here a few months, do some
fruit-picking and a few other odd jobs along the way. And
what about you, Bill? What do you do?'

'Me? I work on the roads, for the RTA at Liverpool. But
I'm on a bit of a holiday meself right now, heading for
Canberra to meet a few friends.'

They were now on the freeway, and the vehicle swept
along the smooth two-lane surface. Bill twiddled with the
radio dial and found some music.

Paul enjoyed listening to Bill talk. He realised that for all
the time he had spent in Sydney, this was the first occasion
he'd engaged in a conversation with someone who had a
'real Aussie accent'. When he mentioned this to Bill, the
driver chuckled.

'Well, I'm not what you would call a true-blue Aussie
going back generations,' he said. 'I was brought up in the
Liverpool area where I picked you up, but my family's from
Yugoslavia.'

'You mean your parents, your wife …?'

'No, not me wife, mate. I'm divorced. I've put married
life right behind me.'

The Englishman stared lazily out of the window at the
rolling, sun-bleached hills interspersed with vast expanses of
eucalyptus forest. It was his first glimpse of Australia beyond
the city, and he was filled with awe at the sheer size of the
countryside. What a contrast this was to the teeming streets
of Delhi and the towering skyscrapers of Singapore. And, as
much as he'd loved Sydney, he'd spent so much time beside
the water that it was a joy to see some countryside.

As they cruised along the highway, Paul was surprised to
feel his eyelids getting heavy. The walk in the heat had tired
him more than he'd realised, and the motion of the vehicle
and the comfortable seat were making him sleepy. But he

also realised how impolite that would seem — Bill had probably picked him up because he needed the company. His thoughts were confirmed as the driver restarted the conversation.

'You always done the same job, mate?'

'No, I've done a few things. Even spent a bit of time in the Navy.'

Bill drove on in silence for a few minutes, then asked: 'What did you do in the Navy: anything secret or specialised, like in the Special Forces?'

'Oh no, nothing as fancy as that,' said Paul, amused. 'I think you'd need to make it a lifetime's career to get involved in anything really specialised.'

'I see,' said Bill, casting a glance at his passenger.

Instantly, Paul was puzzled. He had noticed something strange in the driver's quick look. The warmth had gone out of his eyes. What was the problem? Didn't Bill believe he'd been in the Navy? Oh well, let it drop.

'If you've been in the Services, you must have an opinion about the British troops in Northern Ireland,' said Bill. 'I reckon they ought to get out of there. They've got no right to be there. What do you reckon?'

Paul suddenly felt uneasy. There was a touch of, what was it — aggression? — in Bill's voice, like he was trying to stir him up, get him involved in an argument.

'Oh well, I suppose everyone thinks they're doing the right thing at the time,' he replied carefully.

Bill looked at him again, and Paul saw coldness in his deep-blue eyes.

'What do you reckon about Asians in Australia?' Bill asked, turning his attention back to the road.

Paul was thrown off guard by the sudden change of topic. 'You mean Indians and Pakistanis like we've got in England? Can't say I've seen many in Australia.'

'No mate,' snapped Bill. 'I mean bloody Asians. Chinks,

Japs — bloody Asians. There are millions of 'em here. I mean, jeez, they've been walking all over you. Haven't you seen the little bastards?'

'Oh yes, I certainly have,' Paul said, trying to remain calm.

What was happening? The conversation had changed dramatically from the friendly get-to-know-you chat between driver and passenger of, what was it, three-quarters of an hour ago, to one of downright aggression. He was left with the strong impression that Bill just didn't like him. Was it his accent? The fact that he was a Pom? Or didn't Bill have time for *any* foreigners?

Oh boy, what have I got myself into? So much for hitch-hiking. You save money, sure, but is it worth it for this? Totally on my own in a stranger's car ... a stranger who seems to be getting more and more agitated the further we go.

'Don't be so paranoid,' he whispered to himself. Nevertheless, it would be wise, he decided, to be on his guard. Every time Bill said anything now, there was anger in his voice, as if he had a big chip on his shoulder. Becoming increasingly concerned by the minute, Paul cautiously shifted his eyes to the driver. He now realised that Bill was older than the late 30s he'd first guessed him to be; he would be nearer 50. His bushy moustache certainly gave the impression of a friendly, almost fatherly, figure but the icy glaze in his eyes and the tight lips told a different story. Bill was so pent up ... like a dam ready to burst. Paul looked at the man's arms. Those biceps could bend a steel girder!

Great! Well done, Paul — a nice mess you've got yourself into!

Despite his increasing alarm, Paul still felt dozy. The music, the sun, the rolling shapes of the hills ... just a short nap, he thought, and anyway it might help to ease the tension.

Stay awake! Heed your sixth sense! Something's wrong here!

Another thing now began to worry Paul. He hadn't

thought anything of it before, but it was happening again. As on one or two earlier occasions, the vehicle slowed down and Bill glanced in the mirror as if trying to decide whether to stop. Perhaps this would be a good time for him and Bill to part company, even though they were in the middle of nowhere. 'Come on,' he told himself, 'pull yourself together! You've got a lift — stick with it. You could be waiting out there on the highway for hours.'

'What's happening?' he asked, as the vehicle began to increase speed again.

'No worries, mate,' said Bill. 'We're getting out of range of the Sydney radio stations. I'm just looking for somewhere to pull over so I can put on some tapes. I'll stop in a minute or two.'

Odd, thought Paul. The tapes were right there on the floor between the seats. Why would he want to pull over when he could just reach down for them?

Bill kept looking in the mirror and Paul's paranoia increased, but he again told himself: 'Calm down! This guy's doing you a favour!'

They came up over a rise, and this time Bill guided the vehicle to the side of the road and brought it to a stop. 'I'll just get out and look under m'seat for some cassettes,' he said, opening his door and stepping down.

Paul decided to take the opportunity to stretch his legs, wake himself up, and clear his mind of his concerns. Perhaps this was what they both needed: a short stop to break the tension, although he still couldn't understand what the problem was. As Paul opened the passenger door and moved to jump down, Bill suddenly demanded: 'What are you getting out of the car for? Why are you getting out?'

'Bill,' Paul began, aware of the agitation in his own voice, 'I'm just stretching my legs. If you don't mind.'

Paul stood beside the passenger door for a moment, breathing in the warm summer air.

You'll be okay, you'll be okay. You can walk out of this any time you like. You're in control of your life. But don't be an idiot and give up your lift!

He got back in, closed the door and fastened his seat belt. Bill got in too, then started fumbling under his seat again.

'I'll just have a look under here one more time.' Unable to get his hand right under the seat, Bill got out of the vehicle again and reached in through the open door.

Paul watched casually, but then felt a chill run down his spine. Bill had brought a gun out and was pointing it at him. Dear God, what was going on? This couldn't be happening, it must be a dream — but everything was so clear … right down to the mouth of the black revolver pointing at his chest. He could even see the copper-tipped bullets in the chamber. This was no dream. It was a real, living nightmare. Then Bill's voice boomed.

'This is a robbery,' he said. And, waving the gun, 'You know what this is?'

It's a joke, that's all it is. Bill's having a bit of fun with you, silly. This is his way of warming up the atmosphere between us.

Then he noticed Bill's eyes. Locked on his own. Cold. Determined.

'Calm down, mate,' Paul said, suddenly aware of the dryness in his mouth. 'What's going on? Calm down. What are you doing?'

Get out! Get out of here fast!

He unbuckled his seat belt and reached for the door handle.

'Put that fucking belt back on.' Another wave of the gun turned the order into a threat.

The terrified Paul did as he was told. Bill used one hand to fumble under the seat again, and this time he brought out a bag. Rope dangled from it, and this scared Paul more than the gun. In a strange way, there seemed to be more menace:

14

you could scare someone with a gun, and perhaps nothing more, but a rope somehow signified a greater degree of malicious intent.

That was it. He was getting out.

He flicked off the seat belt, flung open the door, and half fell on to the road. He stumbled to his feet and started running.

After a few metres, Bill yelled: 'Stop, or I'll shoot!'

His heart pounding, Paul spurred himself on. Cars sped past, but he didn't even think about waving any of them down. He just had to get away from this madman. Ducking and weaving, he stumbled on, fearing that at any moment a bullet would tear into his body. Then he heard the crack of gunfire.

My God, he's crazy! Go, go!

Spurred on by fear, Paul dodged across the road and through the traffic, now waving frantically in an attempt to stop one of the vehicles. He needed both distance and refuge — whichever came first. He reached the median strip, a wide patch of grass planted with shrubs that divided the highway, and stole a backwards glance. To his horror, he saw that Bill was right behind him. Powerful hands grabbed at his shoulder. He struggled but couldn't escape as Bill now gripped his T-shirt. Paul knew he was fighting for his life, yet at the same time he couldn't help thinking that this wasn't really happening. Half his mind continued to insist it was a joke or a dream. Then he hit the ground hard, and reality returned with a jolt. He had no hope unless he got away from this powerful man.

You want it to end here, Paul? Get up — get away!

He was back on his feet and running into the road again. He would force the next vehicle to stop even if it knocked him flat: it was worth the risk to escape from this madman.

He saw a large van, a Tarago, moving slowly towards him. It looked like the driver was trying to decide whether to stop or drive around him, but he wasn't going to let it pass — this vehicle had to be his salvation! There was nothing behind it. There was no other chance! He ran straight at the van and could see a woman behind the wheel, another woman in the passenger seat. He dodged around to the driver's side window.

'Please let me in,' he cried frantically, aware of the panic in his voice.

'Go away!' yelled the driver.

'I'm not going anywhere. He's got a gun. Please open the door!'

Joanne Berry had seen most of the drama as she drove along a straight stretch of the Hume Highway. She had been visiting her family in nearby Mittagong and was now heading south-west to Canberra with her sister, Gai Barnes. In the back of the vehicle were her four children and Gai's own youngster.

They were about a kilometre from the turn-off to the Belanglo State Forest, a popular area for bushwalkers and nature lovers, when she had noticed a parked vehicle in the distance — and had suddenly seen two men run out into the road, the first waving his arms in an obvious attempt to stop the cars in front of her. Joanne's immediate thought was for the children. She didn't want to get involved in anything, whatever it was.

As her vehicle drew nearer, she saw the pursuing man, who had his right arm across his chest and his hand hidden in the crook of his arm, catch the first one on the median strip and push him to the ground. They wrestled, then the first man got up and ran back on to the road … he ran right up towards her van and forced her to stop. Joanne became even more uneasy when she saw the fear on his face. Now he was at her side window, pleading to be let in.

'Please!' he cried again desperately. 'Please, please!'

'I'm not having anything to do with this,' Joanne told her sister. 'I've got the kids to think about.'

But she saw how much the man was trembling, and suddenly reached back and undid the door lock. As soon as the young man jumped in, she threw the vehicle into reverse back towards Sydney to get away from his pursuer, then drove across the median strip to drive back towards Sydney on the left side of highway. The other man was already running back to his car: he clambered in and sped off, travelling away from Sydney. Joanne didn't get a good look at his face, but noticed that he was wearing green shorts and a T-shirt, and thought, contrary to what Paul Onions had guessed, that he was about 168 centimetres (5 feet 6 inches) tall. Subconsciously, she also noted that his vehicle was a silver four-wheel-drive with a tyre on the back and a red or crimson stripe on the side.

As the Tarago bounced across the median strip, Paul glanced down the road and had a fleeting glimpse of his attacker turning back to stare at him: Bill's teeth were bared in what Paul thought was an evil grin.

The Englishman had the shakes all the way to the police station at the nearby town of Bowral. He could hardly get the words out as he told his story to the duty policewoman, Constable Janet Nicholson, who took everything down as a formal statement. He had lost his rucksack containing clothing, a camera, an air ticket, his British passport and $500.

But — as he reflected later when he bedded down in the hotel that the police had found for him, and the full reality of the day's terrifying events hit him — he still had his life!

CHAPTER TWO

The shadows were lengthening as Keith Seily and his mate Keith Caldwell from the Scrubrunners Orienteering Club of Campbelltown pounded through the Belanglo State Forest, 140 kilometres to the south-west of Sydney, at 3.45 pm on Saturday 19 September 1992.

Set in the heart of a dairying, fruit-growing and mixed-farming district, it was a beautiful, yet desolate place, comprising some 700 hectares of pine forest, maintained by the New South Wales Forestry Commission, and 2000 hectares of native bushland. The forest is thought to have first been called Belanglo by an 1820s settler who, enchanted by its untamed beauty, gave it a name that meant Good Angel.

Its wildlife — wombats, kangaroos and fabulously coloured birds — now attracted bushwalkers and families in their four-wheel-drive vehicles on weekend picnics. Visitors turned off the Hume Highway some 16 kilometres south of Bowral, the regional capital of the Southern Highlands, then travelled west on an unmade road which led them through the pine plantation to the native bush, some 5 kilometres from the main road.

The tracks through the bushland were stony and steep, but one of the attractions was that visitors looking for peace and quiet rarely saw or heard anyone else, such was the density of the bush. It was a photographer's paradise, the speckled sunlight providing fabulous colours and lighting while on the northern reaches of the native forest in the early morning deep gullies overlooking the Wingecarribee River were often smothered with fog, adding an eerie atmosphere to the silence.

There were chillingly-related named areas, too, like The Ugly Man, Executioner's Drop and Miner's Despair — a combination of names emanating from the 1920s, when the riverside reaches of the forest were mined for coal, and from descriptions applied by orienteering organisations.

Seily and Caldwell were on what was known as a relocation exercise, with Caldwell holding the map — so detailed that it included every termite mound — and leading the way, while Seily studied the surrounding bushland, noting the landmarks and trying to work out exactly where he was in relation to the map.

Their next stop was a large sandstone boulder about 5 metres wide that nestled among the eucalypts and wattles in the forest's north-west section. Located about 40 metres from a rough fire track, the rock had only recently been included on orienteering maps — it was too prominent a landmark for experienced runners, and the rock was far away from the easier courses used by those not so proficient at finding their way through the bush. But orienteering organisations who'd been using the forest since 1976 had begun to include it on their detailed 1:25,000 scale maps — marking it on the legend as a black dot — as the region became more popular with orienteers. In fact, the Belanglo Forest had already been used for two major orienteering events, one in 1988 and another for five days over the Christmas–New Year holiday of 1988–89.

Now, as the two men approached the boulder, a foul smell engulfed them.

'Phew, smells like some animal's copped it,' said Caldwell.

The lower side of the boulder fell away into a shallow cave, hardly deep enough to provide a bushwalker shelter from a rainstorm. It was there, behind a pile of bracken, that Seily then spotted what looked like a tuft of dark fur.

'A wombat,' he thought. 'Found itself a little cave and curled up and died.'

But then he noticed a thin bone and joint protruding from the leaf- and twig-covered mound and immediately changed his mind. 'Kangaroo?' he suggested to Caldwell. Yet even as he spoke, Seily realised with horror that what they were looking at did not match the description of any animal. Caldwell then put into words what had occurred to them both.

'Could it be a person?'

Seily looked more closely and could now see that the tuft of fur was actually hair, cropped relatively short from what he could make out, on the back of a head. He could also see the awkward twist of a pair of arms, locked behind the body's back. He shuddered. It was the first time he had come face to face with human death.

The two men were badly shaken and felt a little sick. But a morbid intrigue rooted them to the spot, and they were transfixed by the shape under the bracken.

Now Seily could see it was the right arm and elbow that had originally caught his attention. There was some skin on the arm and on the back of the head that had turned yellow in its decomposed state. The first bizarre thing that came to mind was that this was the texture and colour of a partially-related cooked chicken.

The person was dressed in a dark top and, while the rest of the body was difficult to make out under the twigs and leaves, Seily noticed a heel of what looked like a Doc Marten's boot. The shocked orienteers stared at the body for several minutes, both of them trying to determine whether the corpse was that of a man or a woman. Short hair, fairly heavy boots …

'A man,' Seily said out loud.

'I think it's a guy, too,' said his friend.

Suddenly, the grim scene and the forest's silence were disturbed by the voices of their four approaching orienteering companions.

'We'd better tell them,' said Seily. 'And then we'll have to get the police down here.'

When the two men broke the news of their discovery to the other orienteers, their friends were as shocked by the report as Seily and Caldwell had been by the discovery. 'Leave us out of it,' their friends said, 'we're not going over there.'

The team headed back to the main track and found their way to an old weatherboard home that orienteers used as a base. Once at the house, Caldwell used his mobile phone to call the local police.

Seily was still shaking. 'Wonder who it could be.'

'Could be anybody,' said Caldwell. 'Heaps of people are missing. But I wouldn't be surprised if that's someone who's been murdered, the way the body was covered over with sticks.'

'Reckon you're right,' said Seily. 'And if I remember, haven't there been some backpackers who've been missing for a while? You never know, this could be one of them.'

Forty-five minutes later Constable First Class Roger Gough and Constable First Class Suzanne Roberts arrived in a paddy wagon, followed by a sergeant in a second car.

Seily volunteered to return to the scene with the officers, getting into the paddy wagon and directing them along the crude track. It was twilight by the time they reached a point close to where Seily thought the boulder was located. The police produced a couple of torches to find their way through the bush. Even the experienced orienteer lost his bearings for a while, leading the officers on a weaving path through the dense undergrowth.

'Sorry about this,' Seily apologised, 'I'm looking for the boulder. Ah, I think I've got it. This way ...'

As the orienteer led them towards the darkening shape, a shudder ran through him. He knew what was there, what to expect, but it was worse the second time around.

Seily waited in the distance as the police bent over the low mound, their torchbeams penetrating the twigs and highlighting the horror that lay below.

On close examination, the officers could make out a pair of jeans as well as the boots that Seily and Caldwell had noticed. After just thirty seconds, the police had seen enough: the orienteers had certainly not been mistaken in their identification of a body. It also seemed obvious from the way in which the corpse had been carefully covered that this was not death by natural causes, or even misadventure such as a snake bite.

Seily watched as one of the officers got on the radio to summon detectives.

'We've got a body here, right in the middle of the Belanglo State Forest ... No, you'll never find it. It's in the middle of nowhere. We're going to have to meet you at the forest turn-off and bring you down here.'

Seily wandered around with the other policemen for a few minutes, his eyes following the shaft of torchlight. It picked out a circle of blackened stones; an old fireplace. He wondered if the person who now lay under the boulder had sat around the fire, unaware of his or her fate.

In the hours that followed, the site was ringed with blue and white tape. Powerful arc lights were set up, and a police photographer's flashlight bounced off the surrounding foliage. Shadows danced on tree trunks as detectives and forensic officers searched the ground near the body for the smallest of clues — a cigarette butt, an old footprint, a discarded match. Anything.

On everyone's mind was one question: who?

The cracking of sticks announced the arrival of more police, and a burly, bespectacled figure in his mid 30s with tousled sandy hair made his way through the scrub. Detective Senior Constable Andrew Grosse was a member of the South West Region Major Crime Squad and was based at Goulburn, 150 kilometres south-west of Sydney and 60 kilometres from the Belanglo State Forest.

The Major Crime Squad deals with all serious crimes, such as armed robbery, assault with a deadly weapon and murder. Grosse had attended close to 200 crime scenes; he was used to the sight of death, and was considered to be one of the best in the business for the meticulous way he went about his work, but he could not deny the loneliness and eerie atmosphere of this bushland scene. From a killer's point of view, it was a perfect place for a murder.

Detective Senior Constable William Dowton, based at Bowral, had driven him here, 4 kilometres along the Long Acre Fire Trail from the main road.

'Whoever did this didn't expect the body to be found,' said Dowton as they walked, stumbling occasionally, over the stones and broken twigs.

'I reckon you're right,' said Grosse.

He followed Dowton through thick bushes and down a slight slope to the boulder overhang. Grosse recoiled at the overpowering smell as he surveyed the branches covering the body. The branches formed a mound, 2 metres long and 60 centimetres high, running roughly from north to south. Through the dead foliage, he could see part of the arm that Seily and Caldwell had noticed protruding from about the centre, and the clump of black hair at one end of the mound.

'Let's start moving some of this away,' said Grosse, after checking that the scientific squad officers had completed their initial investigation of the site.

As he and his colleagues carefully removed the foliage, Grosse noticed that the body was lying face down, with the right arm raised and the hand against the right cheek.

'A woman?' he asked, now that he could see more of the back of the head.

His colleagues nodded in agreement, and pulled away more branches. She was dressed in a navy blue short-sleeved T-shirt, blue jeans, and black leather walking boots. There were three gold rings on the fingers of her right hand, and a silver ring set with a black stone on her left hand. A bracelet encircled her left wrist.

At least they had some distinctive personal items that might help to identify the body.

It was not immediately possible to see the face — apart from lying face down, the head was wrapped in light-brown cloth. Now Grosse understood why the hair had appeared so short; only the lower edges had been visible through the bracken. But he was prepared to estimate, even at this early stage, that the victim was in her late teens or twenties.

Despite his long experience of dealing with all forms of death, the detective winced as he continued to peel away the bracken. The body was in an advanced state of decomposition, with massive insect infestation. Trying not to breathe in the awful stench of death, Grosse looked closely at the back of the T-shirt. It was badly torn, but a closer inspection made him certain that the rips had been made by a sharp instrument.

'Stab marks?' he asked Dowton.

The other detective nodded. 'Looks like it.'

But Grosse was experienced enough not to draw instant conclusions. He knew there was an enormous amount of scientific work to be done on both the body and the area around it. And they still had to find out who it was that lay here.

While the grim examination was being carried out, detectives at the Missing Persons Unit were already sorting through the files of potential victims. Where did they start? Literally thousands of young women went missing every year. Some turned up, but others remained in the files as un-solved cases — although the police knew from experience that many simply started a new life far from the circum-stances they had run away from.

But in recent months missing-people stories with a com-mon link had featured in newspapers and magazines. Several young men and women had vanished while backpacking or hitch-hiking, and they had all abruptly stopped communi-cating with their families and friends.

Like every senior police officer in the Sydney region, Grosse was familiar with many of the cases. The most recent had been the mysterious disappearance of two young British women, Caroline Clarke and Joanne Walters, who had vanished after hitch-hiking from Sydney about five months earlier.

Grosse rubbed his jaw as he moved carefully through the shrubs near the boulder, looking for anything that could be connected with the body. The thought raced through his mind that this could be the body of one of the missing backpackers. He couldn't remember all of their names, but he recalled that in addition to the British women, three Germans had disappeared — a young woman travelling alone, and a man and his girlfriend. And a couple from Melbourne had been missing for, well, he reckoned it must be at least a couple of years now. Grosse paused and leaned against a tree, watching his colleagues search the area around the boulder under the glare of the floodlights. He had a gut feeling that the person lying under the rock was on the list of missing backpackers.

As the meticulous examination of the corpse continued into that Saturday evening, Grosse's instinct was spot on. The body had yielded enough clues for an initial identifi-cation, and the officers at the crime scene maintained radio contact with New South Wales police headquarters. They were soon able to conclude that the clothing and rings on the body matched those worn by one of the missing British tourists, Joanne Walters.

'Two people are going to have a long, sleepless night,' a detective whispered to Grosse. 'Joanne's parents have been in Australia for several weeks trying to find her. They're still here, staying in Sydney.'

Grosse tightened his lips and sighed. Someone would have to give the parents the sad news — and then they'd have to assist with absolute identification. These were the times he hated. Bur he reminded himself that cold, ugly corpses remained living, bright, beautiful people in the memories of their loved ones.

A flashlight beam bounced off the overhanging branches as a police photographer went about his business, and detectives took measurements of the body's location in relation to close landmarks.

Grosse then asked the medical officers, their stark white uniforms injecting a touch of surrealism into the forest scene, to turn the corpse over. The grisly task was completed with great care; there was always the risk that a body could break up.

The detective knelt down beside the figure. The cloth around the head created a bizarre hooded effect, and the front of the T-shirt and the brassiere were pulled up, exposing the breasts and abdomen. In the event of a female's suspicious death, the question of sexual assault is uppermost in detectives' minds. Perhaps the T-shirt had been pushed up as the body was being laid in its shallow grave, but Grosse would never know that. He studied the woman's jeans. The top button was fastened but, ominously, the four lower buttons were undone.

Grosse bit his lower lip. He didn't like any of this. He turned his head and nodded to the medical team; they could take the body away whenever they were ready. It was in the mortuary that the corpse would 'speak' to them. The body would reveal how the young woman had met her fate, and hopefully give them clues as to who had ended her life.

As the detectives in the forest closed down the operation for the night, sealing off the area with crime scene tape and placing a uniformed guard nearby, they were already speculating that another body could be nearby. Joanne's travelling companion, Caroline Clarke, was still missing.

Ray Walters, aged 48, and his wife, Gill, aged 43, had been in Australia for several weeks, searching for their missing daughter. They had checked out the backpackers' hostels in Sydney, and travelled to Mildura, in Victoria. Joanne had sent them postcards from this country town, telling them how much she enjoyed fruit-picking, despite the back-breaking work. They feared the worst, however — it had been completely out of character for Joanne to stop writing as suddenly as she had. Ray and Gill had got nowhere with their inquiries, but had gained some consolation by retracing their beloved daughter's footsteps.

They were now staying with friends in the Sydney suburb of Newtown, preparing to return to their home in Wales, when the police knocked on the door. The officers' grim faces revealed their news before they even spoke.

'I'm sorry to have to tell you this,' one of the detectives said as gently as he could, 'but we believe you should prepare yourselves to accept that Joanne is deceased.'

Gill thought she had been ready for this moment; thought that the passage of time had hardened her to accept news of Joanne's death should that day ever arrive. But she was far from ready: she collapsed in tears into Ray's arms. She was offered a sedative, but shook her head. But the couple did accept the offer of having a policewoman remain with them until dawn.

Early the following morning, a line of police officers drawn from nearby stations moved carefully through the undergrowth around the boulder.

A police caravan had been set up at the top of a nearby hill as a communications centre, but vehicles were kept to a minimum on the approach to a clearing close to where the body had been found. The killer would almost certainly have come and gone in a vehicle, although evidence of tyre tracks could only be established by meticulous examination of the ground.

Constable Suzanne Roberts, who was from the nearby town of Bowral and had been at the scene the evening before, had been warned along with the other officers that another body might well be somewhere in the area. Now, as she approached a large fallen tree trunk some 30 metres from the boulder, she noticed something that looked out of the ordinary. A pile of sticks appeared to have been stacked against the trunk. Then, as she moved in for a closer examination, the policewoman saw a leg protruding from the bracken. Although prepared for such a discovery, her heart pounded as she bent to examine her find.

Denim, probably jeans, covered the leg. The material was torn, and through the rip she could see that there had been some damage to the flesh, as if it had been chewed at by an animal. At one end of the mound she noticed a black leather shoe. Following orders, Constable Roberts touched nothing but stood up and called: 'Find!' This was now a job for the crime scene experts.

Detective Senior Constable Grosse, who had managed to snatch a few hours' sleep after his grim work the night before, was soon back at the scene. In contrast to the previous gloomy evening, the forest was alive with birdsong and rays of sunlight forced their way through the canopy of towering eucalypts.

Grosse was led to the fallen tree trunk. After an initial inspection had been conducted and photographs taken, he noticed, as the branches were pulled away, that the body was lying face down in a north–south direction with the head towards the south.

'Both bodies are lying in the same compass positions,' one of the officers mentioned to Grosse.

'So I've noticed,' said the detective. 'Maybe it's just coincidence. Maybe there's something more to it, some sort of ritual even. But we'd only be guessing. Time will tell … perhaps.'

Both arms were extended up from the shoulders but, as with the other body, decomposition had set in and insects had added to the damage. The woman was dressed in a khaki shirt, blue jeans, black socks and black walking shoes, but there was a sinister addition to the clothing. Wrapped around her head, and leaving only the lower jaw exposed, was a maroon garment of some kind, with a number of small holes in its upper area.

After an initial comparison of rings and clothing with details drawn from the missing persons files, Grosse was in no doubt that this was the body of Joanne's travelling companion, Caroline Clarke.

Grosse moved away to examine the surrounding ground. About 10 metres to the north-west of the body, a number of plants had been broken or forced down as if they had been trampled. Closer to the crude burial site he found six cigarette butts, a piece of cream-coloured plastic and a spent .22 Winchester cartridge case. He took photographs of the items, noted their location, and arranged for them to be collected as evidence.

Grosse looked on grimly and thrust his hands deep into his pockets as, once again, the remains of a young woman were lifted into a body bag to be taken to the morgue. Now it was up to him and his colleagues to find out who was responsible for these murders.

Orienteer Keith Seily had been brought back to the forest that morning, to show detectives the direction from which he and his companion had approached the boulder where Joanne's body had been found. Seily hadn't seen the second burial site, but he couldn't help hearing that another body had been found.

As the police drove him out of the forest, Seily, aware from press reports that several other backpackers were still unaccounted for, asked: 'Could this be the work of a mass murderer?'

There was a moment's silence as his police escorts glanced at each other. Then one of them said: 'You're sharing our thoughts, mate. You should join the force.'

CHAPTER THREE

It is often said that policemen become hardened to their grim work, but it isn't true, thought Grosse. Underneath his calm exterior he was affected by death and murder as much as any decent human being. As he drove home from the forest, he was overwhelmed with helplessness. No matter how diligently he and his colleagues now worked, it wouldn't put life back into those young women. Even tracking down their killer would not relieve the pain that their parents were enduring.

He appreciated their personal agony. Despite his professional, painstaking and often dogged approach to his work, he was also a man of great compassion. It was one of the qualities that made him popular in the force — along with his quick, analytical mind that led to his forming theories and opinions that were often spot on, or very close to the mark. He was already wondering whether two or more people could have been involved in the murders: separating two young women by 30 metres and killing them both would have been a tough task for one person, although he wasn't writing off a single killer yet.

His car swept past rolling paddocks and clumps of thick woodland as he headed south towards the city of Goulburn where he was based. So now, he thought, the history books could add two more names to the list of victims who had died violently in the Southern Highlands, the range of eucalypt-covered hills about 150 kilometres south-west of Sydney. In the old days the murderers had been gangs of bushrangers with their antiquated weapons, but it didn't matter whether villains of the past or present used guns, knives or their bare hands — murder was murder, and these latest terrible crimes would only serve to further blacken the district's name.

Grosse knew something of the history of the area — how, of the many roads carved by convicts from the burgeoning town of Sydney, few had attracted gangs of bushrangers as much as the highway running south-west through thickly wooded hills and gullies.

Named after nineteenth-century explorer Hamilton Hume and now known as the Hume Highway, this road had become Australia's busiest interstate route carrying commercial and private vehicles between Sydney and Melbourne. Major road projects by the New South Wales and Victorian state governments had brought about vast improvements to the hazardous potholed two-lane thoroughfare of twenty years earlier. In fact, road improvements had sped ahead on all the major arteries leading out of Sydney and those which weren't subjected to multi-million-dollar upgrades were maintained on a regular basis.

When there was an accident in which the road surface was damaged, the New South Wales Roads and Traffic Authority — formerly known as the Department of Main Roads — was quick to send repair vehicles to the scene. For example, when two huge articulated trucks crashed on the Great Western Highway at Hazelbrook, west of Sydney, on 12 January 1990, killing two people and tearing up the surface of the highway, special 'road profiling equipment' was immediately sent to the scene. While police took their own photographs, as at all fatal accidents, roads department officials took pictures of the carnage and of the road repairing team at work for their own files. Those tanned and muscle-built road gangers were used to such work and wouldn't have even noticed their photos being taken — it was their job to get the road resurfaced quickly and efficiently and move on to the next task.

The Hume Highway had become a slick dual carriageway that bypassed towns which had so often slowed down interstate traffic. Although shopkeepers complained of losing trade as the new route took shape, the residents were happy to say goodbye to the huge trucks that once clogged up the main streets and shook the buildings. On a good run, the journey between Sydney and Melbourne could now be completed in around nine hours. A far cry from the muddy lane of the 1800s that was a favourite target for highwaymen. In those days there were numerous places to carry out an ambush — and even more in which to hide.

From the small community of Bargo in the Southern Highlands right down to the provincial city of Goulburn 80 kilometres away, the highwaymen had plundered, wounded and killed. One traveller wrote in 1851: 'For a considerable distance, you pass through Bargo Brush, a favourite haunt of bushrangers and a more miserable and cut-throat looking place one would not wish to ride through.'

The notorious bushranger Jacky Jacky rode through the district, as did highway robber Ben Hall and his gang, who sometimes watched the police who hunted them from a place called Hanging Rock. Many of the gangs found refuge in the forest already called Belanglo and which had since been cleared in places by settlers.

Yet for all the fear that the bushrangers created, no-one brought as much darkness to the district as the cruel John Lynch, who was transported from England under life sentence in 1832, but who served only seven years. He went on a murderous spree, axing and stabbing his victims to death and concealing their bodies in shallow graves in the Southern Highlands bushland. The law finally caught up with him and he was arrested and charged with multiple murder. Lynch was hanged for his crimes on 22 April 1842. One and a half centuries later, the sinister shadow of evil that had hung over the forested regions of the Southern Highlands descended once more.

Andrew Grosse was up early the following morning, 21 September, for a gruesome appointment with the pathologist in the morgue.

Shortly after 10 o'clock, with a mask covering his face, he stood in the mortuary of the Glebe Coroner's Court in Sydney's Parramatta Road, staring down at what was believed to be the body of Joanne Walters.

Forensic pathologist Dr Peter Bradhurst started the post-mortem examination. Bradhurst had also requested the assistance of an ondontologist, whose role would be to compare the corpse's teeth with dental charts supplied by Joanne Walters' dentist in the United Kingdom to ascertain 100 per cent identification.

The clothing on Joanne's body remained just as it had been found. Her T-shirt was bunched upwards and the brassiere was still pulled up. Bradhurst set to work, first cutting the T-shirt down the sides in order to remove it.

'This was a pretty frenzied attack,' said Bradhurst as he and his assistants, along with Grosse, stared at the cut-marks in the back of the garment, in the front, near each breast, and in the right sleeve. The highest concentration of cuts, between 25 and 70 millimetres wide, were between the shoulders.

'Now let's find out just how much force he used.'

The pathologist carefully peeled away pieces of skin to expose the bone. 'Chipped and split bone — he used a lot of strength,' observed the pathologist.

Turning to the jeans, Bradhurst first removed a few coins from the rear pocket then saw, as Grosse had at the crime scene, that the top button was fastened but the remaining four were undone. As the mortuary team removed the jeans, they saw that the young victim was wearing no underwear. Grosse wondered how significant this was. A sign that Joanne had been sexually molested, then hurriedly dressed? Time and painstaking forensic work might provide the answer, but there was no guarantee.

Grosse watched silently as a number of loose hairs were collected from inside the jeans. They would go to another forensic scientist who would try to establish if they were from the dead woman. And if not, from whom.

'Right,' said Bradhurst, 'let's have a look at the head area.' His skilful hands reached down to the light-brown cloth still covering the young woman's head. As he pulled it away, two further pieces of cloth could be seen underneath — one appeared to be running through the mouth and around the head, like a gag, while the second piece rested loosely against her cheek.

'Could this have been used as a ligature to strangle her?' Grosse wondered aloud. But he knew Bradhurst wouldn't be able to provide an immediate answer — there was still a great deal more forensic work to be done before any conclusions could be drawn.

Bradhurst set the pieces of cloth to one side, planning to wash them later in disinfectant to prevent further deterioration. Careful examination of the cloth might help identify where it had been made or bought. It could have come from among Joanne's own possessions — or it could have belonged to the killer or killers.

In the partly opened right hand, Dr Bradhurst found some loose hairs and fibres. These were saved, along with fibres and matter from the jeans, shirt and fingernails. They might later prove something — or, indeed, nothing. Samples of the victim's hair were collected, to be sent with the loose hairs for comparison by hair experts and forensic scientists. A vaginal swab was also taken to be sent away for tests.

'I doubt whether we're going to get anything from the swab,' said Bradhurst. 'From the deterioration of the body I'd say we're not going to be able to find any sperm traces.'

Joanne's jewellery was then carefully removed to be sent to her parents.

Bradhurst needed to establish the exact cause of death. It was not enough to assume that because there were a large number of stab wounds to the body, the young woman had died as a result of those injuries. But just how many stab wounds she had received shocked both him and Grosse — Bradhurst counted fourteen to the chest and the neck. Of these fourteen stab wounds, two were in the back on the left side and five were on the right, two were at the base of the neck, three were on the right side of the chest, one was on the front of the chest on the left, and one was on the right side of the neck.

Some of the wounds had left their mark on bones, and Bradhurst was in no doubt that severe force had been behind the blows.

'Any general thoughts?' asked Grosse.

Bradhurst looked down at the human remains of what had once been someone's lively, happy-go-lucky daughter.

'The two pieces of cloth certainly raise the possibility that she was strangled or had suffocated — but whether she was stabbed before or after the cloth was applied, I just can't say.'

Grosse nodded his thanks. He knew it would be of little consolation to tell her parents that she had died from either stab wounds, suffocation or strangulation.

As the search for more clues continued in the forest on the following day, Grosse made his way back to the mortuary to attend the post-mortem on the body of the second victim, generally believed to be that of Caroline Clarke. This time, in addition to Dr Bradhurst and his assistants, experts from the police ballistics unit were in attendance. The holes in the maroon garment that covered the body's head could only have been left by bullets and it was necessary now, as the examination of her remains began, to have the experts on hand.

The mortuary team found some loose coins and banknotes in her jeans pockets, and a red cigarette lighter in the left breast pocket of the shirt.

The maroon garment that had been wrapped around her head, leaving the lower section of the jaw exposed, was a Chinese-manufactured 'sloppy Joe' T-shirt, size L. The holes that had punctured it were about 5 millimetres in diameter, and dark red stains had spread through the material.

As the garment was being removed, Grosse saw two metal fragments — used bullets — embedded in the skull in the forehead area. As he feared, the rest of the skull was full of holes: three entry wounds at the rear base; three entry wounds on the right at the rear; two entry wounds on the left at the rear; an entry wound in the left forehead; a hole on the top of the skull, left of centre and to the rear; two exit wounds to the left side; an exit wound to the right; an exit wound at the base; and an exit wound in the nasal region.

'It's almost as if she's been used for target practice,' Grosse said to himself, sickened by what he had seen.

Dr Bradhurst removed four spent bullets from the brain tissue, and another bullet from the left shoulder. All of these spent projectiles, the ballistic experts agreed, were consistent with .22 calibre bullets.

Altogether, the morgue inspection revealed seven bullets in Caroline's head and shoulder, although she had been shot ten times. The other bullets, it was imagined, were out in the bush.

Grosse then noticed what appeared to be a wound of about 35 millimetres in length in the woman's back. He was able to match this wound with a cut in the rear of her shirt below the right shoulder, leaving him in no doubt that she had been stabbed.

There was also a round-shaped wound, although he couldn't say what had caused it, on the right side of the chest.

In Caroline's right hand, Bradhurst found fifteen head hairs. Had she grabbed at her killer's head, wondered Grosse, or were these from her own head, pulled out, perhaps, in moments of extreme pain?

Soil was scraped from her hands and clothes and this, along with the hairs, was put aside to be sent for further scientific tests.

Body tissue and fingernails were also removed to be dispatched to the Division of Forensic Medicine. The scientists there might find minute clues to the killer's identity under the fingernails — although Grosse was well aware that stories of finding skin from a murderer's scratched face belonged more to fiction novels than to real life.

After examining the stab wound in the young woman's back, pathologist Bradhurst decided that a moderate degree of force had been used — this wound had not caused the same degree of damage to bone as had been found in Joanne's body.

'Any conclusion as to what killed her?' asked Grosse.

Bradhurst shook his head. 'If she was stabbed first, that would have been enough to kill her, and if she was shot first, that would certainly have killed her. But it's impossible to say what came first.'

Once again, Grosse thanked Bradhurst for his work, but kept his true feelings to himself. He was sickened by what the women had been subjected to, and made a private vow not to rest until he had caught whoever was responsible — no matter how long it took.

The following morning, 23 September, Grosse returned to the Belanglo Forest with other officers, one of whom was equipped with a metal detector. This was passed over the ground near the boulder where Joanne had been discovered, but nothing of importance was found. The metal detector was then used in the area where Caroline's body had lain, and 3 to 5 metres north-west of her shallow grave site it beeped. By the time the machine went quiet that day, eight .22 Winchester cartridge cases had been found. Grosse had already picked up a cartridge case when he went to the forest three days earlier, and another officer had also found one, so they now had a collection of ten cartridge cases.

The metal detector was also run over the soil where Caroline's head had rested, and once again the machine beeped. A 30-centimetre layer of soil was gathered up and put into a sieve, and three spent bullets were filtered out. As with the other bullets and cartridge cases, Grosse collected them with gloved hands and placed them individually into clear-plastic evidence bags. The locations in which they were found were photographed and recorded.

The bullets would be sent to the police ballistics unit, where they would be subjected to microscopic examination in the hope that they would reveal characteristics of the weapon which had fired them. Meanwhile, Grosse planned to arrange for a chart to be drawn up, indicating where every item had been discovered.

Neither Grosse nor his companions could be certain of what terrible scenes had been played out in this beautiful forest, but the detective was in little doubt that the British women's last moments of life had been filled with terror.

As the bodies were in an advanced state of decomposition, crime squad officers were aware from the start of the investigation that the passage of time would have given the killer or killers ample opportunity to cover their tracks. These factors would not make the murder hunt any easier, and a great deal of responsibility would be thrown onto the shoulders of the scientific examiners. But Grosse and other senior detectives were reminded of an old forensic saying: 'failure to search is failure to find.' If it meant going over what clues they had time and again, they would do it.

It became obvious to the police team over the following days that they were being spurred on by one particular factor that is normally carefully avoided when investigating serious crime — emotion. There wasn't a man or woman who had gone into the forest to forage around the murder scene who was not utterly disgusted by what had happened to the backpackers.

What monster, or monsters, had brought these two young women into this picturesque bushland and snuffed out their young lives so violently? Had they entered the forest by force, or had they been cleverly lured? Had one been led or ordered to walk in one direction, while her companion was forced to the second location by another assailant? Had one murderer killed them side by side, then dragged them to the places he had already earmarked for their graves? There were so many theories to be tested.

Had the girls been blindfolded so they would be unaware of their immediate fate as the killer raised his weapon — or was it to give them less time to identify the captor or captors?

Caroline's case was especially sinister. Had her head been wrapped with the sweatshirt to muffle the sound of shots, or to stop blood from spurting onto the executioner? And why so many bullets, when one would probably have sufficed?

In the following days, scores of cadets from the police training college at nearby Goulburn spread out around the murder scene. They picked up pieces of paper, discarded cans, scraps of cloth — anything that was not natural to the bush, and which might have a bearing on the killings. The isolation of the burial sites led Grosse and his colleagues to conclude that the perpetrator knew the forest well.

'I'm inclined to think there was more than one,' Grosse told a group of colleagues as they watched the activity in the forest. 'And they had to know their way around here. They've picked a pretty remote region and it was only by chance that the bodies were found. If the orienteers hadn't come by, we might never have found out what happened to those poor women.'

Everyone who used the forest had to be considered as possible suspects, whether they were soldiers on training exercises, pistol-club members, orienteering enthusiasts, or bushwalkers. Another chilling thought was that the killer may have known the area so well that even though he was aware that orienteers trampled through the forest, he knew they never used the boulder as a landmark.

The intense search around the crude burial sites had failed to yield two vital components of the murders: the knife and the gun. Had the murderer kept them, or dumped them somewhere in the forest?

Grosse and other members of the South West Region Major Crime Squad obtained every relevant map that they could find and studied the layout of the forest region. The police experienced problems in finding a good detailed map, but they were able to establish that there were countless places in which to dump a weapon: swamps, creeks and dams and the Wingecarribee River, just 2 kilometres to the north.

One particular landmark caught their attention. The chilling name of 'Executioner's Point' marked a bluff, and less than 1 kilometre from the burial sites there was an area known as 'The Ugly Man'. Detectives checked the names and established they had emerged from geographic features and had found their way onto surveying and orienteering maps over the years. But was there some gruesome connection between the names and the manner of the girls' deaths?

In their friends' home in Sydney's Newtown, Joanne's parents, Ray and Gill Walters, were beside themselves with grief. A small consolation was that the dental charts sent from England had matched the first body's teeth, and so they were thankfully spared the task of confirming that the remains were those of their daughter. If they'd had any lingering hope, however, this was dashed when they identified the rings and other jewellery that had been removed from the body.

They had lost a vivacious young daughter of whom they had been so proud — their beautiful Joanne, a caring young woman who loved children and who had looked forward so much to having youngsters of her own. Nothing that any of their friends or the police officers who called on them in those first dark days said or did could distract them from their grief.

The depth of the Walters' sorrow could be shared by only one other family — Caroline's. In England, Ian and Jacqueline Clarke were driving from a friend's wedding in Surrey to their home in the north of England when their car phone rang.

'Where are you?' asked a police friend, Tony Noble, from Hexham Police Station. 'Can you pull over? I've got bad news.'

They drove to the side of the road and listened with disbelief to what Noble told them. 'Two bodies have been found in a forest. It looks as though it's the girls.'

They had half expected the news. During their anxious months of waiting for word from Caroline, Jacqueline had suddenly said to Ian one day: 'She's not coming back, is she?' And with their suppressed private thoughts now turned into words, they had thrown their arms around each other and wept.

Later, Ian and Jacqueline didn't know how they'd managed to drive the rest of the way home after hearing the terrible news on the car phone. Their reaction was the same as that of the Walters, 20,000 kilometres away. Could they have stopped their daughter from travelling? Could they have done anything to prevent the tragedy? And had their beloved daughter suffered before she met her death?

Caroline Clarke's distraught parents were then left with the unhappy task of arranging to send dental charts to Australia. The second body that had been brought out of Belanglo had to be formally identified.

CHAPTER FOUR

Caroline Clarke and Joanne Walters were somewhat unlikely travelling companions. Although both aged 22, they came from very different backgrounds. Yet the two young women shared a fierce sense of independence and a love of travel. It was these factors that were eventually to draw them together.

Caroline was a convent-educated girl and the daughter of a wealthy Bank of England executive. She had managed to pack more drama into her 22 years than many people experience in a lifetime.

She was slim, with light-brown hair, and was a keen netball and hockey player. She had also proved her ability on the ski slopes of Europe. She decided not to try for a place at university, but to see as much of the world as she could before applying to join the police force.

Once her O-Levels were behind her, Caroline went to Guildford Technical College in Surrey, in the south of England, to take a two-year course in food and beverage studies, and followed this with a temporary job at the Pizza Hut at Guildford. While she was working there, her father Ian was offered a top bank job in the north of England. He and his wife Jacqueline headed north to Slayley, near

Hexham, Northumberland, while Caroline and her brother Simon remained in the family home near Hindhead, Surrey. Caroline Clarke was a big hit at the Pizza Hut. She was promoted to Assistant Manager, and the staff and customers alike found her to be efficient, yet easy-going. When the restaurant formed a social club she became its focal point, and whenever the group went to the nearby Ritz Club, Caroline would challenge the men, and often beat them, at snooker. When she celebrated her 21st birthday on 10 August 1991, Caroline's parents paid for several of the restaurant friends to travel north with her for a big party in a Newcastle club.

Caroline's brother Simon, meanwhile, set off on his own adventures and travelled to Australia. It was from there that he wrote Caroline a number of letters and urged her to follow in his footsteps. He couldn't say enough about the wonders of the big continent down under. Inspired, Caroline told her parents: 'Before I even think about the police force, I just have to go to Australia.'

But there was still much to see before she set out on her big adventure to the Southern Hemisphere. Combining a holiday with a 'trial run' for her planned visit to Australia, Caroline and a 24-year-old friend from the Pizza Hut, Noel Goldersthorpe, bought round-Europe rail tickets.

In August 1991 the pair set off to travel through France, Belgium, Luxembourg, Austria, Hungary and Greece, where they amicably decided to go their separate ways. Noel had found himself a job, and Caroline decided to travel on to Germany, with two German men they had met, in order to visit the concentration camps.

Noel later asked himself what he found so appealing about Caroline. The answers came flooding into his mind: 'That girl knows exactly what she wants out of life and she's determined to get it. She's as rare as a diamond — and far too fast and ambitious for you! What energy, what enthusiasm!'

True to Noel Goldersthorpe's expectations, Caroline returned to England with some extraordinary tales. She had been caught up in the war in the former Yugoslavia, and was ordered from a train at gunpoint. In Amsterdam she had been wrongly accused of not paying a fare, and had been thrown into a police cell without food for twenty-four hours. And in Italy she had been robbed by thieves who gassed the passengers as they slept on a train.

Caroline Clarke stayed in England for just one week before saying goodbye to her parents in September 1991 and jetting off to Australia for her backpacking holiday. She planned to be away for eighteen months, and to return home through Indonesia and Thailand. But she promised her parents that she wouldn't forget them, and said she would write or phone regularly.

Four months earlier, dark-haired Joanne Walters had made the same promises to her parents as she headed off for a working holiday in Australia.

Joanne was Welsh and came from a far more modest background. Educated at a state-run comprehensive school, she was the daughter of a paper-mill worker who lived in a cramped end-of-terrace house. Joanne had trained as a nanny at Bridgend Technical College in Wales, and had no particular ambition except to please the families for whom she worked.

Like Caroline, she had received her travel baptism in Europe, having worked in Sardinia, Rhodes and Italy — and, also like Caroline, her friends regarded her as the life and soul of any party. Joanne had gained eight O-Levels at Maesteg Comprehensive School and, despite her high spirits, former school pals and teachers regarded her with affection and considered her to be a sensible girl. After her college course, Joanne took a job at the Sony television plant at Bridgend and saved hard for her planned trip to Australia.

'You'll have no trouble finding work,' her friend from school, Yvonne Samuel, told her. 'You're just so brilliant with kids.'

'I'm practising for when I have my own one day,' Joanne replied. 'Once I've got all the travelling behind me and done all the things I want to do, I'm going to settle down and raise a family of my own.'

Joanne had decided on travelling to Australia after seeing an advertisement in a British newspaper offering cheap 'two for the price of one' return flights. Her travelling companion was to be Pauline Vuletich, originally from the Shetland Islands, whom Joanne had met in Greece in 1990.

They set off in May 1991, stopping in Singapore for a few days then travelling on to Australia and arriving in Sydney in early June 1991. The young women wandered around the city for four days, then headed for Surfers Paradise, the tourist Mecca of Queensland's Gold Coast. Joanne and Pauline had working visas and intended to find jobs, so while in Queensland they opened bank accounts to deposit the money they hoped to earn. This proved to be a good idea, as they were able to withdraw money without needing to carry traveller's cheques, or to have money sent from the UK.

Eager to see as much of Queensland as they could, Joanne and Pauline hitch-hiked to the Sunshine Coast, north of Brisbane, then travelled further north to the seaside city of Cairns, arriving there in August.

Their travel plans were flexible and Joanne travelled back to Sydney ahead of Pauline, but made a point of phoning her friend when Pauline also returned to the city. They kept in touch, although Pauline planned to visit New Zealand and they would soon be apart again.

Meanwhile, back in England a young Derbyshire woman, Nina Tunnicliff, had also set her sights on a working holiday Down Under. She flew from England on 17 April 1991, and travelled through the United States and Hawaii before arriving in Melbourne. On reaching Sydney in November, she checked into the Original Backpackers' Hostel in Victoria Street, Kings Cross. Five others girls were staying in the same room — one of them was Joanne, who had recently returned from Queensland. Over the following weeks, the two young British women became good friends and explored the city together. They were both on a tight budget, and decided they would save money by leasing a flat together. They found a place in Kings Cross, in Sydney's red light district.

'Hardly a palace,' said Joanne with a grin as she looked around the bleak apartment. 'But hopefully we won't be spending a lot of time here. It'll be fine for a base.'

During their socialising with other backpackers, visiting the local pubs and enjoying a chat in one of the many coffee bars to be found in the area, Joanne and Nina met Caroline Clarke, who had also found her way to Kings Cross. Caroline was staying at a backpackers' hostel, but once a friendship was established she began visiting Joanne's and Nina's place.

'What are you doing about finding work?' asked Caroline.

'I've been doing some nannying,' said Joanne, 'but if you want to travel around a bit, the best place seems to be in Mildura, down in Victoria. There's a vineyard where they'll take you on.'

Caroline was excited by what Joanne told her. She'd heard the same thing about the vineyard. They'd have to take camping gear and sleep out on the property, and the grape-picking would last for only a few weeks, but the money was reasonable.

Together with a Dutch girl they had befriended, Jantina Steegstra, they all set off from Kings Cross railway station and travelled by train to Liverpool, on the city's south-west fringe, on 8 February 1992. The four women walked a short distance to the main road to Melbourne, the Hume

Highway, and split up into pairs, believing it would be easier to get lifts if they separated.

The plan worked well and they all met, as arranged, outside the Mildura Town Hall before making their way to the vineyard at Capagrego Farm, about 17 kilometres from the town. The rural centre of Mildura, perched on the banks of the Murray River, was busy with tourists who had come up from Melbourne and Adelaide to enjoy some lazy fishing and cruises on the river's famous paddle steamers.

At the farm, a tent village had been established by the many itinerant workers who had travelled here to toil under the blazing summer sun. Caroline and Joanne set up their two-man tent, which was hardly big enough for them with all their backpacking gear. But as the days wore on, they were often too exhausted from the grape-picking to worry about the cold nights — or anything else except getting their heads down for a good sleep!

Among those they befriended at the farm was a young Briton, Stephen Wright, from Beckenham, Kent. He had set out from England for a round-the-world trip in late November 1991, and arrived in Sydney in early January 1992. He remained there until early February, when he set off for Mildura. It was natural that, as a fellow Briton, he would strike up a conversation with the British girls, who in turn introduced him to Jantina and another Dutch girl, Resy Arts.

Wright amused them all with his lifestyle — he had a large, blue three-man tent, but it was so crammed with his possessions, including a metal-framed bed, that there was hardly enough room for him to move around. One day, while scrambling around inside with his grape-picking knife, he accidentally stabbed it through the canvas and made a small hole of about an inch and a half in diameter. He intended to sew it up some time, but as a temporary measure he stuck an adhesive label over the hole. But there was always so much to do, including socialising with the other workers, that he kept putting off the small repair task. Certainly he, Caroline, Joanne and Nina were all getting on well together and they agreed that they would meet up again in Sydney if possible.

Hitch-hiking was the normal mode of travel for most of those who had gathered in Mildura. Wright had not tried it, however, and when he set off with a girl friend on 22 March for Melbourne, they headed for the railway station. But Caroline, Joanne and Nina thumbed lifts back to Sydney.

The first thing that Wright did when he later arrived in Sydney was to make contact with the three girls at the Kings Cross hostel where he knew they would be staying. They agreed they'd all had such a good time in Mildura, and that fruit-picking was an excellent way of making money, while getting plenty of fresh air and sunshine, that they would head off to Tasmania where work was on offer in the apple orchards.

'The best way would be to hitch-hike to Melbourne, then get a ferry across to Tasmania,' Caroline told Wright.

He was ready to listen to their advice — the girls had, after all, hitch-hiked out of Sydney to go to Mildura. Wright decided he would try the girls' method of travel, and he and the three young women caught the train from Kings Cross. This time, instead of alighting at Liverpool, Caroline and Joanne suggested they get off one stop further, at the smaller station of Casula. This was virtually on the Hume Highway and they wouldn't have to walk so far.

'There's another advantage in getting off at Casula,' said Caroline. 'It's an unmanned station, so you won't have to pay!'

Wright grinned. He was well aware of how backpackers saved their dollars and cents in every possible way.

Following the theory that smaller numbers mean easier lifts, the four friends split up to thumb their rides —

Caroline pairing off with Nina, and Joanne with Wright. They had little trouble in finding lifts, and met up in Melbourne as arranged on 29 March. They then caught the *Abel Tasman* ferry to Devonport, Tasmania, and started looking for work.

While in Launceston, they decided to purchase some extra camping equipment: Wright bought a portable cooker and Joanne purchased a blue and yellow sleeping bag, because the one she had been using was not warm enough.

A week before the friends decided to split up and head off in separate directions — the English women planned to do some apple-picking — Wright told Caroline and Joanne that he was happy to swap tents. They could have the large blue tent he had purchased in Mildura, and he would take their smaller one because he didn't intend to do any more camping.

On 15 April Nina Tunnicliff arrived back in Sydney and made her way to the backpackers' hostel where Joanne, Caroline and Stephen Wright were already staying, sharing a room, after their excursion to Tasmania. Joanne and Caroline had a new plan — they were heading towards Western Australia to pick melons. Their rough schedule would see them hitch-hiking down the Hume Highway towards Melbourne, then along the Great Ocean Road to Adelaide, from where they would head north to Ayers Rock and then north-west to the Western Australian town of Kununurra.

Nina met up with Joanne and Caroline on Good Friday 1992 — 17 April, and a year to the day after she had set out on her travels from England. The three young women wandered around the city, but Joanne decided to return to the hostel early to pack her things: she and Caroline planned to leave Sydney that evening. It was at 2 pm in Martin Place, in the city centre, that Nina and Joanne said goodbye. Caroline remained in the city with Nina for another hour before she, too, said goodbye and made her way back to the Kings Cross hostel.

They did not leave that evening, although they had informed the hostel that they would be going. In another money-saving exercise, the young women decided to stay in Wright's room for the night and leave early the following morning — early enough to avoid paying. Joanne had another reason for staying an extra night: two days earlier she had met up with her former travelling companion, Pauline Vuletich, who had just arrived back from her trip to New Zealand. At 9 pm on that Friday, 17 April, Joanne, accompanied by Caroline, met Pauline in Darlinghurst Road and, after a few drinks, they made their way to Studebaker's nightclub, one of the major late-night attractions of Kings Cross.

'I'm glad we could get this one evening in together,' Joanne yelled at Pauline above the music. 'We're off to Western Australia in the morning. If I can earn enough money, I'm going to start heading back home through Asia.'

'How're you getting to WA?' asked Pauline.

'If we're lucky, we'll find a driver who'll take us all the way!' laughed Joanne.

Stephen Wright saw the two young women off sometime between 7.30 am and 8 am the following morning. As they'd hoped, they avoided paying for the night's accommodation, and the early start meant they should make good progress with their travels. They informed Wright, as they had told their other friends, that they would take the train from Kings Cross railway station to Casula, as they had all done previously, and start hitch-hiking from there. They would head towards Melbourne and take the coastal road to Adelaide, and then either continue along the southern highway towards Perth, or head north to Ayers Rock and strike out west from there.

Later that morning, close to 10 am, Nina Tunnicliff called at the hostel to check that Caroline and Joanne had got away all right. She hoped to see them again, as did Pauline Vuletich, who also called in at the hostel on that Saturday morning in the hope of saying a final goodbye. Such was the affection that many held for these young women, but Joanne and Caroline had already gone.

Laden down with their backpacking gear, including the blue tent that Wright had given them — the hole he had made with his knife still unrepaired — the two British women walked a short distance along Darlinghurst Road and turned right into the entrance to Kings Cross railway station. They were about to begin the last stage of their travels.

Disgust for whoever had taken their daughter away overwhelmed Ray and Gill Walters, and they wanted the world to join them in their desire to bring the killer or killers to justice. At the same time they needed to purge themselves of the hatred that consumed them, and agreed that while continuing to offer their prayers for the soul of Joanne they had to face the TV cameras.

Only three days had passed since the discovery of Joanne's body when Ray and Gill sat down in September 1992 before Australian and British reporters at the New South Wales police headquarters in Sydney. They would answer no questions, but just shed the venom that was in their hearts for whoever had snatched their daughter from them.

'Whoever did this thing,' said Ray, 'I wouldn't call them sick because sick people can be cured to an extent. These are evil-minded people, and like dogs with rabies there is only one way — they have got to be put down and destroyed. There has got to be some system whereby we destroy these people for their evil genes.'

Gill, her face grey, her eyes blackened by the tear-filled sleepless nights, shared her husband's thoughts. 'These people who have done these things to these girls, they are just proper animals and they ought to be shot,' she said.

It was enough. Ray and Gill stood and walked quietly from the room.

The search continued in the Belanglo State Forest, and police divers joined the hundred-strong team. They plunged into twenty dams, but found nothing they could connect to the crime. Meanwhile, senior New South Wales detectives looked at the cases of other missing backpackers on their files — particularly those of James Gibson and Deborah Everist from Melbourne, Gabor Neugebauer and his girlfriend, Anja Habschied, from Germany, and Simone Schmidl, also from Germany. There were scores of others, some of them foreigners, who were missing or who had overstayed their tourist visas. Included on the list was a 22-year-old Japanese visitor, Naoka Onda, who, on 1 June 1987, left her passport and most of her belongings in a flat she had been staying at in Sydney's Elizabeth Bay and flew to Queensland for a five-day holiday. She spent one night in a hotel there before checking out in the company of a man. She was never seen again.

Detectives raised the possibility of connections between these disappearances, but Sergeant Peter Marcon, head of the New South Wales police Missing Persons Unit, was the first to admit that there was nothing to indicate any strong links between the murdered Britons and the other travellers who were still unaccounted for. There were, of course, some similarities, but not enough to draw any firm conclusions.

The most obvious link was that the Germans, the Victorians, the Britons and the Japanese girl had all vanished after leaving their accommodation in Sydney. Only the movements of Ms Onda did not fit in with the pattern of the others — all of whom had disappeared after setting out to hitch-hike in a south-westerly direction from Sydney, as far as the information available suggested.

While detectives sifted through the missing persons cases, hoping to find more definite connections, Caroline's father finally found the strength, despite his grief, to make a public comment from England.

'Caroline,' Ian Clarke said, 'had been looking for a change of direction and hoped the trip would be a good way of seeing the world. But in doing so she saw the darker side of human nature. She thoroughly enjoyed herself and now we have to look back on the good, happy times she did have. She was full of adventure and did what she wanted to do.'

News of the British girls' fate swept through the backpacker hostels of not only Australia, but the world. British newspapers gave the story prominent coverage, and suddenly every parent in the United Kingdom who had a son or daughter on a budget holiday in Australia was worried. Young travellers wrote or phoned home to assure their families they were all right, and to point out that Australia was still a safe place in which to hitch-hike. The basis of their argument was that all the tourist books and literature published for backpackers said that travellers Down Under did not face the same dangers as those who ventured onto the highways in other countries.

But the managers and owners of Australian backpacker hostels agreed that it was time to be more cautious. Apart from not wanting their lucrative industry to be adversely affected, they agreed that until the perpetrator of the crime was brought to justice he — or they — was still 'out there', and could be looking for more victims. Backpacker hostel operators agreed that it was time to start a database, with owners being required to keep a registry of all tourists and their immediate travel plans. It was also agreed that an educational campaign should be launched, advising the 150,000 backpackers who visit Australia each year that hitch-hiking was no longer advisable. Warnings would be placed in travel magazines, and posters of missing backpackers would be distributed around the country. In addition, the Backpackers' Resorts of Australia organisation decided to work in conjunction with coach companies to ensure that popular destinations were well serviced by buses.

Despite the initial enthusiasm for a registry, Sergeant Marcon at the Missing Persons Unit, and some of the hostel operators, accepted that this would be difficult to implement. Backpackers were usually young people setting out from an organised life in their own country — they were looking for adventure and freedom from the restraints of home. It seemed unlikely that most backpackers would want to be checked up on in this way.

For members of the South West Region Major Crime Squad the murders of the British women led to some hope that if they could find their killer or killers, or at least pick up his or their trail, they might find answers to the other missing backpackers, even though there were no strong connections.

Over the next few weeks, evidence was gathered in great detail.

Filling-station employees at Bulli Pass, on the road to Wollongong, south of Sydney, claimed they saw the British women getting into a white truck on the day they had last been seen. From another 'witness', there came a report of the two women being seen sharing a meal with a young man, beside a white Volkswagen Kombi van in a picnic ground near Bowral in the Southern Highlands.

Every scrap of information was sifted through again and again. The Volkswagen particularly interested detectives. Who was the young man, presumably the driver, that the women were seen with in the picnic ground beside the Box Vale Tramway Walking Track? Detectives put out a statewide, then a nationwide, appeal for him to come forward so he could be eliminated from their inquiries. When there was no immediate response, the arduous task of tracking down every white Volkswagen Kombi owner began.

Detective Senior Constable Grosse was still prepared to link the deaths of the British women with the other missing travellers, and he also believed that others could have been killed and dumped in the forest. The killer or killers had obviously not expected the young women to be found — and may have thought the same about other bodies if he or they had been using the forest as a backpackers' burial ground.

Centimetre by centimetre, police cadets and detectives continued to scour the forest floor, while using the boulder as a central marker. Each man and woman was aware that behind the next bush or termite mound they could find a vital clue or make another grim discovery. But it was an enormous task. With so many gullies, hills and creeks, an army would be needed to cover the forest properly, and there was still nothing more than speculation to suggest that this was anything other than a 'one-off'.

The search eventually wound down. Grosse and his colleagues were satisfied that as far as Caroline and Joanne's murders were concerned they had covered the place of their execution as thoroughly as was humanly possible. What they needed now was a breakthrough — but they knew it was likely to come only as a result of hard work, logic and patience.

CHAPTER FIVE

Sheets of rain swept across the Southern Highlands, but the mist held its grip on the hillsides on that Sunday afternoon in September 1992. Deep in the Belanglo Forest, a tall figure in white stepped through the shrubbery. At the log where Caroline Clarke had been found, the priest, his robes soaked through, paused and bent his head. But at that moment, the man rather than the priest was overwhelmed by the wickedness that had taken place here — and instead of making a silent prayer, he fought against an oath.

'So much evil,' he whispered through clenched teeth. 'So much evil.'

Someone had draped a Union Jack over the log in readiness for the service that Father Gray would soon be conducting. Brushing the rain from his face, he turned and walked the 30 metres to the rock where Joanne Walters' body had been discovered. Here, the Welsh flag, the Red Dragon, had been laid on the stone and flowers had been placed in the shallow grave. The heavy rain clouds only added to the sombre mood, and Father Gray had to take a deep breath and compose himself as he remembered why he was here. They had called on him to drive away the evil, and rekindle the light in lives that had been plunged into darkness.

Gradually the clearing began to fill with police officers and members of the Sydney Welsh Choir and the Australian–Welsh Friendship Club, who had volunteered to sing hymns at the service of remembrance. Some of the vehicles that brought these people to the forest had become bogged on the rain-sodden track, and they had to walk the last 80 metres. Then, as they stood chatting under their umbrellas and the priest lit candles, a silence fell.

Ray and Gill Walters had arrived.

As the couple walked across the carpet of broken twigs and fallen leaves where their daughter had taken her last steps, the sun suddenly broke through, its golden shafts brightening the path ahead. Several people looked skywards as if expecting to see something more.

Gill had trouble walking. She clung to Ray's arm and appeared to stumble here and there, but there was determination on her face as she headed towards the assembled group. This was the bravest thing she had ever had to do.

'We have to give back to the forest the peace it has always known,' Ray had told his wife a few days earlier. 'In doing that, Joanne will herself be able to rest in peace. It's going to be hard for both of us. But we must try to forget what has happened and go through this as a cleansing.'

Yet as they walked slowly forward, Gill stopping for a few seconds as if to gather strength, the questions still raced through their minds. How had Joanne spent her last minutes in this place? Had she cried? Had she been brave ... defiant even? Or, as she walked over this same patch of stony ground, had she stepped out in innocence, unaware of her imminent fate?

As Ray and Gill stood with their 18-year-old son, Jonathan, and Joanne's aunt, Maureen Williams-Jones, Father Gray addressed the congregation of fifty.

'We have come here today, where something wicked

happened, so that this place can be peaceful again and its memories put to rest. Where evil is very strong, and it has been in this place, it does not have the last word. Ray wanted me to say one thing specially. He wants everyone to know the girls loved this place, they loved Australia. They had a good holiday until this thing happened.

'When I first met Ray and Gill I was overwhelmed by the positive way they greeted me, the enormous courage they displayed. I went to give them help and some peace — and pray God I did — but I came away from them feeling really quite inspired. They want justice. Oh, they are angry — but their anger is a holy anger, and the justice they require is nothing that God does not want as much. We pray for that justice and also pray for that person or persons, and pray that God might have mercy on their souls, that they might repent and turn to him and yet be saved; because no-one is beyond the reach of God.'

As the sound of the choir singing 'The Lord's my Shepherd' mingled with birdsong, the grieving couple and their family and friends made their way to the moss-covered sandstone rock where Joanne had lain. Ray bent down under the draped flag and placed a bunch of daffodils at the spot, then stood and wrapped his arm around his wife, as each of them was engulfed in silent prayer.

A few minutes later they stepped slowly through patches of tiny native flowers to the log where Caroline had been found. There Gill, along with Caroline's cousin from Adelaide, Nicola Burge, laid more flowers. Choir members wept as they sang: 'When you walk through a storm, keep your head up high ...'

But through the sadness there was a sense of relief. As Ray gripped the hands of all who had made the journey to the forest, he spoke to one of the mourners.

'Both of those girls loved Australia and I feel we had to come here to say goodbye at the last place they came to. It has helped Gill tremendously to come here. It has given her and me a great deal of inner peace. It came over both of us as we stood there.'

Gill smiled softly through her tears as Ray added: 'We have gained so much strength by coming here today. We have put evil behind us.'

As the Welsh couple made their way back up the track they were watched by two men in light-grey suits. One was Detective Senior Constable Grosse. The other, almost a foot taller, was Detective Inspector Bob Godden, who was now working with Grosse on the investigation. Both men knew they had to come. Not to look for a killer or killers compelled to return to the scene of the crime, but to share the grief.

'This makes me more determined than ever,' said Godden. 'Those people are relying on us.'

In the clearing, with only a few members of the choir remaining, Father Gray closed his prayer book. The sun still shone through the gum trees. The cleansing, it seemed, had been completed. But neither the priest nor anyone else who had prayed there that afternoon could have known the horror that remained.

At the Australian Federal Police Forensic Services Division in Canberra, Dr James Robertson, 44, a softly spoken Scots-born Bachelor of Science and Doctor of Philosophy, laid a single hair under a microscope. It had been found in the partly closed hand of Joanne Walters. The hair might have come from her killer, and it was his job to find out.

He was well qualified for the task ahead. In 1976 he had joined the Forensic Science Unit of the University of Strathclyde, Glasgow, as a lecturer in forensic science, before moving to State Forensic Science in Adelaide in 1985. From then until 1989 he carried out a wide range of forensic casework before moving to Canberra and his current position as Assistant Secretary and Head of the Forensic Services Division of the Australian Federal Police. He had carried out forensic investigations on behalf of prosecution and defence agencies in Australia and several overseas countries and presented evidence on numerous occasions, as well as publishing scientific papers and books.

The division's forensic scientists in Canberra follow a strict procedure for examining hair. They firstly compare samples with a known source — taken, for example, from the body of a murder victim. Usually five or more source hairs are used to cover a range of lengths and colours. The shaft profiles (the shape and length) of the selected hairs are then recorded before the hairs are placed, usually individually, on microscope slides. The colour of the hair and condition of the root and tip are then noted. After completing an examination of the known hair, the questionable hair is then examined separately in precisely the same way.

Dr Robertson and his team of scientists knew from experience it was unlikely that a known hair and a questioned hair would be exactly the same along their entire length. In order to conclude that two hairs could have had a common origin, they should show the same degree of variation, and be indistinguishable at several points along their respective lengths.

Pathologist Bradhurst had snipped a few locks of hair from Joanne Walters' head. These were placed in screw-cap containers and sent to Dr Robertson. The forensic scientist randomly chose a few hairs, ranging in length from 5 to 30 centimetres, from the samples sent to him by the pathologist. Many of the hair roots were atrophied, a condition often seen in hairs that have been removed from a decomposing body. Overall, the hairs were mid- to dark-reddish brown, with the colour of individual hair shafts varying from a true brown at the root end to a reddish brown further along the shaft. In longer hairs, the colour became paler towards the tip.

Dr Robertson had also been sent pubic hair, the roots of which had degenerated or were atrophied. Overall, the hairs were mid- to dark-reddish brown, and the colour of individual hair shafts varied from colourless to mid- to deep-reddish brown.

The forensic scientist then returned to the eleven hairs that had been found in Joanne's right hand. Of these, two were head hairs which appeared to be in the range of Joanne's own head hair. But as his tests continued, he found evidence that he knew would be of great interest to the men from homicide — six of the hairs were very fine, pale brown head hairs. And, in his opinion, they did not match the range of Joanne's head hairs. He would tell the police that if the known head hair sample from the British woman was representative, then it was very unlikely that these six hairs he had put under his microscope came from her.

Two of the remaining hairs were short body hairs. He had not been given any known body hair samples, however, and so was unable to say whether or not they were from the dead woman. The final sample was a pubic hair that was an unnatural blue-grey colour. Dr Robertson felt there was every possibility that the colour was the result of exposure to the environment. Because of this deterioration, he believed that establishing an origin would be virtually impossible.

But he had given the police something positive to work on — six fine pale-brown head hairs that were not from the murdered woman. Were they from her murderer? He certainly couldn't answer that. But he could say with reasonable, although not total, certainty that they were of Caucasian origin — from someone who was of essentially white descent, as opposed to negroid or Asian. If the police eventually arrested a suspect he would be able to compare the suspect's head hair with the six he had isolated.

It would also be important to establish that the six unknown head hairs had not come from Joanne's friend, Caroline Clarke. The women had travelled together, and probably met their fate at about the same time.

But Dr Robertson first had to complete his examination of other hair taken from Joanne's clothing. Four pubic hairs were found in or on her jeans. Comparing them under the microscope with known pubic hairs taken from the body, he concluded that the recovered hairs could have come from her. Two hairs had been removed from the front of the jeans, but these were very short fragments and badly disintegrated — in too poor a condition for him to make any conclusions about them.

Six hairs had been found on the front and rear of Joanne's shirt. One was a short body hair of indeterminable origin, two were almost colourless head hairs, and the remaining three were head hairs that seemed to be in the range of the dead woman's own hair.

So Robertson had discovered nothing more that could help the police. But the six head hairs might well, he decided, be all that they needed to pinpoint the killer once a suspect had been found.

Dr Robertson then turned to the hair samples collected from Caroline Clarke. As source hair, he had been given hairs from her head and pubic region. The root ends of many of the head hairs were atrophied, but in individual hairs he was able to see that the colour varied from a pale-brown at the root end to a more yellow-brown towards the tip. The pubic hair was a light- to mid-brown colour, varying along individual hair shafts from colourless at the root to a light- to mid-dark brown at the tip.

Having established a pattern for Caroline's source hair, the scientist examined the fifteen hairs recovered from her right hand. They varied from fragments of 1 to 2 centimetres in length, to hairs that were nearly 17 centimetres long. All of the strands fell within the colour range of Caroline's head hair, and Dr Robertson could find nothing to indicate that they were from a third party. And he also determined that the strands found in Joanne's hand did not include Caroline's hair.

So the only clue — or rather mystery — that he could give the police from his tests and observations were six light-brown hairs, the source of which remained unknown.

'We're all going to have to wait until someone is arrested and I can make a comparison of head hairs before I can do anything more to assist in your investigations,' Dr Robertson reported to Grosse in a phone call.

At Goulburn police headquarters, Grosse tucked his chin into his hand and sighed. 'Patience,' he told himself again. 'Patience ...'

Paul Douglas, a machine worker at the Boral industrial depot located a short distance from Sydney's famous Rosehill Racecourse, had read about the discovery of the bodies in the morning paper, then, like many other workers at the huge complex, followed the progress of the police investigation. It was on all the front pages and given prominence on the six o'clock TV news. He chatted to his mate, Paul Miller, about it all.

Douglas had known Miller for about three years and they'd become even better mates since Miller had started working the same shift in 1991. Douglas got on all right with Miller, although he was amazed at how the other man was able to keep working considering all the dope he smoked.

Paul Miller was a burly, keep-fit fanatic — he could do 100 press-ups at a time. He sometimes grew a moustache, sometimes a beard, sometimes made his hair darker with a rinse, at other times a lighter brown.

Miller would bring a bong to work and would draw cannabis through it. Douglas could always tell when Miller had been hooked up; normally he was a pretty quiet kind of bloke, didn't say much at all, but after using the bong, well, he could talk virtually non-stop for eight hours. Rabbit on about anything during their meal breaks, or if work was a bit slack … cars, women, bloody politicians, you name it, Miller wouldn't stop. But only if he was on cannabis. With the odd nip of whisky thrown in for good measure, if the smell on his breath was anything to go by.

Miller was pretty audacious, too. With a handful of other workers, he would swing it so that he could finish his shift an hour or two earlier than his official clock-off would show. It was just a matter of getting someone else to clock off for him. Just as he would cover for someone else.

Still, Miller was a good friend. He was always on hand to fix up a mate's car if there was anything wrong with it and Douglas enjoyed having a beer or two with him after work. Once, Miller drove him to his brother Walter's home in the Southern Highlands and they both had a pleasant afternoon with Walter and Walter's wife, Lisa.

Miller also took him to a bush property he'd bought not far from Walter's. 'I'm going to build a house here,' he said. Douglas was impressed, although he thought it was a long way from the main road, some 40 kilometres or so.

Meanwhile, Miller was living at his mother's place in Guildford, which Douglas was familiar with because he'd taken his car there for Miller to have a look at.

In September 1992 they were both on the afternoon shift working with some equipment called an unloader and Miller had obviously been on the bong, the way he was talking incessantly. They started chatting about the topic that was running hot in the papers, the discovery of the British girls' bodies. One of their mates was there, too, but he wandered off, leaving just Douglas and Miller.

'There are two Germans out there,' said Miller, the drug driving his words. 'They haven't found them yet.'

Douglas didn't know what to think about that. His friend had obviously been on the bong. He didn't reply.

Some two or three weeks later, they were working at the unloader again during the afternoon shift, Miller showing all the telltale signs of having been drawing on his bong. They talked a bit more about the murdered British backpackers. 'There are more bodies out there,' said Miller. 'They haven't found them all.'

Douglas remembered what Miller had said once before. He shrugged. What was he expected to say?

The two men continued their daily tasks or, in Miller's case, his frequent rorts, smoking dope, drinking alcohol and getting off work early if he wasn't covering for someone else. Miller's mood swung from quiet to talkative, which became a characteristic of the man. He was happy to talk about anything if his mind was fuelled.

One day, in the meal room, they got chatting about rape cases. Miller's mood seemed to be 'normal'. The two men agreed that rapists were getting off pretty lightly because the justice system, well, it just wasn't up to it. 'Stabbing a woman is like cutting a loaf of bread,' Miller suddenly said, for no apparent reason.

Douglas was disturbed by the comment. There was nothing frivolous about it. Miller seemed to be deadly serious.

Under the influence of cannabis, Miller chatted a lot to all the fellows at work. One man who had his ear was Des Butler, who trained him at the Boral industrial plant after being introduced to Miller there in November 1989. Like Douglas, Butler became friendly with Miller, whom he found easy to get along with, although he was well aware of the other man's penchant for drawing on the bong fairly regularly.

They had a few drinks together after work and on one occasion Miller asked if he'd like to go out shooting with him. As with Douglas, Miller took Butler to his brother Wally's place, where he also met Wally's wife. Then Miller took him to his bush property; showed him around, talked about the house he was going to build there.

Butler also read in the papers about the British women being found in the forest. During an early evening shift shortly after the publicity, while he and Miller were working together at the unloader and Miller was affected by hashish, Miller said during a general conversation about the murders and about other missing backpackers: 'I know who killed the Germans.'

Butler didn't say anything. He just didn't believe his workmate. He'd been on the bong, hadn't he?

CHAPTER SIX

The murders of Caroline Clarke and Joanne Walters shocked the nation. There was a general feeling that, particularly to restore Australia's reputation as a safe place for tourists, the killer or killers of the young overseas travellers had to be caught — and quickly! But detectives had little to go on apart from the width of the stab wounds, which gave some indication of the size of the knife used on Joanne, and the bullets. The ballistics experts worked overtime, concluding from the spent bullets that some, at least, had passed through one barrel and then another — a sign that a silencer had been used. More work would have to be carried out to establish the type of weapon that had fired the bullets, and the only clue would come from the impact of the firing pin on the cartridge. Weeks of tests lay ahead.

Almost one year later, on Tuesday 5 October 1993, John Springett, a resident of the Southern Highlands, strolled through the sparsely furnished rooms of the old weatherboard house that orienteering groups use as a base in the Belanglo State Forest. Located beside the track running into the forest, the house had been fitted out with a kitchen and double bunks, and could accommodate twenty people at a push if it was necessary to stay the night during an orienteering contest or mapping exercises. As treasurer of the Southern Highlands Orienteering Club, Springett took it upon himself to keep a check on the old red-roofed building. At around 1.30 pm he heard a vehicle pull up and wandered outside to investigate.

'You got a phone here, mate?' asked the driver, a man in his mid 30s.

'I've got a mobile,' said Springett. 'Something up?'

'There certainly is. Jeez! I got a skull wrapped up in a towel on the front seat,' said the man. 'I was looking for firewood and bang, I came right across it.'

Springett handed the man his phone and listened as he reported his grim find to the Bowral police. When the conversation finished, Springett started walking towards the driver's red ute to have a look at the object, but was interrupted by the ringing of his phone. It was the police, ringing back to check that the call had been genuine. Springett told them that although he hadn't seen the skull, the man appeared to be deadly serious.

As they waited for the police to arrive, Springett learned that the man often went into the bush looking for firewood. 'I can imagine the police get all kinds of suspect calls, and I didn't want them to treat this as a hoax,' the stranger explained. 'I thought that if I marked the place and brought the skull out to show them, they'd know for sure that I wasn't mucking them around.'

Springett reckoned that made a lot of sense, although he wondered what the police might think about the skull being moved.

'I tell you, I'm really glad I was alone,' the ute driver went on. 'I've got two young girls who love to go bushwalking, and I wouldn't have wanted them with me when I found it.'

At Bowral Police Station, where the police had returned to more routine work as the months had drifted by without any strong leads to the killer or killers of the two British women, the immediate reaction was predictable. Another backpacker.

In a replay of the activity of eleven months earlier, local policemen Senior Constable Christopher Roberson and Detective Constable Stephen Murphy sped to the forest, where the ute driver was waiting. He introduced himself as Bruce Pryor, a potter who lived in the district, handed the skull over, then led the two police officers deep into the forest, passing a track leading to the place where Joanne and Caroline had been found.

'Just through there,' said Pryor, pointing towards the base of a tall tree.

Although a thorough search had taken place about a kilometre away, around the bodies of the British women, Roberson and Murphy became aware as they made their way through the wattles and gums just how easy it would be to walk past something unusual here without seeing it — even something as large as a body. If a body was in a decomposed state and covered in bracken, you would need virtually to trip over it to know it was there. And this was a bare skull — indicating that it had lain in the forest for much longer than the British women's bodies — and the stench of death would have long faded away.

Pryor led the policemen to where he had found the skull.

'You shouldn't have moved it, mate,' he was told. 'You should have left it exactly where it was.'

'But I can show you the exact spot,' said Pryor, in no doubt about the police annoyance.

The officers looked at the place where the skull had been found — the ground was slightly depressed and discoloured. But the skull was not all that Pryor had found. He had also discovered a human bone — a femur.

'My wife's a radiographer, so I know something about

human anatomy,' he said. 'As soon as I saw the bone, I knew what it was.'

The policemen relayed an urgent radio message to Sydney and other police stations in the area, and later that afternoon Detective Senior Constable Andrew Grosse returned to the now familiar forest.

'I'm getting to know this place well — for all the wrong reasons,' said Grosse as he greeted other police. 'I just hope this is the last time we find anything like this. One thing, if we find more bones and they're hidden under sticks, we can probably look at a connection with the English girls.'

With others, he began searching the area where the skull had been discovered and, as expected, they found a number of sticks and bones. From decaying clothing collected nearby — including what appeared to be a summer frock — the police became reasonably certain that the remains were those of a woman.

Three female backpackers were still missing, but only one, Simone Schmidl, had been travelling alone. If this *wasn't* Simone, there was a chance the body was either that of missing Victorian backpacker Deborah Everist, or German traveller Anja Habschied.

In the cases of the two couples, the body of the dead woman's travelling companion could be close by. These first police officers on the scene recalled how the British women had been found — covered in twigs and lying 30 metres from one another. Was it possible that another body lay within a similar radius of this latest find?

As the site around the skeletal remains was taped off, the police fanned out into the forest. Within two hours, at 4 pm, a scientific detective made the discovery that they had all been expecting. A second skeleton was found about 25 metres from the first. Lying near it was an old piece of dark material which looked like it could be from a hat — could this be part of the black hat that James Gibson, Deborah

Everist's boyfriend, usually wore? It was decided, however, to leave everything untouched and make a thorough examination of the area at first light on the following day.

On the following morning, Wednesday 6 October 1993, Andrew Grosse helped to carefully remove the undergrowth at what was thought to be James Gibson's burial site. The body, reduced to a skeleton, was wearing blue jeans and a green shirt and was lying on its left side in a foetal position, with the head tucked in against the upper chest. There was a ring on a finger and a chain and pendant around the neck.

'We've got enough here to give us an early identification,' Grosse told his colleagues as they stood in a semicircle around the remains. From above, birds sang, but hardly anyone noticed. The detective sighed. 'I don't think it's too outrageous to assume that the other bones will be those of the girlfriend, Deborah Everist.'

At the other crude grave, Grosse stared down at bones and a number of vertebrae. It seemed certain that the remains had been disturbed, possibly by wild animals. There was no skull, as this had been found elsewhere by Bruce Pryor. A silver-coloured charm necklace with a crucifix attached and a multi-coloured stone bracelet led Grosse to believe that he could well be looking at Deborah's remains.

At the South West Regional Crime Headquarters, near Parramatta, in Sydney's west, Detective Sergeant Steve McLennan was sickened by the grim news from the Southern Highlands. He had initially been put in charge of the specific inquiry into the Clarke–Walters murders — a separate role to that of Grosse, who was embracing what was turning out to be a mass-killing inquiry.

McLennan was also concerned that the double-murder investigation into the British deaths had been long and slow, and no firm leads had emerged. He understood how difficult it was for people to cast their minds back five months — between the time that the British women had disappeared and when their bodies were found. Now, with the latest discoveries appearing to be the bodies of the missing Victorians, who had not been heard of since the end of December 1989 — almost four years ago — they would be asking the impossible.

Although disturbed by the discovery of two more bodies, McLennan was well aware that this new development could help the investigation into the British women's murders. There would now be more to work with, more chance of establishing a pattern, and more hope of finding matching clues. Killers made mistakes — such as unwittingly leaving behind 'evidential fingerprints' in the form of bullet casings, the size and type of blade used in a stabbing, and the severity and angle of a knife thrust.

On 6 October, McLennan, a burly figure in his mid 40s and distinguishable by his shock of silvery-white hair, walked through the gum trees with the local Coroner, Mr Ian McCrae. They crouched down to examine the two sets of remains that had been under guard through the night. McLennan estimated that the distance between these bodies and where the British women had been found was between 750 metres and 1 kilometre.

'I'm not assuming anything,' McLennan told McCrae, 'but it looks like there has to be a connection between the two pairs of bodies.'

'I agree,' said McCrae, 'but I think we both know we have to keep an open mind until firm evidence can be found. In the meantime, I have no doubts whatsoever in concluding that we're looking at two murder victims.'

Carefully, they walked through the scrub. Scraps of clothing lay around the area, including some shredded, knotted pantyhose. Had one of the victims been tied up? The knots in the nylon suggested that this might well have been the case.

McLennan stared down at the stripped corpse of what

was believed to be Deborah Everist. 'I hate to think what these poor folks went through,' he said.

As scores of police moved into the forest and started searching — turning literally every leaf over — in what McLennan ordered to be a thorough 'heads down, bums up' operation, a young man driving home through Melbourne tuned into the news on his car radio. When 25-year-old Tim Everist heard that two more bodies had been found in the Belanglo State Forest, his reaction was instant: 'This is it. It's them.' For nearly four years he and his family had expected this news ... four terrible years of anxiety since his sister Deborah and her boyfriend, James, had vanished after setting out from Sydney to hitch-hike back to Melbourne.

Tim's mind went back to the time when the young couple were making their plans to head off for Sydney in December 1989. He'd heard how James had given his mother a reassuring grin as he packed his rucksack on that balmy evening just after Christmas.

'We'll be okay,' James had said in answer to his mother's concerns about hitch-hiking. 'It's really safe if you travel as a couple. The problem with you, Mum, is that you've been watching too much TV.'

But Peggy Gibson patted the family dog, Perot, and remained unconvinced. It was true that James travelled frequently, using his smile and his easy-going charm to win him a free ride, and he'd never run into any problems. Now, with the Christmas and Boxing Day festivities over, he was preparing to head off again from the Gibson family's home at Moorooduc, a beachside community on the curved finger of land known as the Mornington Peninsula, south of Melbourne. Peggy wasn't at all happy about it — this time he would be undertaking one of his longest journeys, hitch-hiking first to Sydney, 855 kilometres away, before thumbing his way back down the highway to a conservation rally at

75

Albury, midway between the two cities. And he'd be taking Debbie, who had never hitch-hiked in her life, with him.

James was a familiar figure at conservation and anti-logging protests. He was tall and slim and was made even more distinctive by his long brown hair worn in a ponytail, and his black wide-brimmed felt hat — a hat which caused some people to liken him to a rangy gunslinger from a Clint Eastwood Western. Like many of his generation, James was determined to save the planet — to stop wood-chipping, prevent the slaughter of whales, and keep Australia green. Conservation was his guiding light. He went on wilderness walks, camped out in the bush, read constantly about environmental issues, and fought bushfires as a volunteer with the country fire brigade.

James was also an adept painter who had adorned the walls of his bedroom with his works, and he'd proudly shown his mother some of his modern clay sculptures. He was 19 years old and looking forward to starting a sculpture course at the Chisholm Institute of Technology. Yes, James really had his life together.

But, as Tim later learned, something was worrying Peggy Gibson. She couldn't define it, but a niggling feeling told her that James, for all his experience, shouldn't be hitch-hiking this time. But she'd also conceded that maybe he was right. She'd been watching too much TV, and had perhaps seen too many fictitious murders and kidnappings. And the real ones mostly happened overseas — wasn't Australia the safest place in the world to hitch a free ride? This was one of the reasons why low-budget backpacker hostels were opening up all over the country. Besides, as her youngest son had reminded her more times than she could remember, he would not be travelling alone. Debbie would be with him, and she had a sensible head on her shoulders.

Tim choked back tears as he drove through Melbourne, as a vision of his bubbly sister danced in his mind.

Petite, dark-haired and attractive, Debbie had grown up in the city of Frankston, also on the Mornington Peninsula. She was 19 when she disappeared, the same age as James, and although sharing the same interests as her boyfriend, she was more outspoken. With her striking blue eyes ringed with dark mascara, a cute fringe, trademark dangling earrings, and bubbly personality, Debbie's friends always described her as vivacious.

Despite the contrast in the couple's personalities, the Everist family and their friends regarded them as a perfect match. As their bond grew, so did the friendship between their parents — along with a curious telepathic interaction between the mothers. As Peggy Gibson became increasingly concerned about James making this particular trip, Pat Everist was also worried about her daughter setting out on the venture. And that was in spite of Debbie's telling her that she and James would be getting a lift with friends once they'd reached Melbourne by train.

Pat had a lot on her mind on that evening of 27 December as Debbie sorted through the clothes she would take, picking out a handful of summer dresses to pack into her small overnight bag. While Pat was inexplicably concerned about Debbie's journey, she also had to carry the burden of knowing that her husband was terminally ill with cancer.

'It's only a week, Mum,' said Debbie, 'and then I'll be home. I promise I'll call often, so you'll know I'm okay.'

Tim later discovered that just before Debbie left she made a quick decision — to borrow his sleeping bag in his absence. It was quite new, and green with a cream lining: she probably thought, he told himself, that he wouldn't mind because it would be for only a few days.

On the following morning, 28 December 1989, James and Debbie were driven to the Frankston railway station by their respective parents. They all arrived at 9 am, as arranged, and the mothers watched with suppressed anxiety as the teenagers bought their tickets for Melbourne, where they would really begin the journey to Sydney. As usual, James was wearing his black hat, and he carried his red pack. Inside was a small camping stove; the canvas fly he used instead of a tent; his new 35-millimetre camera, an all-black Ricoh with a 50-millimetre lens, which he'd bought to take pictures of his trip and the rally; and some clean clothes. For security, he'd marked his name on the top of the backpack and also inside.

It was the middle of the Australian summer and Debbie, aware that it would be hot on the highway, had decided to set out in a cornflower-blue floral cotton dress. As far as clothes went, she was certainly different from James — he liked to dress for the bush, Debbie for the town. Anyway, neither of them expected to be tramping for miles along the Hume Highway that ran between Melbourne and Sydney. With the school holidays well under way, there was a lot of traffic about and they hoped to find an easy lift and be in Sydney by that evening.

True to her word, Debbie phoned home the next day. Mrs Everist was watering the garden when the phone rang.

'Hi, Mum. Just calling to say hello and that I'm okay.'

'How was your trip?' asked Mrs Everist. 'Are you enjoying yourself?'

'We're having great fun. We're making the most of our time. We've already been out on a boat around the harbour.'

In the background, Mrs Everist could hear James talking to someone.

'I'll call you tomorrow, Mum, to let you know what our movements are. Take care. Love you.'

But Debbie didn't call. Mrs Everist rang Mrs Gibson. James hadn't phoned home either. Despite their initial concerns, both families assumed that the young couple were having such a good time in Sydney that they just hadn't got around to making the phone calls. And they had preparations to make for the return trip to Albury for the conservation rally.

When three, and then four, days passed with no further phone calls, however, Peggy Gibson, Pat Everist and their families became concerned.

'Any news?' Mrs Everist asked James' mother.

'Nothing,' said Peggy Gibson. 'We can only assume that there's no phone where they are. We'll probably get a call as soon as they can get to a phone.'

Every time the phone rang, they expected it to be James or Debbie. But there was still no word.

One week went by, and then two. By now Peggy and Pat were beginning to panic. They called each other frequently, hoping that one of them had heard something.

'Should we call the police?' asked Mrs Everist, noticing the concern in her voice.

'It's difficult to know what to do,' said Mrs Gibson. 'If we call the police in and they're all right, we've wasted everyone's time. But it's a worry.'

Like many other parents faced with a similar dilemma of sons and daughters not staying in touch, they were reluctant to involve the authorities unnecessarily — and end up embarrassed because their children had been perfectly all right, and had simply been enjoying themselves so much that they'd neglected to phone.

Peggy and her husband Ray decided to set a deadline: their daughter Mary Ann's wedding on 21 January. James had been looking forward to the event, and he would certainly be back in time. But it was with heavy hearts that the couple watched their daughter say 'I do'. James had not turned up.

At the Everist home, Pat watched her husband's health decline as he worried about Debbie and his cancer advanced relentlessly. Pat and Tim knew that something must have happened to Debbie — she was fully aware of how sick her stepfather was, and should certainly have called to ask about his health. It was definitely time to call the police.

The Gibson and Everist families provided the Missing Persons Unit with all the relevant details — photographs, physical descriptions, and what the young people had been wearing when they had last seen them. They also described what other clothes had been taken, as well as James' camping gear and camera.

The families were all too aware, however, that thousands of youngsters vanished every year, and that the faces of the missing peered out from police station notice boards. Some had been unheard of for years; others had only recently been added to the array of black and white portraits. These were the people for whom there was genuine concern: thousands of other names remained in the files. The police hoped that these were kids who had merely run away from home, and would eventually turn up alive somewhere.

Tim Everist had been living away from home, but moved back in with his family to help his mother nurse her dying husband. Meanwhile, Pat prayed that her daughter would call to brighten those dark days. Friends rallied round, copying photographs of the couple and distributing them up and down the highway on pamphlets that boldly featured the word 'MISSING'. Shopkeepers, truckies and postmen looked at the faces and scratched their heads. No, they couldn't help, but they'd certainly keep an eye out for them.

Three months passed before Peggy Gibson received a phone call in March 1990 that set her heart pounding. The news was ominous. Someone passing through the ruggedly beautiful Galston Gorge, near the northern Sydney suburb of Hornsby, had come across a red backpack. It had contained only a tin of sardines and, although the area where James' name and address was written had been roughly cut from the top of the bag, the same details were written inside on the bottom. The bag was passed to the police at Hornsby.

Stories appeared in the newspapers about the discovery and the link with the missing Victorians. In Hornsby Michael James, a company director, was alerted to the articles by his wife — with good reason. On 31 December 1989 Mr James, a keen cyclist, had been riding up a steep narrow hill running through the gorge when he found a Ricoh camera dumped and damaged in a ditch. He had kept it, but had made no use of it. Mr James' wife put two and two together and suggested that the camera was probably linked to the discarded backpack. He called the police.

Detectives showed the camera and backpack to Mr Gibson, who travelled from Victoria to look over the items. Sadly he conceded that whatever fate that befallen the young man, and probably Debbie, it had struck within twenty-four hours of her making the 29 December phone call to her mother.

Police cadets clambered over rocks and pushed their way through the lush undergrowth of the gorge. They had been told to be prepared to find two bodies. But this initial hunt revealed no further clues to help solve the mystery of the missing couple, and senior officers decided to mount a full-scale search of the rugged region.

The detectives involved in the case remained open to all possibilities, however. Had the couple fallen to their deaths while climbing cliffs, with their gear later plundered by someone who had found it? They might have been victims of foul play. They could have committed suicide in a bizarre youthful pact. Perhaps they had decided not to return to Melbourne for some unknown reason, and dumped their belongings to avoid being identified. Based on the strong relationship that the young people had with their families, the last scenario was almost instantly dismissed. So, too, was any suggestion of a suicide pact, given that they had so much to live for and had shown no such suicidal tendencies. This left the police with two possibilities: accidental death — or murder.

As plans were being made to start the big search — involving 160 police, volunteer firemen and the State Emergency Services — black clouds rolled in and torrential rain lashed the gorge. It was far too dangerous for anyone to tackle the slippery slopes in those conditions. The search was postponed. A few days later, the same thing happened again. Finally, in April, the search got under way, but nothing was found that could shed any light on the missing couple. They had simply disappeared into thin air.

Peggy Gibson was not content to sit back at home and wait: she wanted to see the area for herself and perhaps come up with some suggestions. She travelled from Melbourne to Sydney, and stared down over Galston Gorge's eucalypt-covered slopes and steep cliffs into its gullies and creeks. 'How could they find anything down there?' she thought.

Like the Gibsons, Tim and his mother and friends refused to give up hope. Pat Everist, now grieving over the death of her husband after he had finally succumbed to cancer, softly smiled her thanks as everyone assured her that they would keep searching, keep asking around, until it was certain that Debbie and James would not be coming home.

'We can't just give up hope that they'll come home,' Mrs Gibson told her husband.

At the Everist home, Tim was telling his mother the same thing. 'We'll swamp the area with requests for help,' he added. 'Somebody must have seen them. Perhaps someone knows something but hasn't read the papers or seen it on TV. We can't rely on chance — we've got to try harder ourselves.'

More pamphlets were prepared. T-shirts were printed with coloured photographs of the teenagers, and these were distributed with the help of friends and volunteers along the east coast of New South Wales. The families were now banking on James' distinctive black hat as the trigger to spur someone's memory. Although the police tried to hide their pessimism from the two families, they did warn them that they were becoming less optimistic of finding the couple alive.

Once or twice Peggy tried to face up to the possibility that James and his girlfriend were dead, but immediately pushed the thought to the back of her mind. She would not entertain such a thing until someone brought her proof that she would never see her son again. 'Let that day never come,' she whispered.

Now, as Tim Everist drove through Melbourne, his initial shock at the news on the radio turned to angry thoughts.

Some bloody psycho is out there on a thrill kill. Why my sister? Poor Debbie, she never went hitch-hiking and the first time she tries it she walks straight into the hands of a maniac!

Just after Tim reached his mother's house, the New South Wales police phoned to inform the family that they were reasonably certain the bodies in the forest were those of Deborah and James. When a similar call was received at the Gibson home, Peggy sadly picked up the thick scrapbook of press cuttings about numerous missing hitch-hikers, including her son, and gazed at photos of James in that silly hat of his. It seemed like only yesterday that she had seen him wearing it as he waved goodbye to her at the railway station.

Dear James. So gentle, so caring, so intent on doing good for the world, and his life has been snuffed out before his dreams could be realised.

With two missing people from their state almost certainly dead, the Victorian police called up the computerised missing persons files that they had compiled, and which covered the entire country. Looking for similarities with the New South Wales murders, they examined twenty-five cases of people who had gone missing or been murdered while hitch-hiking, walking on public roads, or waiting for public transport. There had been only three arrests, which meant there were several killers — or even more sinister, just one — still at large.

Among the unsolved cases were the murders of John Lee, aged 14, and Fiona Burns, aged 15, who had set out from Adelaide in October 1990 to hitch-hike to Melbourne. Their bodies were found about 100 metres from the main highway, both had been stabbed to death and, like the Belanglo victims, they were found some distance — 50 metres — apart in bushland.

There were many others whose whereabouts remained unknown. Included in this category were 22-year-old Carmen Verheyden, last seen hitch-hiking at Casula, in Sydney's south-west on 11 March 1991, and nurses Deborah Balkan and Gillian Jamieson, who disappeared from the Parramatta area of Sydney in 1980.

Now that four bodies had been found in the forest, the phrase 'serial killer' was on everyone's lips, particularly in the wake of the movie *The Silence of the Lambs*.

But Chief Superintendent Clive Small — who had now been appointed to head the Belanglo murder investigations and to co-ordinate work already done by Grosse, McLennan and other detectives — was not prepared to speculate that a lone crazed killer was seeking out a particular type of victim.

This tall, veteran career officer had been selected to head the Belanglo task force because of his thirty years of experience, during which time he had collected numerous commendations and citations. The holder of the prestigious National Police Medal, awarded in 1981, it was Small who reopened investigations into the wrongful arrest and charging of former scientific officer Harry Blackburn, who had been accused of rape. Small's inquiries had cleared Blackburn and, following a Royal Commission into the affair, Small was rewarded with a commendation.

In 1992 the prominent detective received a commissioner's commendation for his services within Task Force Omega, which investigated the circumstances surrounding the shooting of police officer Michael Drury and uncovered police corruption. In addition, Small had won widespread praise for his organisational skills during royal tours, the Pope's visit and Australia's bicentennial celebrations.

Over the years Small had become a firm believer in using computers to fight crime. At a criminology conference in Canberra in 1992 he spoke with pride about how computerised techniques were used in the Liverpool area, where he was stationed.

'There are some similarities in these murders, that's true,' Small now told a group of detectives at Bowral. 'The indications are that we're heading in the direction of a common offender or offenders, but until we have more evidence we must continue to treat these as two incidents that *may* be connected.'

News of the latest discoveries in the forest that the locals knew so well spread rapidly through the Southern Highlands. By coincidence, police and residents had arranged a community meeting in the Bowral Town Hall for the evening of 7 October — just two days after the Victorians' bodies had been discovered — when the Clarke and Walters families would thank everyone, via videotape from the UK, for their continued support, and ask for their vigilance so that the murderer or murderers could be brought to justice.

In the Glebe mortuary in Sydney, a silver ring was removed from James Gibson's hand, and a silver chain and pendant lifted from his neck. The zipper on his jeans, which was coming away from the clothing, was, strangely, in the down position. The forensic pathologist, Dr Bradhurst, found cuts, presumed to be knife marks, on the chest — one in the sternum and another slightly lower. There were marks, too, under the right arm — on the fifth and sixth right ribs. The eighth left rib was fractured, and there were marks to the fourth, fifth and sixth vertebrae in the middle of the back.

The manner in which James had died shocked even the hardened investigators involved in the case. The knife that had plunged numerous times into his chest and back had been driven with such force that it chipped, cut and gouged his bones. Whoever had wielded the knife had been as strong as an ox — or drawn his strength from madness. Detectives were sickened as they could not help imagining the harmless young man's last moments in a lonely forest far away from help.

The cause of Deborah's death was not immediately obvious. True, her skull, which had been disturbed but not damaged by the potter, Bruce Pryor, had been fractured and the jaw broken and, although these injuries would certainly have rendered her unconscious, they were not thought to have brought about instant death.

As the pathologists probed, however, they found evidence of a single stab wound and several slicing-type injuries to Deborah's body — as if she had been struck by someone lashing out with a machete. There was little doubt that blood had flowed liberally in that patch of forest almost four years earlier, and one terrible question now emerged. Had Deborah, her skeleton revealing no other evidence of a fatal blow, been left to bleed to death?

In any case, Dr Bradhurst was in no doubt that there had been a sexual aspect to the young couple's murders.

The knots in the pantyhose, found some 4 metres from her body, suggested that Debbie had been tied up. It was clear to him that there had been a bondage aspect to her death, and the fact that the zipper on James' jeans was down, with the top button still secure, also suggested a sexual element.

Every detective had his private thoughts, but they all agreed on one point. The killer was unspeakably cruel and sadistic. But were they dealing with only one murderer? The fact that both pairs of victims were not found side by side suggested that they had been led or forced to separate areas by two or more people.

In the case of the British women, one had been shot numerous times, while the other suffered multiple stab wounds. Two weapons ... two murderers? Similarly with James and Debbie — he had been stabbed with a knife; she had been smashed about the head and face and cut with a weapon, a machete perhaps, that caused slashing injuries.

Skill, luck and gut feelings all play a part in crime investigation, and Superintendent Small and other senior officers now had strong deep-down feelings that the Belanglo State Forest held yet more terrible secrets. A new and extremely thorough search of the forest was the only way to find out.

CHAPTER SEVEN

To help with the intensive search, specially trained cadaver sniffer dogs were brought down from Brisbane to supplement the forty police officers who were already crawling through the bush. The area to be searched was 4 kilometres long and 400 metres wide — an enormous task, but it could be completed with patience, and the police were prepared to give plenty of that. If those gut feelings were correct and there were other bodies in the forest, the victims were certainly beyond help now. But there was still a need for urgency: no-one was forgetting that a killer — or killers — was still at large, and if there were more bodies to be found, there could also be more clues.

The search technique was designed to cover the apparent pattern that the murderer or murderers had followed. He or they had dumped the victims no closer to a fire trail than 50 metres and no further away than 200 metres. Lines of police covering this corridor moved shoulder to shoulder through the bush, often on their hands and knees. Others followed, overlapping the ground that had already been covered. The search was so effective that two teeth which had been separated from Debbie's skull were found in the bracken. Whenever anything of note was found, searchers yelled 'Find!', and all activity stopped until the item had been collected and placed in an evidence bag.

On Monday 1 November 1993 the horrors of the past were repeated. Approximately 1.5 kilometres from where the remains of the Victorians had been found four weeks earlier, and 40 metres from the Miner's Despair fire trail, Constable Martin Roullis, taking part in a line search, came across three bones, one of which he thought might be a human leg bone. Close to a small tree he saw a brown hiking boot — then a human skull. He called for a senior officer. Now, a more detailed examination revealed a skeleton, lying face down against a large fallen branch, and loosely covered with branches and foliage. The state of decay did not allow an immediate identification of sex or age, but one thing was certain — the body had been in the forest for between two and three years, suggesting that the victim had died after the Victorian couple and before the British girls.

On 2 November Detective Senior Constable Andrew Grosse rushed — once again — to the forest.

'I've been waiting for this,' said Grosse as officers led him from the fire trail and through the low scrub to a pile of branches. Underneath, he could clearly see a human skull, three bones, and a pair of green shorts. As the bracken was removed from the body, which was lying on its stomach in a north–south direction with the head towards the north, Grosse had a clearer view. There was a purple headband around the head, bearing the words 'Compact-O-Mat'. He could also see decayed remains of clothing around the upper chest area, and a leather band with multi-coloured stones — a Maori carving — around the neck. A search of the surrounding area produced nothing of assistance to ballistics officers.

On the following day, in the mortuary that had already hosted four bodies from the Belanglo Forest, pathologists prised a ring from one of the fingers and carefully removed the necklace. These items, along with hiking boots and clothing found near the body, helped to identify the victim as Simone Schmidl, a lone German traveller who had gone against the advice of her friends and set off to hitch-hike from Sydney to Melbourne in early 1991 to meet her mother. Ominously, when found she was wearing no underwear beneath her shorts, leaving the examiners to wonder whether she had been sexually molested. The pathologist found digging-type marks on the vertebrae and ribs — and more of these marks on the back of the vertebrae at the top of the neck, at the top of the spine, and on right and left ribs — indicating that she had been stabbed.

Twenty-one-year-old Simone Schmidl, known as Simi, had worked at a variety of jobs in her native Germany, saving up for what she told friends would be a trip of a lifetime, travelling around Australia and New Zealand. She knew the risks involved in hitch-hiking, which is why she never tried it in Germany. But Australia and New Zealand were different: she'd bought travel books that said the two countries were probably the safest in the world for backpackers and hitch-hikers.

Following the separation of her parents, Erwine and Herbert, in 1986, Simi had been living with her mother in Regensburg, Bavaria, but she kept in touch with her father and often went on holidays with him. Although their vacations were usually in hotels, Herbert had no doubt that his only child would have preferred camping out. In 1988 she set off for a holiday in Canada and Alaska, and if the travel bug had not bitten her before, it certainly did then. She wanted to visit as many far-flung corners of the world as possible, which was why Australia and New Zealand particularly appealed to her.

'There's no doubt I've got the travel bug,' she told her father. 'I've learned so much from meeting different people.

And you've got to move around at street level — no big hotels or anything like that. If I could afford it, I'd spend the rest of my life travelling around the world.'

As usual, Simi sought her father's advice on what to buy as she made preparations to head off for Australia and New Zealand. Herbert, anxious that she should have only the best, narrowed down to two the choice of stores they would visit for Simi's travelling and camping equipment. The prices there might be a little higher, but the quality of their wares was superior. Herbert also knew quite well one of the storekeepers, Georg Wolf, so there was an additional reason for not shopping around.

Wolf, an assistant at Sports Tahedl, watched the father and daughter as they checked over a number of camping items and pored over catalogues. Simi liked bright colours so when she saw a Salewa-brand backpack with a lilac and blue pattern she had no hesitation in choosing it. Simi purchased a Salewa-brand sleeping bag and cover. She also liked the look of a blue Vau de Hogan tent but the store did not have one for immediate sale, and so she had to place an order for it to be delivered from the manufacturers. She and her father watched Wolf fill in the order docket. Two weeks later, in that European summer of 1990, Simi returned to pick up her tent, and signed her name at the bottom of the purchase docket.

Wolf — who also provided Simi with a cooking set, made up of two aluminium pans, two orange-coloured plastic cups and a gas ring, a Hi Sierra daypack as well as two Compact-O-Mat straps for securing camping equipment — asked her where she was going on holiday.

'Australia, New Zealand, mainly,' she said. 'I'm really excited. At least now I've got all the gear I need.'

On 29 September 1990 Herbert and Simi Schmidl headed for the Regensburg railway station. Loaded down with her backpack, sleeping bag and tent and daypack,

Simi's exciting journey to the Southern Hemisphere was about to begin. As she was about to board the train to travel to Frankfurt, where she would catch the flight to Sydney, Herbert raised his camera and took a snap of her, a solidly built young woman — close to 76 kilograms — filled with anticipation of the adventures ahead. He took a second photo when she was on board, then waved goodbye as the train pulled away. Simi was wearing a blue jacket, and her unruly mass of dark-brown hair twisted into dreadlocks was swept up, as usual, under a headscarf, one of the main features of her appearance. She gave her father a final big hug, her eyes sparkling behind her big, round metal-framed glasses. There was no need for a picture this time — that final vision was to live with Herbert for ever.

On the flight to Sydney, Simi began chatting to another German traveller, 20-year-old Jeannette Muller, and they struck up an instant rapport. As neither had any definite plans, apart from an intention to visit New Zealand, they agreed to travel together. Simi invited Jeannette to stay with her at the Sydney home of a friend, Kristine Murphy, who Simi insisted wouldn't mind putting her up as well. Simi had travelled through Alaska with Kristine in 1988, and was well aware of how open and friendly the Australian woman was. Simi told Jeannette they'd be able to have the best part of four months together before she had to meet her mother, who was planning to come to Australia in late January to join her for a holiday.

For a week, the two new friends used Kristine's home in Coronation Avenue in the western suburb of Guildford as a base while they went out exploring the harbour city. Like other backpackers, they headed to the beaches and wandered through Kings Cross, the city's colourful nightlife district. Simi loved it there. With its bustling bars, the flashing neon lights of the sex clubs, fast-food outlets and Italian coffee shops, it lured overseas travellers like moths to a lamp. Villains rubbed shoulders with undercover police, and Japanese tourists walked right through the middle of it all with their cameras. Now and again, a fight would break out, or a wallet would be deftly lifted. It was all part of the Kings Cross scene, and if you were a backpacker you had to go there to experience the pulse of the city.

In early October, Simi and Jeannette set out to hitch-hike to Melbourne. They took a train from Sydney to the nearby satellite city of Liverpool, and then walked the half-kilometre to the start of the Hume Highway. They had no trouble getting lifts to their destination. In Melbourne, the young women decided to share the cost of buying an old Datsun 180B and drive it to Queensland.

'Do you think it will get us there?' laughed Simi.

'We can only pray,' replied her friend. 'We'll test it on the run to Sydney and make a decision whether to go on from there.'

They headed back up the Hume Highway without incident and called in on Kristine and her mother.

'The car didn't let us down,' Simi told Kristine. 'Now we're going to give it the real test and take it to Queensland. I must say it's so much better to drive yourself. You can go where you want and it's a lot quicker than hitch-hiking.'

'Well, if you come back this way, you know there's a bed waiting for you,' said Kristine.

Simi and Jeanette set off on the main highway north. Although they had friends in Brisbane who would put them up, the two women camped out on occasions. At Noosa Heads, on the Sunshine Coast, Simi snuggled into her sleeping bag and hammed it up as Jeannette took a photo of her.

Towards the end of November, Simi and Jeannette called on Kristine in Sydney again. This time they were on their way back to Melbourne — to leave the car with friends who would sell it for them. They then hitch-hiked back to Sydney to stay with Kristine and her mother once more.

'We've come to know the Hume Highway very well,' Simi told the Murphys. 'I've arranged to meet my mother in Melbourne for a holiday after Christmas, so I'm going to have to go back down again — I could probably do it with my eyes shut now.'

But first there was one other adventure to be enjoyed — the trip to New Zealand. They loved their new destination, but the heat that the German girls experienced while travelling the New Zealand roads in summer resulted in a decision to buy water-bottles. They found a couple of tough plastic containers, which fitted into strong green fabric pouches, in a camping shop. Simi used a marker pen to write 'SIMI' on the bottle's side and the cap.

They travelled all over New Zealand, sleeping out in Simi's tent and cooking up meals on the gas stove. The two friends often sat by their tent chatting, and Simi would sometimes smoke her favourite brand of cigarette, Marlboro. She fell in love with a necklace she saw for sale featuring a Maori carving, and wore it constantly — regarding it as her lucky charm. Shortly before Christmas, Simi rang her father and his second wife to pass on her good wishes and to let them know that all was well.

On 19 January 1991 the two friends flew from Auckland to Sydney and once again made their way to the suburb of Guildford, where Kristine and her mother accommodated them. The Murphys loved hearing the stories of the young women's travels, but were concerned when they realised how much hitch-hiking they'd done.

'You girls have taken some terrible risks,' said Kristine, softly reprimanding them.

'It's okay,' Simi assured her. 'And I hope you're not going to get upset when I tell you that I'm going to hitch-hike to Melbourne to meet my mother.'

'Don't do it, Simi,' said Kristine. 'You can push your luck too far. You never know who's going to pick you up.'

'It's perfectly safe,' said the carefree guest. 'Nothing happened to Jeannette and me in New Zealand and we've been just about everywhere. Anyway, if you read the travel books they'll tell you that Australia is the best place to hitch-hike!'

With her mother due to arrive in a few days, Simi was anxious to save what remained of her dwindling finances. She told the Murphy family that she could hardly afford the bus fare to Melbourne, which was why she intended to hitch-hike.

'Please don't do it,' implored Kristine. 'I'll lend you the money for the fare.' Jeannette, too, was unhappy about Simi travelling alone. True, they had walked many kilometres through New Zealand, but there had been two of them. Jeannette also offered Simi the fare to go by bus to Melbourne.

'Thank you, all of you,' said Simi. 'But I've made up my mind. I'm going to hitch.'

In a final attempt to persuade her friend to take the bus, Kristine searched through the travel sections of a number of bookstores in the hope of finding a guide that warned against hitch-hiking in Australia. But every book she opened emphasised that this was one of the few countries that was safe for hitch-hikers.

Dressed in a bright-yellow singlet, green shorts and hiking boots, Simi set out from the Murphy home at 8.15 am on 20 January 1991, heading for Guildford railway station. Although she had traveller's cheques, her Australian currency amounted to no more than $20.

Jeannette accompanied Simi part of the way to the station, and felt sad that they were parting after having so much fun together. She knew that Simi would take the train to Liverpool and then walk to the highway, just as they had done three months earlier.

Simi was very excited. A new phase of her travels Down

Under was about to begin, and she couldn't wait to meet her mother, who was due to arrive at Melbourne airport three days later. They would then set off on their planned camper-van holiday.

Simi and Jeannette said goodbye near a newsagent's shop, close to the railway station. Simi promised she would ring Jeannette and her friends from Melbourne after she'd met up with her mother. Then she turned and headed off, her colourful rucksack bobbing up and down on her back. It was only later that Kristine Murphy and her mother learned that the trains were not running that day — bus services were operating instead, taking travellers from the station to their various suburban destinations.

Motorist Jeanette Wallis couldn't fail to notice the backpacker heading south along the beginning of the Hume Highway near Liverpool. The traveller was loaded down with so much gear, including a bedroll on top of the backpack, that Mrs Wallis could see little of the person from behind. As she overtook and stopped at some traffic lights, she looked in her rear view mirror and saw that the tourist was a solidly built woman. She was struck by her mass of hair — 'messy hair' was how she described it later.

'That's dangerous,' she thought. 'A woman hitch-hiking on her own like that. She shouldn't be doing it.'

Mrs Wallis pulled into a nearby McDonald's and when she came out to continue her journey there was no sign of the backpacker. But she thought so much about the tourist, travelling on her own along the highway, that she mentioned it to her husband when she got home.

Erwine Schmidl was full of happiness. It had been months since Simi had set out from their home in Regensburg and now, as the 747 flew over the centre of Australia shortly before dawn on 23 January, Erwine was longing to hear about her adventures before they began travelling together. Her fears for her wandering daughter had diminished. Simi had accomplished her wish to travel around Australia and New Zealand, and her prediction that all would be well had proved to be correct. All that worry for nothing!

Erwine waited patiently in the long immigration queue at Melbourne's airport, and put up with another frustrating wait until her baggage came around on the carousel. Then she was quickly out through the doors and into the arrivals area, her eyes scanning the crowd for that distinctive mop of hair and the trademark headscarf or band.

Families hugged and kissed all around her. Erwine's fellow travellers laughed and shed tears of happiness as they greeted their loved ones and posed to have their pictures taken. But gradually they all drifted away and Erwine was left standing alone.

Where was Simi?

Erwine hung around the airport for hours, waiting for her daughter. With an increasing sense of alarm, she took a taxi and dropped her bags at a friend's house. They waited for the phone to ring — waited for Simi, full of apologies at being held up, to call. But it seemed that Simi had vanished. Erwine telephoned Sydney and fired anxious questions at Kristine Murphy and Jeannette Muller. Was there anything, she begged to know, that might have caused Simi to change her plans about going to Melbourne? Had she been sick? Could she have been injured in an accident? But even as Erwine asked the questions, she knew that only the most serious circumstances would have stopped her daughter from meeting her, or at least arranging for someone to get in touch. They all knew it.

Simi became another statistic in the missing persons files of the New South Wales and Victorian police forces. Her mother, now broken-hearted and physically sick — she had been vomiting and stricken with nervous twitches — returned to Germany.

Between 1988 and the discovery of Simi's body, almost twenty other people had gone missing in Australia while hitch-hiking. And, going back to 1972, the Missing Persons Unit at Parramatta had amassed more than 600 unresolved cases. Under these circumstances, it was understandable that, until the discovery of the bodies, detectives had not been spending much time looking for a connection between the disappearances of the Victorian backpackers and that of Simone Schmidl. Although it certainly looked as though some mishap or tragedy had befallen James Gibson and Deborah Everist, and now Simi, more than a year had passed since the couple had vanished, and the only link was that they and Simi had all intended to hitch-hike from Sydney to Melbourne.

Four months after Simi disappeared, a pair of round metal-framed spectacles and a sleeping bag were handed in to police. The items had been found dumped in the bush at Bright, 75 kilometres south-east of the Hume Highway on the lower slopes of Mount Buffalo in Victoria. Photographs of the articles were sent to Simi's mother and as far as she could tell, they belonged to her daughter. But the detectives handling her case thought it curious that Simi might have been so far off the main highway, particularly as she had been travelling to a deadline in order to meet her mother.

Erwine hoped that the glasses and the sleeping bag were a case of mistaken identity. She sat by the phone ... and waited.

In Regensburg, almost three years later, the broken-hearted Mrs Erwine Schmidl heard the news that Simi's body had been found. 'The police always told me to expect the worst, but right until now, right until the end, I hoped she would still be alive,' she said to a friend. 'I can't even imagine that this is her body and that someone murdered her — it's a nightmare.' Frightened and confused, Erwine closed her door on the world.

The police were now convinced that they had a serial killer or killers on their hands, and the ever-cautious Detective Superintendent Small was ready to publicly acknowledge the fact.

'We have every reason to believe that all the murders are connected.' The killer or killers, he told journalists at a search command post close to where the bodies of the Britons had been found, knew the Belanglo State Forest extremely well, but it was impossible to say whether he or they were locals. 'The reality is we do not have any prime targets in this matter at this stage.'

Although many other people were missing, the police now turned their thoughts to two particular backpackers — Anja Habschied and her boyfriend Gabor Neugebauer. Because they had vanished under mysterious circumstances — like the other victims, they were backpackers who had suddenly stopped contacting their families and friends — Small, Grosse, McLennan and other officers had a terrible feeling that their corpses also lay in the forest.

'I'm doubling the search team,' Small told his immediate subordinates. 'I'm increasing manpower to eighty. I want every inch of the forest covered.'

To expedite identification in the event that bodies were discovered, dental records of the German couple were rushed to the command post.

There was an expectant atmosphere as the lines of police moved slowly and carefully through the scrub. Everyone involved was sure that there would soon be another cry of 'Find!'

CHAPTER EIGHT

They wore studs in their noses, believed in the New Age and shared the same environmental ideals as Victorians James Gibson and Debbie Everist. And, like their compatriot Simi Schmidl, Munich University students Gabor Neugebauer, aged 21, and his girlfriend, Anja Habschied, aged 20, had read many travel books and decided that Australia was a safe place in which to hitch-hike.

He was tall and handsome, recently released from conscription in the German Army, and very fit. She was strikingly attractive and had a particularly distinctive streak of false red hair that was skilfully woven into her own and flopped forwards over her face. They had an easy-going attitude to life and wanted to see as much of the world as they could.

There was something else apart from their shared interests that bound them together — they were very much in love, so much so that their friends and families thought they didn't notice enough of what was going on around them. As they planned a trip to the far side of the world, they became even more involved with one another. But they wanted to get every detail right, determined to enjoy as much of the world as they could on what funds were available to them. Surrounded by maps, they sat in Gabor's flat and pored over routes through Indonesia and Australia. Finally they hit on a plan, deciding to travel through Indonesia, hitch-hike around the east of Australia, and then, on their way home to Germany, fly from the northern city of Darwin to the Indonesian island of Bali.

Unlike most young travellers to Indonesia, who relished the beaches, the temples, the availability of hashish and the nightclubs, Gabor and Anja did not enjoy their stay, because they didn't like the food. They found it too spicy and in particular they missed fresh milk and other dairy foods. It was a relief, then, to fly into Brisbane, Queensland, in December 1991, and to enjoy the abundance of familiar foods. They then travelled north to the city of Cairns, where, like Simi who had been there nearly a year earlier, they mingled with other young tourists on the waterfront, and wrote postcards and letters to their friends and parents. It was quite possible that they had not heard of the disappearance of the Victorian couple, or of Simi Schmidl. And with dozens of other travellers hitch-hiking up and down the east coast — and finding everyone who gave them a lift to be anything but threatening — there was no reason for them to fear this method of travelling around.

It was from Cairns that Anja penned a loving letter to her mother, Mrs Olga Habschied. Anja had kept in touch regularly, sending postcards and letters and occasionally ringing. She described some of their adventures and wrote of the plan to travel south to Sydney. Passing on greetings to her grandparents, and adding an extra kiss for her cat, Molle, Anja made a point of telling her mother how kind the police had been when Gabor had lost his money belt as they travelled through Queensland.

'The fellow we were travelling with put Gabor's money belt, with our airline tickets, on top of the car. It was not until 400 km later that Gabor noticed he was missing his money belt. The Richmond police went 60 km up to where we had slept and looked for it.'

Anja recounted that the police had found the money belt and posted it 'Express' to Cairns.

'Really unbelievable. They drove those 120 km for us and searched for an eternity in the heat on our behalf. That day did not seem to be our lucky day. The evening before, we left a good, expensive pot standing next to the car. In the morning it had disappeared. How could anyone have taken it? We were 60 km from the nearest town. Perhaps it was a kangaroo! One sat near us and watched us during our search for the pot that day. That wasn't all that happened that day. We were faced with a flat tyre, too. However, I did learn how to change a wheel.'

Anja told how she and Gabor had learned Sydney was the place to be at Christmas, mentioning that there was going to be a huge beachside party for foreigners. She was referring to the traditional Christmas Day gathering of locals and tourists — a large number of whom came from Europe — on Sydney's Bondi Beach. For Northern Hemisphere travellers in particular, eating Christmas lunch in the summer sun at the seaside was a novel alternative. They dragged sofas on to the sands, set up portable TVs, kept their drinks cool in fridges, even if there was no power, and celebrated into the early hours of Boxing Day.

Anja and Gabor may not have known exactly what to expect, but, having found a reasonably priced backpackers' hotel in Victoria Street, Kings Cross, they were looking forward in any case to exploring the rest of Sydney which, Anja noted in a letter, 'is said to be very beautiful'. With the festivities over, however, they would have to rush back to the north of Australia to catch their pre-paid flight from Darwin to Bali.

'It's going to be a little difficult after Christmas because we will need to travel the 4100 km to Darwin without stopping. Unfortunately, everything you want to see in Australia lies so far away and if you want to see something you have to spend a lot of money. On the first of January, then, we will fly back to Indonesia

again. Once again, we'll have to go through a difficult adaptation from the good-tasting food here in Australia to the milkless Indonesia.'

The letter reached the Habschied home two days before that Christmas of 1991, but while the letter was travelling from Australia, it seemed that something sinister happened to the loving couple.

Just twenty-four hours after Anja's parents read her words, the phone rang at the Neugebauer home in Munich. It was Gabor, calling from Bondi. Despite the earlier enthusiasm expressed by Anja, he did not seem excited at the prospect of joining in with the huge beach party the following day. In fact, there was an edge to the young man's voice which alarmed his father. Gabor sounded agitated. His voice seemed strangely distant.

'We want to get out of Australia,' he said — not once, but twice. There was a hint that he and Anja had struck trouble of some kind, but Gabor did not have time to elaborate. The phone went dead.

Yet neither Gabor nor Anja seemed to be unduly agitated when they spoke to staff at the backpackers' hostel just before Christmas. They came and went with other young overseas travellers but paused to tell the staff and other backpackers that they were going to travel north to Darwin.

'Why leave on Boxing Day? Why not stay around for the rest of the Christmas holidays?' one of the staff members asked.

'We've only got a few weeks of holiday left,' said Anja. 'And anyway, our seats are firmly booked to leave Darwin on New Year's Day.'

On Boxing Day morning Anja and Gabor settled their bill and headed off up the street. The next and final part of their journey was about to begin.

Gabor and Anja did not catch their flight from Darwin on New Year's Day. Gabor's mother, Mrs Anke Neugebauer, had sent her son a Christmas parcel with cookies and vitamins, to be collected in Darwin. It was never picked up.

A Darwin couple claimed they saw them on 1 January, and said that the young people missed their 8 am Garuda flight to Bali by only two hours after travelling up from Sydney. And another report later studied by police said that the young woman seemed downcast when she and her boyfriend checked into the Overland Caravan Park outside Darwin at 10.30 am. According to the park's proprietor, Joe van der Meulen, they looked tired and dirty. He also reported that they left the caravan park on the following day in a tan-coloured station wagon with three men.

Their tickets remained unused, and no new bookings were made.

Did Anja and Gabor really make it to Darwin? Or were the sightings cases of mistaken identity? What was behind Gabor's agitated phone call to his father? These were the questions that police immediately asked when the couple's worried families finally raised the alarm — but they knew that the answers would come only with time and patience.

But time brought only misery. The Christmas parcel that Mrs Neugebauer had sent to Darwin was returned to her five months later. And Gabor and Anja never wrote or rang again.

On 4 November 1993 the Belanglo Forest revealed another of its dark secrets — and ended the mystery of what had happened to Anja and Gabor almost two years previously. It was only three days after Simone Schmidl's body was found that the now familiar cry of 'Find!' resounded through the eucalypts.

Working with a team about three-quarters of a kilometre from where Simi's body had been discovered, Sergeant Nail Smith found a woman's brown leather sandal. He notified the search leader, then continued picking his way through the bush. Some 10 metres further on and about 25 metres to

104

his right, the sergeant came across a partly burned log, on the far side of which was a stack of small logs ranging in length from 1 to 4 metres. Smith and another officer pulled the logs away to reveal a skeleton, apparently that of a female, judging by the clothing, but there was no head. It seemed to Smith and his colleagues that no animals had disturbed the remains — chillingly, the corpse had been covered without its head.

'Keep searching this area,' Smith and his colleagues were told by their senior officer. 'All the bones we've found in the past have been disturbed, so you'll find the skull somewhere.'

But as the search continued, there was no sign of the skull in the immediate area.

Detective Senior Constable Grosse knew the forest well by now. He had also learned not to be too shocked or surprised by the ghastly revelations that it held. After being notified of the discovery of the headless corpse, he'd been told by radio that a second body had been found, some 55 metres away. As he drove along the winding bush tracks on that November day in 1993 he was already envisaging the pattern — a log, sticks, a corpse. And he was right.

'Looks like we've found the two Germans we've all been expecting to turn up here,' a sergeant told him as Grosse stepped from his car. 'There are enough clues to tell us who they are.'

Grosse was guided towards a large fallen tree about 30 metres north of a fire trail and lying in a north–south direction. On the tree's western side there was a pile of sticks and forest debris. Underneath lay the headless remains of the body which was to be later confirmed as that of Anja Habschied, chest against the ground and the feet pointing towards the south.

A few metres south-west of this grave site, Grosse was shown the brown sandal, and he was then led through the scrub in a south-westerly direction, across a track, to a place where a large log lay in an east–west position. A pile of sticks and bracken had been built up beside it. In the foliage Grosse saw a number of bones and decomposed clothing — the remains, as it was to be proved, of Gabor Neugebauer. Fifteen metres to the west of the skeleton Grosse was shown a plastic bag that appeared to contain an airline ticket and other papers.

'I need another look at the first site,' he told one of the accompanying detectives. 'But I don't think any of us are in any doubts about the links with the others, are we?'

'We can't find the head, Andrew,' said one of his colleagues. 'There may have been a lot of disturbance by animals, but I can't see them carrying off a head.'

Grosse crouched down over Anja's remains. He noted that the skeleton was clothed in a halter-neck top that had rips and tears around the neck region. There was no lower body clothing or shoes, but a couple of coloured bands encircled her wrist, and on the ground beneath the disarrayed wrist bones — disturbed, it seemed, by animals of the forest — he found a gold-banded watch, still in the closed position. The watch hands had stopped at 5.35, but that meant nothing. The watch could have stopped at any time over the past two years.

Returning to where the second body lay, Grosse gazed sadly at the bones protruding through the bracken. As the twigs were pulled away, he saw that the skeleton, dressed in shorts and a shirt, was lying on its stomach with the head towards the east and the right side of the skull against the ground. Fabric was tied around the face, and further investigation revealed that there was also fabric in the mouth, as well as a small round hole in the skull behind the left ear. Grosse reached down and carefully withdrew a silver ring with a knurled edge from the finger bones. One of Grosse's colleagues, Constable Jason Donnelly, arrived with a metal detector and ran it around the area. The machine beeped as it passed over the skull, and both policemen realised what this probably indicated — a bullet, or bullets, in the head.

As the remains were lifted into a body bag, ballistic police moved in to search the area but found nothing of any relevance. But everyone was grimly reminded, yet again, of the unspeakable acts of cruelty and barbarism that had occurred here.

The post-mortems confirmed all that Grosse and his companions had suspected. Gabor had been shot six times in the head — three times in the left side, and three times in the base of the skull at the rear. A piece of cloth had been stuffed into his mouth to gag him, while another piece of material had been tied around his head, apparently to further muffle his cries. And Anja had been decapitated with a single blow to the head by a very large, sharp weapon. Whoever performed this barbaric act would have used tremendous force.

Who was the monster, or indeed monsters, responsible for such wickedness? This question again haunted the police officers, many of whom had sons and daughters of the same age as the victims, as they spread out around the crude burial sites that had concealed the bodies of the German lovers for almost two years.

Approximately 160 metres from where Gabor's body had been found, the searchers discovered nearly fifty spent .22 cartridges that were consistent with the Winner brand, along with an empty Winner box that had contained fifty rounds. But there was much more to come: forty-six spent .22 Eley-brand cartridges and an empty fifty-round Eley box. Bullet fragments were found lodged in trees and embedded in plastic bottles scattered around the site. It was as if the area had been used as a shooting gallery.

In the same part of the forest, police found a pair of pink

jeans that were identified with almost 100 per cent certainty as Anja's. Inside the jeans, as if just stuffed in, was a piece of pinkish-coloured cloth, knotted and wrapped so that the front formed a V, similar to the masks worn in cowboy films. A blindfold, Detective Grosse surmised as he examined the material. A restraint-like item made from a leather leash, a window sash cord and a plastic pull-tie was also found in this area.

Why had their captor apparently fired nearly 100 rounds, at the risk of raising the curiosity of others who may have been in the area? Had a silencer been used? But why so many shots, when ultimately 'only' six bullets had been pumped into Gabor's head?

And, even more puzzling, where was Anja's head? A thorough search of the area had failed to locate it, and the experienced policemen agreed that no animal would have carried a head away and hidden it. So many questions — would there ever be any answers?

By now, Grosse was spending most of his days in the forest, sifting around the crime scenes. He wanted to know about everything that was found. Empty sherry bottles were scattered around the areas where the various bodies had been discovered; one officer found some looped wire; and another discovered pieces of black electrical tape that had been looped into the shape of handcuffs. Personal belongings were collected and placed into evidence bags — everything from black underwear found near the remains of Deborah Everist; to a silver chain necklace with a green stone attached, discovered 60 metres south-west of where Gabor's remains had been found; to a fading black belt engraved with the words 'W Germany' which was located near what were believed to be Anja's pink jeans.

Grosse's attention was drawn to marks on a tree near the Everist–Gibson site. On removing the bark from around the damaged area, he discovered a number of embedded bullets, which he gouged out and put aside, to be sent to the Forensic Ballistics Unit.

Chief Superintendent Clive Small, the man in charge of Task Force Air — the codename given to the murder hunt because the victims had all disappeared into thin air — now called a meeting of the senior officers involved.

'Everyone's been working very hard, but there's still a great deal more to be done before we can say our work in the forest is over,' he said. 'We cannot assume there are no more bodies out there.'

The cadaver-sniffing dogs they had been using were getting sore feet from trudging through the prickly undergrowth, so special leather booties were made for them. The men's and women's backs ached, too, but the search for clues and more bodies would continue in a strict grid pattern, kilometre by kilometre, until every leaf had been overturned.

There wasn't a person involved who was not overcome by the gruesome task assigned to them. Some felt they were walking through a graveyard where the souls of the departed still roamed, awaiting release through a Holy Man's blessing. The searchers were ordinary people, assigned from police stations around the Southern Highlands and spending each night at the Goulburn Police Academy. At the end of a day during which a corpse could have turned up behind the next bush, it was virtually impossible to expel their sombre moods. One officer even bathed in disinfectant each night in an attempt to rid himself of death's taint.

In Germany, Gabor's and Anja's parents received the news in much the same way as the relatives of the other victims. 'It was what we were expecting,' said a tearful Mrs Anke Neugebauer. 'Of course, we held out hope, but deep in our hearts we knew that with no contact after all this time, something terrible had happened to them. We've mulled over Gabor's last phone call to us, when he said he had to get out of Australia as quickly as possible. We don't know if there's a connection between that call and their murders. Perhaps we'll never find out.'

Like Erwine Schmidl, who had kept in touch with the Neugebauers, Anke and her husband Manfred had held out a slim hope that the missing Germans were being held against their will — perhaps in a remote farmhouse. 'But when I heard that Simone's body had been found, my hopes collapsed,' said Anke. 'And now, just days after hearing about Simone, we've been told they've found Gabor and Anja. Whoever is responsible must be very sick. Only a sick person could do something like this. I know you don't have the death penalty in Australia, but he should be locked up for life.'

Officially, Chief Superintendent Small and the men of Task Force Air were saying little about the profile they had built up of the person or persons responsible for the murders. In fact, Small was against profiles because they put a certain picture in the minds of investigating officers which might be completely wrong.

But there was enough of a pattern to reveal that the killer or killers owned a four-wheel-drive vehicle, probably had a gun licence, and knew the main highways running to the north and south of Sydney well. The discovery of James Gibson's camera and backpack at Galston Gorge, north of the city, and the dumping of the bodies in the Belanglo Forest much further south, suggested someone who travelled up and down the roads regularly. As the killings had occurred over a two and a half year period, between late December 1989 and April 1992, it was clear that the suspect or suspects had been active on the road during that period, and probably before and after those dates as well.

Something of the killer's character was also beginning to

emerge. Each of the victims, apart from James Gibson, who had been on his side, had been found face down — lying against a rock or a fallen tree and covered by a canopy of branches. Some officers thought that there was something ritualistic about the way in which the bodies had been left, while others believed the positions of the bodies suggested a neat and tidy mind. Close to each discovery, detectives had found a circle of blackened stones that had been used as a bush fireplace, and a large quantity of ashes had been found in each fire site.

And there were all those sherry bottles, all bearing the name of McWilliams. Had the killer or killers entertained the victims around a glowing fire before they were coldly executed? Or had the captives been forced to drink the alcohol so they would be stupefied or even more helpless?

Certainly the perpetrator must have exuded enough charm to give his potential victims the confidence to step into his vehicle as they hitch-hiked down the highway. Had he then driven them under duress, perhaps at gunpoint, into the forest? Or had he persuaded them that the forest held secret wonders — waterfalls, a rare bird colony, a perfect camping spot surrounded by grazing kangaroos?

Many criminologists and psychologists painted their own pictures of the murderer. Professor Paul Wilson, Dean of Arts at Queensland's Bond University and one of Australia's leading criminologists, had little doubt that the manner in which the murderer disposed of the bodies had strong ritualistic overtones. The murderer was rational, well organised and unlikely to stop killing. He chose backpackers because they were vulnerable — they did not know the area or the community and, as outsiders, their senses were not necessarily attuned to the intentions of people they met.

'This killer is calculating and ruthless, killing for perverse sexual pleasure and probably taking trophies from his victims,' Professor Wilson told journalists eager for his views. 'I would be very surprised if there wasn't a sexual motive, though that doesn't necessarily mean sexual intercourse. It could simply be a sexual thrill of dominating a woman, particularly with a man involved. The fact that he has, in most cases, targeted couples indicates he is very confident and very, very dangerous.'

The fact that most of the backpacks were missing, along with various personal effects, led detectives to agree that the killer had taken 'trophies' from his victims. They believed that *when* they finally caught him they would find mementos of the murder spree.

One by one the experts came up with their picture of the killer, generally agreeing that he would be fit and strong, quick-witted, and probably single.

Paul Mullen, Professor of Forensic Psychiatry at Melbourne's Monash University, believed the killer worked alone and was unlikely to be involved in a stable relationship. He believed the man had a long history of pre-occupation with killing, power and sadism. 'Police have to hope that this is the sort of person who has done something less grotesque in the past and that they have a record of it,' said Professor Mullen, when asked for his observations.

Professor Richard Ball, of Melbourne University's forensic psychiatry unit, felt that the killings were sexually inspired, although the murderer might not necessarily have had sex with his victims. 'These kind of lust murderers, like Jack the Ripper, are expressing their complex psychopathology in a very angry, hostile, mutilating way and at the same level, a sexual and pleasurable way,' he said.

Forensic psychologist Tim Watson-Munro believed that the killer would appear totally normal on the outside, and the chances were high that he was married or in a stable relationship. 'We are dealing with a predatory serial killer who I think is quite aware of what he is doing. He is bad rather than mad.'

Former FBI investigator Robert Ressler, who introduced the expression 'serial killer' to the world, volunteered his opinion that repeat murderers act to satisfy a lust for power and sexual kicks. They are so proud of their work that they will return to the scene of their crime and certainly keep trophies. One of the criminal experts who helped establish the FBI's Behavioural Science Unit, featured in *The Silence of the Lambs,* Ressler found it interesting that couples had been targeted in the Australian murders. Most serial killers chose single victims. 'You're dealing here with a very confident murderer,' observed Ressler. It was important, he advised, to try to get inside his mind.

It was already clear that this killer was filled with self-confidence. Even to the point that he not only knew he would be able to lure young backpackers to their deaths, but that he could murder them all in the same forest and bury them there without fear of being caught while he was carrying out the crime.

Other portraits of the killer, drawn up by forensic psychiatrists in Australia and overseas, revealed a man who would have obtained a thrill in forcing one of his victims to inflict injury or death on the other. It was also generally agreed that the killer was an older rather than a younger man — probably someone in his 40s or older. He would have an easy manner when talking to his potential victims, but once he had them under his control he would demand that the women act submissively, fulfilling his need to exert sexual control. His kicks would come from specific reactions from his victims, such as fear or passivity during his sexual assaults.

The experts were also generally agreed that it was common for well-organised serial killers to boost their feeling of control by using restraints such as ropes, pieces of clothing, handcuffs, gags and blindfolds. Such killers then often complete their violent fantasies with torture, mutilation, evisceration, dismemberment and other perversions beyond the imaginings of a decent mind. The serial killer is also usually the first-born in a family, or someone who would certainly have younger brothers and sisters over whom he had grown up with a sense of seniority and power.

Chief Superintendent Small studied all these psychological assessments carefully, but was reluctant to present the public with a possible profile. As with his own men, he felt that people would develop a stereotyped idea and discount alternatives. He was also aware of the need not to create hysteria, but at the same time he needed the public to be fully aware of the gruesome murders so that everyone remained alert.

Every scrap of information given to the search headquarters at Bowral was now fed into a computer, with Small holding high hopes that clues to the killer's identity lay somewhere among this enormous amount of data. Some of the information was astonishing — people had named their friends, and one man even accused his father of being the murderer. Basic information concerning the history and geography of the Southern Highlands also went into the computer — the development of housing estates; the extensions to freeways; the bypassing of Mittagong and Berrima, towns lying near the Belanglo State Forest, in recent years. This seemingly irrelevant information could, however, have some bearing on the movements of the killer.

And among the calls which jammed a special backpacker murder hotline were stories of narrow escapes from drivers who 'must have been the murderer'. Other tales told of prowling cars and trucks, and vehicles that had been parked suspiciously. Two girls reported that they'd had a frightening encounter while hitch-hiking south along the Hume Highway in 1988. The driver had taken them off the highway and onto a bush track, where he made sexual advances. They said they were lucky to escape. It was another story to follow up — two more minds to probe for the tiniest details.

But among the most fascinating pieces of information given to the murder team was a statement by a former resident of the Southern Highlands, Mr Alexander Milat, who had since moved to Queensland. He claimed that during Easter 1992 he was in the Belanglo State Forest with a friend, and that they saw two girls answering the descriptions of Joanne and Caroline being abducted by two men in a four-wheel-drive. As with any such information, detectives worked quickly to check it out, and the man whom Mr Milat named as his companion said he was unable to confirm the report. Alexander Milat's claims were filed away, among all the other reports that might or might not have a future bearing on the case.

With the New South Wales state government increasing the reward for the killer's capture to $500,000, and Sydney's *Daily Telegraph Mirror* newspaper offering a further $200,000, there was a great deal of incentive for someone to turn the murderer in if they had any suspicions. At the South West Region Major Crime Headquarters at Parramatta and in a room adjoining Bowral Police Station, a special team of detectives methodically pieced together the facts, rather than psychologists' assessments, that would help to build a profile.

The killer owned one or two weapons, so he was probably a hunter; he knew the Belanglo Forest well, so he either lived locally or went to the bush regularly; and he had a four-wheel-drive vehicle because no ordinary sedan or truck could negotiate the forest's rugged trails. He was charming enough to win his victims' confidence; and strong enough to overpower them and tie them up. And he was methodical — separating the bodies of friends by about the same distance, and leaving a kilometre between the bodies of the British women and the Victorian couple, and a kilometre between the corpses of Simi Schmidl and those of her compatriots Gabor and Anja. Some detectives speculated that if only one man was involved he may have drugged his victims, making it easy to cope with two people on his own.

The murder toll of seven sent reverberations right to the top of the police force, and Assistant Commissioner Bill Galvin announced that 300 more police would be drafted in to assist the eighty already searching. This would make it possible for the entire forest and its 30 kilometres of fire trails to be covered, in addition to the hectares that had already been searched.

As the turning over of leaves and branches continued and police officers were being called in from all around the Sydney region, the 'ballistics boys' came up with a break-through. One of the murder weapons, the one that had shot the bullets into Caroline Clarke's skull, was a .22 US-made Ruger and relatively rare in Australia. Telltale semi-circular markings on the shell casings found near Caroline's body pointed to this type of gun — a semi-automatic rifle with a barrel about 10 centimetres shorter than a normal .22.

The police decided to search for the weapon in the Southern Highlands first, given that the killer seemed to know the forest well. Teams of police spread throughout the area, knocking on the doors of all 2000 registered gun owners in the Bowral district and seizing Rugers so that markings on fired cartridges could be compared with those found in the forest. Bowral opal dealer John Tereghy readily produced his Ruger when police called on him. 'This is the sort of gun we're looking for,' he was told.

While the search for weapons was initially aimed at the Southern Highlands, police noted that around 600 Ruger rifles were registered in New South Wales, and they made preparations to check every one of them. The Australian Federal Police offered to give Task Force Air a copy of an Australia-wide register of 2000 licensed Ruger owners, compiled after the former Federal Assistant Police Commissioner, Mr Colin Winchester, was shot dead with a similar weapon outside his Canberra home in 1989.

The Task Force officers were keeping details of the type of weapon for which they were searching under wraps, and were very concerned when details of the gun were revealed in a Sydney Sunday newspaper. They feared that if the killer read the article, he would almost certainly dump or hide the weapon and, if questioned, come up with a plausible story to explain its disappearance.

On Tuesday 16 November 1993, almost 400 police officers sat down in a forest clearing near the command post and bowed their heads to observe a minute's silence. The search of Belanglo was over, and this was a pause of respect for the young people who had lost their lives there. Father Barry Dwyer, a police chaplain, led the searchers in 'The Lord's Prayer' and in prayers for the victims and their families.

'We are reminded of the fragility of life, as we remember those seven young people whose life was brief and who died in such tragic circumstances,' said the chaplain as the men and women who had worked so hard listened, some close to tears.

They and their senior officers were now confident that, having combed the native forest over the past six weeks, there were no more bodies or clues to be found.

The search commander, Inspector Fred Brame, stepped forward to offer his praise. 'This is one of the largest searches that has been carried out in this country and you have demonstrated your professionalism and dedication throughout,' he told the assembled men and women. 'We had a number of objectives put to us, one of which was to gather evidence for the investigative squad, so hopefully the people responsible for this will be arrested. And hopefully we have removed the lingering despair of the parents of those seven young people found in this forest.'

But there was one more search to undergo — a hunt through Galston Gorge, north of Sydney, where James Gibson's camera and backpack had been found. More than 100 officers had already been assigned for the task, which would begin on the following Monday. However, the search was to yield nothing more to help the police in their hunt for the killer, but it left senior officers satisfied that they had now thoroughly investigated both areas that the killer was known to have visited.

The vital question now was whether the perpetrator, who would have read of the discovery of the bodies and watched the searches on television, would strike again. Had he watched the events of recent weeks with heart-pounding excitement? Or with fear that he might have made a mistake, and the police would be on to him within hours? As far as Chief Superintendent Small was concerned, it was essential to find the murderer and lock him away before he could kill again. The danger periods were during the school holidays — all seven victims had gone missing during the Christmas–New Year period or at Easter.

'We are very aware that the killings have happened in the school holidays,' said Small to a group of crime writers. 'This may be significant, but we just don't know.' It meant, however, that anyone who was thinking of hitch-hiking during school holiday times should abandon those plans — or take the utmost care. 'Hitch-hikers should tell people where they are going and when they expect to arrive, and should warn people at the other end that they are coming. They need someone to raise the alarm. We cannot give any assurances that the person who has committed these crimes has been able to stop. Certainly, you do think about the viciousness, violence and cold-bloodedness of the crimes and you do wonder what sort of person could do this. These are not spontaneous killings; they are very much planned, face-to-face meetings. The victim is confronted and time is spent

118

with them, getting to know them before the murders.' Looking at the murder sites, the distance from the main road and the nature of the killings, it is clear that a good deal of time was spent committing the murders and burying the victims.'

By Christmas 1993 — an anticipated danger holiday time — detectives had sifted through the records of 15,000 motor vehicles, including 6000 Kombi vans, that might have had some significance as a result of public information. Detectives had also inspected more than 2000 firearms in the Southern Highlands, and another 600 in other parts of New South Wales. So far, however, they had failed to find the .22 Ruger that had ejected the shells found near the body of Caroline Clarke. And more than a handful of police were prepared to speculate that the gun had already been well and truly disposed of.

There was also the question of how and why the victims had ended up so deep in the forest. The conclusion was that they had been driven there in a four-wheel-drive vehicle, and this theory tended to rule out the mystery Volkswagen Kombi van beside which two women, thought to have been the British travellers, were seen in the Southern Highlands picnic area. Although the van's driver had not been traced, the feeling was that he was either keeping low because he did not want to be innocently drawn into a murder inquiry, or that he was not aware the police thought he might be connected. In any case, detectives were now convinced that a cumbersome vehicle like a campervan with its low clearance could not have negotiated the rough tracks leading to where the bodies had been found.

The murders had other repercussions. Although many New South Wales politicians were already aware of the rising murder toll, and that the rate of unsolved killings had tripled since the late 1960s, they were stunned by the state's murder statistics. In fact, in over 2500 murder cases between 1968 and 1992, the perpetrators had got away with it in 250 cases. And it was getting worse. Between 1990 and 1992, fifteen in every 100 murders remained unsolved, compared with only six in every 100 between 1968 and 1970.

As an explanation, senior officers told politicians that the early figures were smaller because the police had had twenty-five years to solve those crimes, whereas there had been a relatively short time in which to solve more recent murders. Nevertheless, the politicians became increasingly outraged as they studied whatever crime statistics they could get hold of. What came as no surprise was that the statistics revealed that murder remained male-dominated, with men more than six times more likely to kill than women. Shooting was the most common murder method, but there had been a significant increase in the use of knives and other sharp implements. The number of killers aged between 30 and 44 had gone down significantly since 1968, and more than two-thirds of killers were now aged between 15 and 34.

What the police were well aware of, statistics or no statistics, was the fact that while more than 80 per cent of killers murdered family members, friends or acquaintances, only about 17 per cent of homicides involved killers who were unknown to their victims. As far as the backpacker murders were concerned, it seemed fairly clear that the murderer fell into the latter category and the victims had not died at the hands of someone previously known to them.

Anxious to get the killer off their highways, the New South Wales government pushed senior officers hard for an arrest. The message raced down through the ranks. And the murder investigation became the biggest of its kind in Australian criminal history.

CHAPTER NINE

Paul Douglas was worried. Quite honestly, he didn't know whether he should go to the police — shop a mate — or just pass it all off as a coincidence. But over and over his mind kept going back to those strange conversations with his workmate at the Boral depot. Douglas looked through the newspaper stories again, the ones that told of the discovery of the Germans' bodies. Maybe it was just a coincidence. But what if it wasn't …? Finally he picked up the phone and rang his local police station. It was late November 1993.

'I don't want to waste your time,' he explained, 'but it's to do with these murders in the Belanglo State Forest. It's about this chap I used to work with …'

Douglas went on to explain that up to two months ago, he was working with a man called Paul Miller. Miller wasn't at Boral any more, but there were a couple of things the other man had said that were now playing on his mind, considering all the talk recently about the murders.

In later interviews with the police, Douglas told his story as best he could remember. He spoke of Miller's claims that 'there are more bodies out there', how he had referred to the police not finding the Germans yet, and recalled Miller's comment that 'stabbing a woman is like cutting a loaf of bread'.

Police had received hundreds of tip-offs, many of them leading nowhere, others showing enough promise to warrant further inquiries. The information from Douglas certainly had potential, but it could, like so many other tip-offs, come to nothing. Certainly, it was worth following up. Paul Miller should be quietly checked out.

In England, Paul Onions thumbed through the newspaper clippings that he'd been keeping and read them yet again. He'd first taken an interest in these Australian murders in September 1992 when he had read about the discovery of the British women in the forest. He'd checked the map, and from what he could work out the grave sites were not far from where he'd fled for his life almost three years earlier — from the man who had called himself Bill. Well, he'd given the police a full description of the incident, and no doubt they would be in touch with him if they believed there was any connection.

It was now November 1993, and the British papers had been full of the horrific discoveries of five more bodies. He was surprised that no attempt had been made to contact him, because he was now convinced there was a link between what had happened to him and these other hitch-hikers.

Onions rang Australia House in London, and was eventually given the number of someone to speak to at Task Force Air in Australia. On 13 November he rang the New South Wales police and was put through to an officer. He retold the story of the attack on him by a man called Bill.

'I've just got a feeling that what happened to me is linked with these murders,' said Onions. 'I don't know the area very well, but it looks like it was pretty close to where I had the gun pulled on me. Anyway, I gave all the details to the police in Bowral at the time.'

The Englishman's information was among hundreds of reports that had been made to the Task Force. It took a great deal of time to follow all of these up, and it wasn't until February 1994 that Paul Onions' story became the focus of attention. It had taken three months for the report to reach the ears of Chief Superintendent Clive Small and his senior investigating officer, Detective Senior Sergeant Robert Benson, but when they heard about Onions' call from the UK they agreed that this was both intriguing and serious. Aided by Detective Stuart Wilkins, they began to track down Onions' original report — and the officer who had taken down the details.

The Bowral Police Station occurrence book revealed that the report had been dealt with by Constable Janet Nicholson, who had since been transferred twice: to the south-western Sydney suburb of Camden, and then to nearby Campbelltown. In the course of moving from one police station to the other, she had disposed of unwanted records. Constable Nicholson knew that the details of Onions' report would remain in the occurrence book, but as several years had passed and nothing had come of the reported incident, she'd considered it unnecessary to keep the original statements. No-one involved in the original investigation to find the man who had attacked Onions could have realised just how important that incident was to be in years to come.

Constable Nicholson was grilled by the Task Force detectives. They were becoming increasingly convinced that an incident in which a man had produced a gun and rope in the attempted hold-up of a backpacker near the Belanglo State Forest was of prime importance. While she was unable to produce the statement that she had typed up, Constable Nicholson did have her police notebook. On page 47 were the key facts that she'd jotted down after Onions had come bursting into the Bowral Police Station, accompanied by the woman who had driven him there. She remembered his arriving at 3.20 pm and being very upset. He had given her a jumbled account, which she couldn't follow, of a man and a gun — she'd asked him to calm down, and he was gradually able to give her details of the incident.

'Immediately after getting a reasonably clear picture from Mr Onions, I contacted the police centre at Goulburn and gave them a description of the offender,' she told the Task Force officers. 'According to Mr Onions, he was a burly man in his 40s, with a big moustache and driving a silver four-wheel-drive.'

Constable Nicholson recalled taking Onions into the interview room to get a detailed statement from him. He was still upset and, as he spoke, pausing on one occasion to show her a rip in his T-shirt collar — a result of his struggle to escape from his attacker — his voice rose and he appeared close to tears. In order to get a description of the weapon that the man had produced, Constable Nicholson remembered unbuckling her own service revolver and showing it to Onions.

'It was something like that,' she recalled him saying. 'But I think yours is a bit smaller.'

The Task Force officers asked Constable Nicholson to have another hunt around for the original witness statement that she had typed up in Onions' presence. In any case, the investigating detectives had the occurrence book entry, which the constable had written up from the facts in the statement.

In the bustling operations room at Bowral Police Station, with maps of the forest on the walls, the location of the bodies and police coming and going, Chief Superintendent Small was dismayed that the report of this important occurrence had not surfaced until now. While he was aware that it would have been buried among all the other reports and tip-offs that had poured in, he was concerned that this particular incident had not received earlier attention. He had a gut feeling about it. A man threatening a hitch-hiker on the Hume Highway warranted special attention, and the fact that the reported incident had occurred south of Bowral, and not far from the Belanglo State Forest, elevated it to a priority category.

Small realised that a great deal of work now lay ahead for himself and the Task Force team, but he was convinced that if they could find the man who had pulled the gun on Onions, they could have their backpacker killer. He also knew, however, that personal feelings were not enough to convict. As much as he believed in his own intuition, the only thing that would ultimately matter in court was hard evidence.

It was imperative to bring all their information together and build up a more detailed profile of the assailant who had terrified the young Englishman. The offender had provided personal details of himself to Onions, but were they real? For the time being Small had to gamble that they were at least partly true, and it was at least known that the man had a strong Australian accent, a four-wheel-drive vehicle, and probably a driving licence. It could not be assumed that the vehicle was his, although the fact that he was familiar with the cassette player and the radio made this likely.

Small also reasoned that if the driver was the backpacker killer, he would have had no reason to give Onions a false description. This man was very confident, and would not have expected Onions to escape and tell his story. But of course Onions *had* got away, and the incident would probably have scared the offender enough to lie low for a while.

The police went over the relevant dates. Onions had been attacked on 25 January 1990, just three weeks after the last known sighting of the Melbourne couple. There were then no reported disappearances, or at least none that fitted into the Hume Highway–backpacker category, until Simone Schmidl vanished almost exactly a year later, on 20 January

1991. Virtually another year then passed before Gabor and Anja disappeared around Christmas 1991. But it was then only a further four months before the British pair were last seen alive.

Small was certain that these young women had died on the day they were last seen alive — they were found wearing the clothes they had left Sydney in, and the Belanglo State Forest was only a couple of hours out of the city. It was reasonable to assume that the women had reached this area on the same day as when they had set off. There had been reported sightings of some of the victims after they'd been seen in Sydney, but the Task Force officers had discounted these because of their dubious nature.

Small was intensely aware of the importance of pin-pointing exactly when all the victims had last been seen. If and when they apprehended anyone, the question of alibis would naturally arise. Small reminded himself that what was most significant, however, was that all of the murdered backpackers had vanished during holiday periods — around Christmas or Easter. Even when Simone Schmidl disappeared, on 20 January, many people were still on holiday — and she had vanished on a Sunday, a non-working day for most people, anyway.

Small and his officers also knew that, as a general rule, violent stabbing and gunshot murders, particularly those in isolated places, were committed by unskilled or semi-skilled workers, or by someone who was unemployed. The nature of such attacks, which often suggested that the killer had played with his victims to some degree, did not normally conjure up a white-collar worker in the minds of the homicide men. And in the case of the backpacker murders, the weapons that had been used — two different rifles, a Ruger and another type of .22 according to the ballistic officers, along with a sharp knife and possibly a machete — suggested someone who hunted.

The Task Force head and Senior Sergeant Benson once again studied the maps of the forest on the operations room wall. Apart from the similar ways in which the bodies had been covered, with branches resting against a log or, in Joanne's case, against the boulder, there was the distance that separated those who had travelled in pairs — they had all been found about 30 metres apart.

But to Small, the most significant point was a pattern that had emerged with each set of killings. Gibson and Everist, the first victims, had been buried deep within the forest. Simone Schmidl had been murdered closer to the Hume Highway, while Neugebauer and Habschied had been found even nearer to the main road. Then, Small assessed, the murderer had decided he was getting too close to the pine trees, which forestry workers frequented, and had decided to return deeper into the forest to murder Joanne Walters and Caroline Clarke.

'I have no doubt this offender knows the forest well,' Small told his subordinates. 'In order to find his way around, he must have been there a number of times, and he almost certainly used a four-wheel-drive.'

Small also believed that the killer's confidence had grown — if the clues left in the forest could be relied upon, this man seemed to have spent a great deal of time with his victims as the murders continued. In the case of the Germans, items were spread over several hundred metres and shells had been found some distance from the bodies, suggesting time had been spent firing a weapon. Small did not believe the Germans had been killed where the bodies were buried — he was convinced they had died where the empty cartridge cases were discovered. And the way in which they had died, with Gabor being bound, strangled and shot and Anja being decapitated, also suggested a lengthy period. Covering the bodies, too, would have taken considerable time.

With Joanne Walters, Caroline Clarke, Simone Schmidl, and Anja Habschied the fact that they had no lower clothing on suggested sexual interference, which would have involved time. Whose cigarette butts had the police found? They could have been the killer's, or from one or both of the women — a red cigarette lighter was found in the pocket of Caroline's shirt. In any case, the murderer had lingered long enough for a number of cigarettes to have been smoked by someone.

One of the many calls that had been received by Task Force Air was from a local resident who suggested: 'Have a look at the Milat family — they're a pretty weird bunch. They've got guns and they go shooting.'

Being 'weird' did not make anyone a suspect, but the name had come up once before, when Alexander Milat had reported seeing the British women in a four-wheel-drive in the forest with two men. This information had been treated with scepticism by Detective Senior Sergeant Benson, who did not believe that the combined speeds of Milat's vehicle and the approaching four-wheel-drive would have allowed him to get a good look at the occupants.

Numerous names were being checked, and among these the Milat family now became part of the general investigation. Initial inquiries revealed that there were ten brothers and three sisters; a fourth sister was deceased. The father, who had migrated from Yugoslavia, had died some years earlier but the mother, Mrs Margaret Milat, was still alive and living in the Sydney suburb of Guildford. Many of the brothers were scattered around the south-west Sydney area, with some living in the Southern Highlands.

The first step was to ascertain whether there was 'anything known' about the family — whether any of them had been in trouble with the police, or been involved in any other investigation. Detectives found records of numerous motor vehicle offences, but also others that were more serious, including an arrest for rape, an armed robbery, and breaking and entering.

Discreet inquiries were made at the Roads and Traffic Authority (RTA) — Bill had told Paul Onions that he worked for 'the roads'. They discovered that an Ivan Milat had been working for the RTA — then known as the Department of Main Roads (DMR) since late 1989. Certainly he was working there in January 1990, when Onions was attacked — and what was more, he was on an accrued day off on 25 January, the day of the attack.

Detectives went back further, to the firm that had employed Milat in 1988, a road-sweeping company. Mr John Waylon, director of the company, told police he remember-ed Milat. He had been acquainted over the years through work on the roads, and when Milat asked Waylon if there was a job going with his firm, Waylon had happily taken him on. But he had asked to be employed as Bill Milat, because he said he was trying to avoid a 'domestic situation'. Waylon took this to mean that Milat was trying to avoid a former wife or partner. Waylon considered him to be a model employee, always courteous, always on time. But he stayed at the sweep-ing company for only two months before giving in his notice in November 1988 and going to work for the Boral company in the plasterboard section at its factory next to Rosehill Racecourse.

Police established that Ivan Milat had once again been employed at Boral under the name of Bill Milat, filling in his employment form with the birth date of 9 July 1947. His own birth date, police found out, was actually 27 December 1944.

Police continued checking into Milat's movements and found that when he left Boral after eleven months of employment, he went to work for the RTA, this time under his own name of Ivan Milat.

His worksheets showed that he was off on 30 December

when James Gibson and Deborah Everist went missing, he was not at work when Onions was attacked, and he was not working between 19 and 21 January 1991, covering the day on 20 January when Simone Schmidl had set out to hitch-hike from Sydney to Melbourne. Milat was on leave between 23 December 1991 and 21 January 1992, when Anja Habschied and Gabor Neugebauer vanished. Milat's time sheets also showed that he was off work between 17 and 21 April 1992, when Caroline Clarke and Joanne Walters went missing.

When the RTA depot was closed down, Milat, like all the other workers, was paid off and he was immediately hired by the concrete manufacturers Readymix, a firm he was still working for.

Detectives dug deeper into Milat's background and found he was no stranger to the police. In June 1962, when he was only 17, he had first come to their notice for stealing from a house and he was put on probation for a year. Within two months he was back before the courts, charged with breaking and entering while still on probation and was committed to an institution for six months.

He learned no lessons. In October 1964 he was convicted on two charges of breaking and entering and stealing, for which he was sent to jail for eighteen months. Shortly after his release he was convicted of stealing a motor vehicle and other items. He was sentenced to two years in prison, but was released on parole in April 1967. Within four months he was back before Liverpool Court charged with being an accessory after the fact to stealing, and was sent to jail for three years with an eighteen-month non-parole period. Police read on. Milat had so far proved that he was a robber who was snubbing his nose at the system.

Milat's criminal record then began to show a very bad side. In April 1971 he was charged with the rape of a woman in a field off the Hume Highway, but he had absconded while on bail. In June 1971 a charge was issued against him for robbing a store while armed with a shotgun. Three days later, on 27 June 1971, a charge was brought against him for bank robbery at Canley Heights, in Sydney, while wearing a stocking over his face and armed with a sawn-off rifle and a shotgun. Milat fled to New Zealand. His accomplices, including his brother Michael, were given long jail sentences. In 1974, when Ivan Milat was brought before the courts, he was found not guilty of the rape and armed robbery charges.

Further discreet conversations with workmates at Readymix established that although Milat now drove a red Holden Jackaroo four-wheel-drive vehicle, he had previously sat behind the wheel of a silver-coloured Nissan four-wheel-drive with a white roof and a red and blue stripe on the side. What was more, he was extremely possessive about the vehicle, so it was unlikely that he would have allowed anyone else to use it.

One other line of inquiry had been continuing while the investigation into Ivan Milat was being undertaken — detectives were looking into the background of Paul Miller, the man who once worked for Boral and who had boasted to a workmate before the Germans were found that he knew who had killed them. Licences for cars and motorcycles were carefully checked. Addresses staked out. Detectives' hearts pounded when they found out that Paul Miller was a pseudonym. The man's real name was Richard Milat. He was a younger brother of Ivan Milat. And, until moving to an address in the Southern Highlands, he had lived at 55 Campbell Hill Road, Guildford — the same address that Ivan Milat had been living at before he moved west to his present address in the suburb of Eagle Vale, near Campbelltown.

Detectives agreed that Ivan Milat was shaping up to be a 'very good suspect'.

CHAPTER TEN

Chief Superintendent Small was convinced that they were closing in on a man who would be able to answer a lot of questions about the attack on Onions and, because of his belief that there was a connection, about the backpacker murders. But he and other senior detectives were well aware that they needed to find out a great deal more about Milat. Building up a profile of a suspect without alerting him would be no easy task, but they eventually drew up a detailed picture — going right back to the day that Ivan's father had clumsily met his future wife ...

Stijpan Marko Milat literally bumped into the woman who was to give birth to his fourteen children when he knocked her over while riding his bicycle in 1934. Furious, she didn't want to hear the apologies in his heavily accented English as they picked themselves up from the road. But Stijpan was eager to make amends and at his insistence, amid his exaggerated gesticulations, she finally agreed to go out on a date.

A Croat from what was then a united Yugoslavia, Milat had migrated to Sydney to work as a farmer after serving with the British Army in Europe in World War I, or so his sons boasted to their friends. His dedication to King George V earned him the right of residency in Australia, where he intended to start an industrious life. Margaret was only 19 years old when they met, and a little concerned about getting too involved with a foreigner who was twenty years older, and whose name she couldn't even spell. But she believed he had admirable qualities and, despite the advice of girlfriends who were going out with boys of their own age, she accepted his marriage proposal.

They set up home in a rural area west of Sydney, in Kelly Street, Rossmore, in a house previously owned by Milat relatives — Benedikt, a market gardener, and his wife, Kata. It was here in a small weatherboard house on a slightly undulating landscaping — unbearably hot in summer and bitingly cold in winter — that the first of the next generation of Milats were to begin their days.

Anxious to make himself more 'Australianised', Stijpan changed his name to the English equivalent, Stephen. He worked long hours in the vegetable patch surrounding their home, pausing only to wave to the occasional passing neighbour. There were only a few other houses in Kelly Street, mainly occupied by migrant families, and even today the mixture of homes that stand there — some are modern brick monuments that reflect Mediterranean taste, while others are simple wooden or fibro abodes that have seen little or no restoration for decades — are well spaced by large blocks of land. By the early 1950s, with six youngsters already on their hands, Stephen and Margaret decided it was time to move closer to Liverpool, the nearest large community, which would later establish itself as a city.

Their new home was a small timber house in Junction Road, Moorebank, about 30 kilometres from Sydney's centre. They had, in fact, moved just a few kilometres, from the west side of the Hume Highway to a little over a kilometre to the road's east. Like the house in Kelly Street, the second property was perched in the middle of a vast wasteland that had been divided into vegetable allotments. The tall, muscle-bound Stephen believed that with a lot of hard work there was good money to be made in market gardening, but as a backup he started keeping a few cows, goats and chickens.

Their firstborn in Kelly Street had been a girl, Olga, the first of the fourteen Milats to be delivered at Liverpool Hospital. Three other sisters came along, Shirley, Margaret and Mary. But what delighted Stephen most were his ten sons: Alexander, Boris, Ivan, William (Billy), Michael, Walter (Wally), George, Richard, David and Paul. He was determined to bring them up to appreciate the value of hard work.

In those early days the house was full of children, chickens clucked outside, and their mother toiled night and day in the kitchen. There was lettuce everywhere, the pickings of the flourishing allotments that Stephen tended lovingly. Coming from a Catholic country, he sent all his sons to Liverpool's Catholic Patrician Brothers High School, where their greatest victories were won not in the classroom but in playground and after-class confrontations. The Milat boys were always in trouble — whether for answering back after being scolded during lessons, or trying to steal another boy's girlfriend. Each brother followed the ambitions of his elder — and that was to get through school as quickly as possible and out into the world.

All of the Milat children 'did it tough', but they weren't so different from many of the other big families who grew up in that district. In the Milat family the kids all had to muck in, from the youngest to the oldest. The brothers and sisters either had to help their father when they came home from school, or assist their mother with the washing up and laundry. On Saturdays, there was a choice of getting up at 4 am to help their father, or staying in bed a bit longer and then doing the household chores. There was no way that any of them could escape from being asked to do something around the house.

The Milat sons often became involved in fights, and caused enough consternation in the neighbourhood to result in the police visiting the house frequently. Their mother was very protective, but Stephen was ready to give his kids a belting if he thought they were in the wrong. These were the rules and the Milat brothers, who were usually the troublemakers, readily abided by them and took their punishment when it came.

One by one, the ten sons found a job, labouring mostly, then met a girl and got married. Some of them left home to go off and live with a girl or a wife, but then came back again after something went wrong. Brothers and sisters were coming and going all the time, it seemed to the neighbours. Special bonds were formed within the Milat clan, with each person being closer to one brother or sister than the others. Ivan Milat's bond was with his brother George, ten years younger. Ivan took George under his wing, and made sure he knew that the basic rule of life was to learn how to look after himself.

In the early 1970s, at about the time when George left school, Margaret and Stephen Milat sold up and moved to Campbell Hill Road, Guildford, in Sydney's industrial west. Ivan continued to keep an eye on George after the family moved into the three-bedroom weatherboard house.

Ivan, with his interest in fitness and body-building — despite his love of junk food — was by now regarded as the tough guy of the family; all of the brothers were in firm agreement about that. He would take George out to the back yard and teach him how to fight. He lived by example, always doing his push-ups and weight training, keeping himself really fit, and he was all for giving someone a hiding if they deserved it. But he always told his brothers that they had to stop before a fight went too far.

'If you want a helping hand bashing someone, I'll help you if I can,' Ivan (the police learned) was to often tell George, 'but don't expect me to fight all your battles for you.'

Ivan constantly emphasised the need for George to be able to look after himself. The Milats had earned quite a name for themselves, and there were a lot of people around the district who didn't see eye to eye with them. But those who knew Ivan realised that he didn't want his younger brother to become aggressive — he just knew how tough things could be, and wanted George to be able to stay on top of a situation.

They were a close family in many ways, but in other respects they argued a lot. They all put it down to the fact that there were so many of them. Christmas time in particular emphasised the size of the family when, as teenagers and young adults, they all tried to sit around the table. There was hardly enough room to breathe.

As each of the Milat children grew up, their parents' problems did not diminish. The brothers would tell their friends how David, the second youngest, was about 12 or 14 years old when he mischievously rang Qantas and threatened to blow up a plane unless they provided him with a big ransom, a getaway jet and a 'couple of hosties to go with it'. The police didn't have any trouble finding him because he had used the phone at home. The police treated it as a childish prank, but David got a really bad thrashing from his father over that one.

The local police knew all of their first names and middle names off by heart. Their parents lost count of the number of times that the police would give them an escort home, dump them in front of Stephen, and say something like: 'And guess what your son has been up to tonight?' It almost always ended up with their father handing out a smack across the ear.

Milat senior lived a pretty tough life, but a good one, and died in the early 1980s at the age of 86 after three operations for bowel cancer.

None of the Milats ever tried to pretend that they were saints. The brothers were into joy riding, assault, abuse, driving without a licence — the everyday kind of crime that police have to deal with in a tough working-class suburb. George, despite being under the watchful eye of Ivan, was no angel either, and he received a good behaviour bond for driving a getaway car in a break-and-enter when he was 19. The local police were aware, though, that George often took the blame for things that his brothers had done.

Cars brought them all a lot of problems. The Milat brothers had seemed destined for trouble on the roads since the day their father knocked down their mother with his bike. Cars became a natural part of their lives. Cars and guns — it was part of growing up. They were Milat accessories, just as they were accessories for all the other young fellows in the area. All of the Milat boys used to go out shooting feral animals in the bush, and they needed cars to get there.

'Look after your cars, because without a car you won't be able to move,' Ivan would tell his brothers.

Ivan used to fix up vehicles himself. He had Fairlanes, big custom American jobs, Holdens and Zephyrs, and he really looked after them. If it meant spending a week on a car to smarten it up, Ivan would do it. He'd wash it, change the oil, vacuum it, polish it, take the hub cabs off, steam it — sweating over the car until it looked as though it belonged in a showroom.

The whole Milat family knew that Ivan liked his cars to look as flash as he did. And Ivan loved dressing up smart. He always wore his hair at a reasonable length, always kept himself clean, his face was always shaved, and he spent a long time in the shower. He was so clean and meticulous about his appearance that he could make himself look like a millionaire. He put the same care into his cars and tried to make sure all his brothers did the same, but cars still brought them bad luck.

George, to Ivan's dismay, ran into trouble on the road, although it wasn't when he was at the wheel. One day, when doing some road work for the Water Board, George heard a car crash over the hill and ran straight out on to the road to see what he could do. Another car came up over the hill, didn't see him, and hit him. George was 27 at the time, and he was off work with a crippled leg for four years.

The Milats lost their sister Margaret through a car crash. As they all repeated for years afterwards, it was so damned stupid! She was 16, George was 17, and brother Wally was 18. The three of them had driven off from the house in Guildford in a Valiant Pacer, red with deeper red stripes, with Wally driving, Margaret in the front passenger seat and George in the back. They were only doing a speed of about 50 kilometres an hour, but the car slid on the wet road, smashed head-on into another vehicle, and Margaret banged her head against the windscreen.

When George saw the trouble his sister was in, he ran in a panic all the way home, almost a kilometre. He told his mother there'd been a terrible crash down the road. Ivan was out the back at the time and jumped into his car with George and went to the crash scene. While waiting for an ambulance, Ivan helped out as best he could, but they could all see that Margaret was in a bad way. At the hospital, she was put into intensive care but she died. Bloody stupid loss, they all said. Riding down the road with her two brothers and then she was gone, just like that.

Then there was David. He was now brain damaged, the Task Force officers ascertained, after two bad car accidents. He had no memory. Requests by his family to carry out a simple chore were forgotten within a minute or two. And that was in addition to losing the use of his arm. The Milat brothers, police learned, often told their workmates about how David had been drinking and smoking dope back in 1984 when he had a row with his girlfriend and got on his motorbike and roared off. It was a big motorbike, a 900 cc Kawasaki — a Kwaka, as it was known in the district — and he was so stoned that he fell off on the straight and banged his head. Even though he was wearing a crash helmet, he suffered brain damage. All of the brothers reckoned it was pretty strange that the accident happened almost a kilometre from the house, the same distance away that Margaret was killed.

David started getting blackouts when he came out of hospital and became worried about driving, so he sent the police a letter, telling them about the problem, and handed in his licence. Some time later, the police returned his licence — or at least that's what the Milat brothers told their associates. David started driving an orange 180B Datsun, but blacked out one day as he was going through Liverpool. He hit a truck, wiped out the side of his car, and badly damaged his right arm. David couldn't do much with his arm now, except swing it like a propeller from the shoulder as something of a party trick.

Ivan spent years working for the Water Board, joining them right after he left school, but he also helped his father out with the market garden. After leaving the Water Board he worked at yard cleaning — an essential job while a new house is being built, as yard cleaners pick up all the rubble and clear the site. Ivan also helped one of the brothers doing brick cleaning.

All of the Milat men did heavy manual work — even their father worked on building foundations after leaving the market garden business. Then he started stone masonry, and proved to be good at this too. The Milat father was very meticulous, always had been, and, detectives learned, Ivan often told his workmates that he got his obsession with cleanliness and keeping things in order from his father.

Ivan took George on yard cleaning jobs for a while. George smoked, but nothing like Ivan. George would tell his friends he'd never seen a man smoke like his brother. Ivan wouldn't touch alcohol but he could smoke four cigarettes in the time that George got through one. But Ivan remained fanatical about keeping his body in good shape, even though he smoked and the food he ate was hardly nutritious — fish and chips, hamburgers, chiko rolls, dim sims. Ivan, it was clear to all who knew him, was far more interested in cars than what he ate.

Ivan's cars attracted the girls and he went out with a lot of them over the years, but it was Karen that he really fell for. The problem with this was that she was going out with someone Ivan knew and had become pregnant by him. The police were to learn that, on seeing Karen's unhappiness, Ivan announced one day, 'I'm taking her,' and that was just what he did. Ivan, so the story went, had simply felt sorry for her. Ivan and Karen got married in the mid 1980s — the family didn't take much notice of the date, because none of them went to the wedding, according to what family members told their friends. Ivan, the police understood, had been involved in a family feud over something and he didn't ask any of them. He told his mother where the wedding was going to be, then said it had been cancelled. Karen had her baby long before they were married, and they lived for a while at the Milat family home in Guildford, before getting a place of their own in the western suburb of Blackett.

Guns and knives were both a hobby and tools for the Milats. They used the guns to go shooting feral animals for dog food, and then they'd skin them with their special skinning knives.

Wally was keen on guns, just like Ivan, and they went out shooting together on countless occasions — often to the Wombeyan Caves area. When Ivan was working on the roads he was away from Monday morning until Friday night, but he really enjoyed his weekends, either cleaning his car or heading off into the bush. He always kept his guns shiny and clean and knew how to use them — people often described him as a real expert. In between his work and hunting weekends, Ivan had a string of girlfriends before he went out with Karen. Picking up 'sheilas', as he called them, was part of his entertainment program, but there were bad feelings between Ivan and his younger brother Wally when Wally became suspicious that Ivan was having an affair with his wife in the early 1980s.

This incident had angered Wally, but that was the least of his problems — he almost lost his life in a freak accident with a bullet. Unlike the meticulous Ivan, Wally didn't worry about how old his ammunition was and, what's more, he liked to make his own bullets. His brothers were always telling him that he put too much charge in them, and one day their warnings came home. A hammer fell off a shelf and hit one of Wally's home-made bullets and, because it had so much charge, it exploded loudly, hurling a piece of shrapnel into Wally's right eye. The doctors fought to save the eye but weren't successful, and he ended up getting a glass one.

George, the police established, would often tell his friends about Wally's accident, but he could never remember which eye his older brother had lost. To help his recollection, he would stand with his left foot forward and pretend to hold a rifle, in the way that Wally would stand before the accident. Since then, police learned, Wally would have to look through his left eye when holding a rifle, with his right foot forward.

Chief Superintendent Small carefully read through the documents and police intelligence that had helped to create a picture of Ivan Milat. There was nothing there that decisively ruled him out as a suspect — quite the opposite in fact. In addition to his criminal record, Milat went shooting, and he knew the Southern Highlands. Added to Paul Onions' description, everything seemed to fit in. It was time to put Ivan Milat under surveillance — and talk in detail to the young Englishman who had escaped with his life from the man called Bill.

CHAPTER ELEVEN

Joe Maric, who lived next door to Ivan Milat and his sister Shirley Soire, spotted it when he set off for work one morning: a plumber's van parked on a street corner. Then he kept seeing the van around — on and off for several days, but not always in the same place — and one of Joe's neighbours noticed an electricity van cruising around. The plumber's vehicle and the electricity van seemed to change places sometimes. This went on for weeks, until Joe and other residents of Cinnabar Street, on the Eagle Vale housing estate, in Sydney's south-west and just 350 metres from the Hume Highway, decided that something was up.

'What do you reckon?' asked one of Joe's neighbours. 'There's the vans, and I've noticed the same Holden Commodores cruising around the estate and even the same BMW motorbike.'

'I reckon someone's planning something,' said Joe. 'Could be a gang planning a series of robberies, trying to work out who's at home in the daytime, something like that.'

'I'm going to call the police,' said Joe's neighbour.

If the operation being planned against Ivan Milat was ever in danger of being 'blown', it was in the four months from January to May 1994 while police were keeping him under surveillance. They were watching him at work and at play, snapping photographs of him whenever it was safe to do so.

When the Eagle Vale estate resident telephoned the police, he was told quite openly that the vehicle he had reported was probably a police vehicle. Another neighbour was told not to worry because the cars were part of a major surveillance operation. If the residents had noticed that something was up, it would have been surprising if Milat himself had not been suspicious, especially as he was followed whenever he left for work in the early hours of the morning in the concrete-mix truck he left parked outside the house.

Ivan Milat and Shirley Soire were joint owners of the house at 22 Cinnabar Street, Eagle Vale. The four-bedroomed house was brick, had a tiled roof and a double garage to the left of the front door, and was estimated to be worth $186,000.

As police watched number 22 and the man who occupied it, they took note of his every physical detail. The 49-year-old was certainly well built, with bulging biceps. He sported a moustache which ran down the sides of his mouth into a stubbly beard which had not been allowed to grow below his lower chin. He had greying sidelevers running to the level of his ear lobes and dark hair which was greying at the sides. He had narrow, blue eyes and a tanned complexion, earned from the days he spent working in the sun. But his height was shorter than the 178 centimetres (5 feet 10 inches) estimated by Paul Onions — he would be closer to 170 centimetres (5 feet 7 inches), police guessed.

Some of the surveillance photographs showed Milat with his lips bared, like in a grin — the same kind of grin that Onions described of the man who attacked him on the Hume Highway. In time, the police realised that the 'grin' was simply the way Milat held his mouth, revealing his teeth.

Over all, detectives were excited by the similarities in

Milat's general appearance and the description provided by Onions. As well as talking to the Englishman, they were going to need to talk to Joanne Berry, the motorist who had picked Onions up as he'd fled for his life along the highway. She had had only a glimpse of the attacker, but she'd already told police that he was about 168 centimetres (5 feet 6 inches) tall — closer to the height of the man they were now watching.

Inquiries had also established that Milat had once driven a silver-coloured Nissan four-wheel-drive — another aspect of Milat's profile which needed to be thoroughly checked. But they had not been able to trace any record of his holding a gun licence. Nor could they find any record of a motorcar driving licence — at least not since the early 1970s — yet he was driving a red Holden Jackaroo four-wheel-drive. Sometimes he rode a Harley Davidson motorbike.

Detectives needed a photograph to show to Onions, and although they had started taking surveillance pictures of Milat, they needed a good, clear, close-up. Not that they would have been able to have got hold of it, but he was actually proudly posing for a photograph in January 1994, as the secret investigation into his background began. He dressed up for the photograph: a cowboy outfit, a leather belt with a holster and gun slung around his waist, a wide-brimmed hat, and a shiny Texas Ranger badge pinned to his chest. The picture was taken in his lounge room and showed Milat, with a long Mexican-style moustache, surrounded by weapons and ammunition.

For a good close-up of the man in whom they were extremely interested, detectives had to look elsewhere. One possible source was a passport photograph — but had Ivan Milat ever applied for a passport? When he fled to New Zealand in 1971, to escape a charge of raping a hitch-hiker, passports were not necessary for Australian citizens travelling to that country. Checks were made with the Department of

Immigration, and detectives couldn't believe their luck — not only had Milat obtained a passport, he had received it as recently as 1989. His height on his passport application was said to be 178 centimetres (5 feet 10 inches). The photograph that accompanied his application showed a man with a moustache that reached down to the sides of his mouth.

Detective Stuart Wilkins, a Task Force Air member, contacted Paul Onions several times during April 1994, going over the Hume Highway incident in detail, and concentrating on the description of the offender. On 2 May, the Englishman was secretly flown to Sydney and put up in a hotel and given time to get over jet lag. Two days later, he travelled with Detective Wilkins and Detective Sergeant Graham Pickering to Liverpool, where he identified the stretch of road he had walked along before he had seen the Coca Cola sign. He now learned this area was Casula and the newsagent's he had purchased a drink from was known as Lombardo's. From there, he and the police travelled down the highway along the route that 'Bill' had taken. Onions told them to pull in to the side of the road at a particular point — it was where the driver had pulled the gun on him. The place was 900 metres north of the Belanglo State Forest turn-off.

The following day Onions, nervous about the whole affair yet anxious to help the police in their efforts to find his attacker and, perhaps, the backpacker killer, was taken to the video unit at the New South Wales police headquarters in Sydney, where he was shown a number of photographs of men with moustaches — thirteen in all — as they appeared on a TV screen. When face number four appeared, Onions suddenly yelled: 'That's him! That's the man who robbed me!' He had picked out Ivan Milat. But, to be certain, the Englishman went through the faces several more times, working the remote control himself.

Detectives knew they would have to move in on Milat at

some stage, but they still needed to act with caution while going about their background inquiries.

Although Ivan Milat had called himself Bill at two workplaces, police were aware that he also had a brother three years his junior and whose name was Bill. They had to be absolutely sure they were locked onto the right suspect. Inquiries were made into Bill Milat's background and they established that he had lived for a number of years in Bargo, in the Southern Highlands, and had been married to Carolynne Milat for more than twenty years. Bill, detectives ascertained, was not as sturdily built as Ivan, had a short moustache and thinning dark hair. His appearance did not fit in with the description provided by Onions. But had Ivan been using Bill's identity? Certainly when he had applied for a job at Boral in 1988 he had filled in the form under the name of William and had stated he was born in 1947 — the same year as his younger brother William.

Ivan had not owned a motor vehicle licence in his own name since 1971, and he had not obtained a shooter's licence until 1991. But had he possessed weapons, illegally, before then? That was something the detectives hoped to find out — and urgently.

Despite learning that Ivan and Bill Milat were two different people, detectives decided nevertheless to pay a 'courtesy call' in the near future on William in Bargo and find out whether he had been driving a four-wheel-drive Nissan on the day of the attempted kidnapping of Paul Onions. Always, they were aware that inquiries they made about Milat could leak back to him, but that was a chance they had to take. In making their inquiries, they had to show their hand to some extent.

Among Ivan Milat's workmates at the old DMR was Anthony Sara, who started at the depot in 1989 and got to know Milat when they were both being trained to use some road levelling equipment. Police tracked him down in April

1994, and although stunned at their approach for help in their inquiries into Ivan Milat, he agreed to tell them what he could.

Their work, Sara revealed to detectives, took them around a 300-kilometre radius of Sydney, which entailed staying in motels. As their friendship developed, Ivan took Sara to meet his mother at her home in Campbell Hill Road, Guildford, where he was also introduced to two of Ivan's brothers: Richard, and the brain-damaged David. Richard, Sara noticed, called Ivan 'Mack'. He had driven with Ivan to the small community of Hilltop, where he was introduced to brother Wally and his wife Lisa. Sara recalled Ivan telling him how the family owned a block of land near Wombeyan Caves in the Southern Highlands and it was there that they sometimes went shooting. Ivan said he had a 'quite a few' guns and showed Sara photographs of two of the weapons; Sara thought they were an SKS and an SKR.

As their friendship developed and Ivan talked about guns, Sara became interested in weapons and accompanied him to a gun shop at Horsley Park, in Sydney's western suburbs, where Milat had looked at a shotgun and purchased $400 worth of ammunition. Some time later, Sara told the police, Milat had told him that 'I have got that "shotty"', a reference to the shotgun he had been looking at.

As detectives talked to Sara, who continued to admit his unease about discussing his former workmate, he revealed that one day in the early part of 1992 as they were travelling in an RTA vehicle along the Hume Highway past the Belanglo State Forest, Milat remarked: 'You'd be surprised what's in there.'

'What was your response?' detectives asked Sara, their curiosity deeply aroused.

'I said something like: "What, snakes, kangaroos, that kind of thing?"' But, Sara told the police, Milat didn't answer his question. He continued talking about work. But it could have been because Milat hadn't heard the question — he seemed to have hearing difficulties at times. The police pressed Sara. Was the remark made before September 1992, when the bodies of the English women were found? Yes, said Sara — it was only later that he had read the news about the backpacker murders.

Sara went on to tell the police what else he knew about Ivan Milat. He was very proud of his Nissan four-wheel-drive, which he traded in for a red Jackaroo in about 1992. Sometimes at work he had seen Milat with a bowie hunting knife and he was always talking about guns. Around about June 1992, Milat had started going out with Chalinder, a short, dark-haired woman of Indian descent, whom he referred to as Cylinder because he couldn't pronounce her real name. Also in 1992 he had started talking about a house in Eagle Vale, in which he had a half share with 'a bird I have known for years, Shirley'.

The interview with Sara was over. In time, police were to learn that Sara phoned Milat three weeks after the interview, about getting some work. In the course of their conversation Sara told Milat: 'I've been contacted by a couple of detectives about the Belanglo State Forest.'

Again, Milat didn't respond, Sara was to tell police. He continued talking about work, just as he had when Sara had asked the earlier question when they were travelling past the forest.

While inquiries were continuing into Ivan Milat's background, detectives were also looking carefully at Richard Milat, the man who had called himself Paul Miller at the Boral complex and who had boasted about the police not finding the Germans in the Belanglo State Forest.

They obtained a photograph of Richard, established that he was Ivan's younger brother, and in order to ensure that it was indeed he who had been working at Boral and had made the boasts, they took the picture to Lawrence Aked, the company's human resources manager. They also showed him a photograph of Ivan Milat, the man they believed worked at Boral under the name of Bill Milat. Aked told the police what they expected to hear — the photo of Richard Milat was the man who had worked at Boral from early 1988 until June 1993. And the photograph of Ivan Milat showed the man he knew as Bill Milat.

'All their lives they've been confusing police and covering up for one another, and they're still throwing spanners into the works,' said one detective after the identities of the photographs had been confirmed.

Apart from planning a visit to William Milat in Bargo, Task Force Air detectives also put Alexander Milat on their list of family members to be called on. They wanted to know what Alex would now have to say about the incident he had reported — the incident in which he claimed to have seen two women, who he believed answered the descriptions of the English backpackers, in a vehicle in the Belanglo State Forest.

Chief Superintendent Small and his officers were well aware that any relatives contacted by the police might phone Ivan Milat and tell him, just as Sara had, so detectives obtained official permission to set up a telephone intercept on Milat's phone line to listen to his reactions to any calls he received.

On Saturday 21 May Detectives Brett Coleman, Royce Gorman and Mark Feeney called at the Bargo home of William and Carolynne Milat, Ivan's brother and sister-in-law. Deborah Milat, William's daughter, who was in her early 20s, answered the door.

'I'm sorry,' said Deborah, 'my parents have gone away, but can I help you?'

'It's all right,' replied one of the detectives, 'we just want to see your father about a traffic matter involving a four-wheel-drive vehicle, a silver Nissan Patrol. We want to ask him about Mr Ivan Milat registering cars in your father's name.'

'I'll tell him you called,' said Deborah.

Later that day she spoke to her father, who told her to contact her uncle Ivan and tell him what had happened. She rang the Cinnabar Street house throughout the rest of the day but received no response. Finally at 8.30 pm her uncle's girlfriend answered. Chalinder Hughes told Deborah that Ivan was in the shower, but that he would call back.

Fifteen minutes later the phone rang at Bill's home, and Ivan asked: 'What's wrong?'

'Dad told me to call you and tell you that the police know you've been registering your cars in his name,' said Deborah.

'Don't worry about it,' said Ivan. 'They know it was registered in your dad's name. Now, how's little Matthew [Deborah's baby son] …'

On that same day, 21 May, Detective Senior Sergeant Robert Benson and two other detectives, acting on the orders of Chief Superintendent Small, walked up to the front door of a house in Dulong Road, West Woombye, a small hill community 20 kilometres inland from the popular Queensland coastal resort of Maroochydore.

In many respects the area resembled the surroundings of the Southern Highland township of Buxton, where Alexander Milat and his wife Joan — the name she preferred to her first name, Elizabeth — had lived for a number of years before moving north in late 1992.

Alexander Milat interested the police in two respects: first, the curious statement he had made about seeing the British women being abducted, and secondly, the timing of his move to Queensland, which had occurred a short time after the bodies of Joanne Walters and Caroline Clarke had been found.

When Mr and Mrs Milat had shown the officers into the

151

dining room, Sergeant Benson asked if she had any camping equipment that may have been given to her by someone in her family. She asked them to wait a moment, left the room and returned after a short time with a backpack in lilac, pink and black colours.

Benson looked on in contained astonishment as Mrs Milat opened the top flap and indicated the initials 'IM' on the inside of the flap. He examined the initials carefully, noting that the M was intersected by the I. The backpack, she said, had been given to her by her brother-in-law Ivan before she and her husband moved to Queensland. Sergeant Benson passed the backpack to one of his equally surprised companions — they had not expected what looked like vital evidence to fall so easily into their hands.

IM — Ivan Milat? It seemed certain that the initials stood for his name. But, the sergeant reflected as he returned to the police car, there was more to the article than Ivan's initials. He believed that the pack, a Salewa brand, was very similar to the one that Simone Schmidl had been carrying when she disappeared.

'There's something else,' said Detective Senior Constable Stuart Wilkins, one of the officers who had taken Paul Onions back to the Hume Highway and who had now accompanied Benson to Queensland. 'I'm willing to give evidence on oath to this effect — that Joan mentioned, in passing, something about serial killers keeping tokens like backpacks.'

The net was closing in around the man who lived at 22 Cinnabar Street. While detectives were working in the Southern Highlands, talking to Deborah, and visiting Alex and his wife in Queensland, other officers were watching Milat himself as he went about his work on that Saturday 21 May. They followed him as he rode his Harley Davidson motorbike to the Readymix depot at Rosehill, then kept a discreet distance as he went about his tasks that day with a workmate on a road profiling machine at two locations around Sydney. They watched with interest when Milat, the road work finished, drove a company truck towards Casula, where at 1.27 pm, detectives noted, he stopped off at the newsagent's where Paul Onions claimed he had first met his attacker. Later, after picking up Chalinder from her Sydney home, he drove with her to the depot where he completed his daily tasks and drove with her in the company truck to his home, stopping off at a KFC fast food outlet before arriving home at 7.38 pm. He did not go out again.

But at about 2 am on Sunday, his brother Bill phoned him from his weekend holiday location. Bill, who seemed to have been drinking, told Milat that the police had called on him during the previous day and asked about the Nissan.

The assault began the next morning, in the final hour of darkness. At 6.40 on that cool morning of 22 May 1994, a convoy of police vehicles, some disguised as they had always been, as tradesmen's vans, screamed into the Eagle Vale housing estate and blocked off Cinnabar Street, leaving just enough room for a white vehicle, filled with commando-style police of the State Protection Group, to speed through. The Toyota stopped outside number 22.

Inside the house, Ivan Milat and his girlfriend Chalinder — Ivan's sister Shirley was not at home — were disturbed by the insistent ringing of the telephone. Milat picked it up. The caller was police negotiator Detective Sergeant Wayne Gordon, parked in a police vehicle a few streets away and out of sight of the house. A sleepy-sounding Milat answered.

Gordon, calling Milat 'mate', told him who he was, that a search warrant had been issued and that armed police had surrounded the house.

Milat was told to leave the house and walk down the street with his arms out in front of him, well exposed, 'for the safety of yourself and whoever's in the house with you' and he would be met by members of the State Protection Group.

'They'll be dressed in black. They will be armed and I want you then, at their direction, to lay face down on the ground,' said Gordon.

'Okeydoke,' said Milat, but after three minutes he had failed to come out. So Gordon phoned again, asking Milat and his girlfriend to walk out of the front door separately.

'Hang on, hang on,' said Milat. 'Well, what, you're tellin', you know, like, I, I just assumed you were someone from work ringin' up.'

'No, mate,' said Gordon. 'I'm from the police. It's no joke. This is real.'

'Why didn't you knock on the bloody door or something like that?'

Gordon, an expert negotiator in counter-terrorism, hostage and suicide situations, told him that it was police procedure to ring the occupants of a house before a search.

Milat laughed, then said: 'Hey, I'm just lookin' out the window. I can't see anybody.' And he asked whether the police wanted him and his girlfriend to walk out 'lookin' like an idiot or something'.

Gordon, insisting again that it was no joke, told him once more who he was.

Milat said: 'Well, that doesn't mean anything to me.'

Once again, Milat was told to leave the house and walk out of the front gate and turn left.

'We haven't got a gate,' Milat said. Then he added after a further brief conversation, his voice stuttering: 'It, it, it strikes me as slightly weird, but anyway, I'll play your little game.'

Shortly afterwards, when it was suggested Miss Hughes could follow him out, he said: 'I think we'll just walk out together. I'm not real keen on this.' But he said he would be 'out in a second'.

More than two minutes passed, with the front door remaining closed. Gordon made a third call.

Miss Hughes answered. 'Yeah, we're comin' out now,' she said. 'He's just trying to find the keys. He always loses them in the morning.'

Finally Milat opened the door.

Senior Constable Ray Duncan was one of two black-clad figures, wearing reversed black baseball caps, from the State Protection Group standing on each side of the house. Others were positioned nearby. Duncan was armed with a Remington A70 shotgun and a self-loading pistol. He was ready for anything. He and his colleagues would not have been called in unless plain-clothed and uniformed police were confronting a dangerous situation. The State Protection Group team had been warned that the man inside the house was a gun fanatic and there would certainly be weapons inside. Duncan's finger had been on the shotgun trigger from the moment he had silently approached the house.

Now, from Duncan's position beside the garage, he heard the telephone ring inside the main premises. Shortly afterwards he heard a door leading from the house into the garage open, followed by a car door opening and closing.

Duncan, who was being kept closely informed of the telephone negotiations by radio transmitter through a small earpiece, saw Milat step out onto the lawn ... saw Milat turn towards him ... heard him exclaim 'Shit!', as he noticed the heavily armed black-clad figure beside his garage.

Then Duncan and his colleague rushed at him, yelling: 'Get down! Get down!'

As Milat dropped to his knees, he was pushed face down onto the grass. In an instant, the barrel of a shotgun was jammed against his head while his hands were jerked up behind and looped plastic restraints, known as flexicuffs, were pulled tight around his wrists.

Unmarked police vans sped up to the house, disgorging more State Protection Group officers, this time wearing army greens and carrying pump-action shot-guns.

As Milat lay on the ground he was approached by Detective Sergeant Stephen Leach, a powerfully built officer with neatly cropped hair and beard, who showed him a search warrant and told him the house was going to be looked over.

A State Protection Group team went through the premises first, making sure it was safe for other officers to enter. Milat was hauled to his feet and led back inside. There were a few initial questions Leach and his colleagues wanted to ask him in relation to the attack on Paul Onions and the murders of the backpackers.

By now the neighbours were out in the street, some in their pyjamas and nightgowns, stunned at the arrest of the man they had all regarded as a good-natured, hard-working resident who kept the house, the lawn, his red four-wheel-drive Holden Jackaroo and his Harley Davidson motorcycle in immaculate condition. Now the mysterious activities of various vehicles in the district in preceding weeks was explained, although the target of the police surveillance was still a surprise. Milat was so highly regarded and trusted that he would play with the local children and give them rides on the mini-bike and go-kart that he kept. And he had once promised an unemployed neighbour that he would keep an eye out for a job for him.

One of the officers who walked into Milat's home moments after it was given the 'all clear' by the State Protection Group team was Detective Senior Constable Grosse. They were about to start looking for any property that might link Milat to the Belanglo Forest murders. And not just guns. What else, nobody knew. Matching bullets, perhaps, even some ropes ... only a thorough search would give up the secrets the house may or may not hold. It was planned that the four-bedroom premises would be searched systematically, one of the officers being instructed to note where any item thought relevant to their inquiries was found.

In Milat's bedroom Grosse found in a built-in cupboard a metal tin containing thirty-eight .22 bullets, and on the shelf an unused 12-gauge shotgun cartridge. He also collected a 12-gauge buckshot cartridge, a rifle telescopic sight, and a tin of 500 air rifle pellets.

In a bedside table he found an envelope containing foreign currency: NZ notes, what looked like a Greek currency note and Indonesian money. Simone Schmidl, he recalled, had been to New Zealand, both the English women had been to Greece and the Germans Gabor and Anja had been to Indonesia and were planning to return. The bedside table also contained a postcard sent from New Zealand from a man called Jock and addressed to Ivan Milat. But the text, inviting Milat to come over to New Zealand some time, began 'Hi Bill'. Detectives made a note to try to trace the writer and ask about his association with Milat. Grosse also found a driving licence with Milat's photograph but issued in the name of a brother, Michael Gordon Milat.

As the search of the house continued, Detective Senior Constable Peter O'Connor climbed a ladder in the garage and hauled himself through a manhole into the attic. The beam of his torch swept over the rafters, then down into the wall cavity. Something white caught his eye — a plastic bag. Even lying flat, he couldn't reach it, so he climbed back down and found a stick. This time he was able to pull the bag up. It contained rifle parts — a trigger assembly, a spring and guide and bolt assembly, and a .22 calibre rifle magazine — and a piece of cloth. When Grosse was shown the parts, he wondered whether they were from a Ruger rifle. He would leave it to the experts to confirm that.

Grosse went into the garage through a door leading

from the central hallway, and noticed a red Holden Jackaroo four-wheel-drive vehicle, registration number QBY 388. He found packets of bullets in the pockets of a green jacket in the vehicle and spotted a blue nylon Salewa-brand sleeping-bag cover in the garage.

Back in the house one of Grosse's team showed him a Salewa-brand sleeping bag. Already at this discovery, detectives were beginning to discount the sleeping bag that had been found in Victoria and which had been thought to belong to Simi. Her mother had accepted that the sleeping bag discovered in Victoria had belonged to her daughter, but here was a similar-looking article carrying the brand name Salewa, rare in Australia.

Moving meticulously from room to room and through the garage, detectives found a piece of silver-coloured piping in a shoe box which they decided to pass on to forensic police — it looked like it might be a home-made silencer; a .22 Winchester bolt action rifle under the bed of Milat's sister, Shirley; a box of .22 Winchester rapid fire bullets between the mattresses of Shirley's bed; photograph albums containing pictures of Milat with roadmaking machinery and firearms and of him in the vicinity of the house as it was being built; a Ruger-brand receiver (the housing around the bolt) in plastic wrapping inside a boot in a hallway cupboard; a map of the city of Newcastle, north of Sydney; and a map of the Belanglo State Forest and surrounding areas.

Other interesting finds included black electrical tape; an unused passport, issued in August 1989, in the name of Ivan Milat, with the photograph showing Milat with a moustache; and an Olympus camera. Onions had been carrying an Olympus camera when he was forced to flee from 'Bill's' vehicle. Caroline Clarke had also had one of the same make.

As the search was going on, Detective Sergeant Stephen Leach informed Milat, who was now handcuffed with metal cuffs and sitting on a couch in the living room, that he wanted to ask him about the murders of the backpackers.

Milat replied: 'I don't know what you're talking about.'

Describing the attack on Paul Onions, Leach asked Milat what he knew about it.

'I don't know what you're talking about,' Milat again replied. He gave the same answer when asked what he knew about the deaths of the seven backpackers.

'I've been told that you own hand guns and rifles,' said Leach.

Milat's response was: 'Whoever told you that, tell them to come and give them to you.'

By now, Leach had been handed bullets found in the bedroom. He showed them to the arrested man. Milat said he used them to go shooting at his brother Alex's place at Buxton in the Southern Highlands and that he borrowed his brother's weapons on those occasions.

He was asked again about the incident involving Onions.

'I had nothing to do with it,' he said.

'Mr Onions has identified you.'

'It wasn't me.'

Had he ever been to the Belanglo Forest?

'I know where it is,' said Milat. 'I've driven down a dirt track that goes past it.'

'When was that?' asked the police officer.

'A long time ago — in the mid 80s.'

Shown the rifle parts from the wall cavity and asked what they were, Milat replied: 'Looks like something out of a gun.'

'Have you seen it before?' asked Leach.

'No,' said Milat, adding that he had no idea how the parts had got there.

When asked who had been in the ceiling, he replied: 'You blokes and the builders.'

Shortly before 9 am, Ivan Milat, a jacket over his head, was led handcuffed to a police car and driven to Campbelltown Police Station for further questioning. He was taken into an interview room where, as the video camera ran and an audio recorder made a separate recording, Sergeant Leach asked him further questions about the incident on the highway and the bodies in the forest.

Although Milat exercised his right not to answer any more questions, when invited to comment on the gun parts and how they got into the wall cavity, he replied: 'I wouldn't have a clue. I presume youse had them.'

After further conversations, during which Milat questioned the accuracy of notes taken by police in relation to conversations at the house, the road ganger was charged with the armed hold up of Paul Onions near Berrima on 25 January 1990.

The Eagle Vale house had been one of seven to be hit that morning by teams of police headed by officers from Task Force Air. All the others were occupied, or had been owned, by members of the Milat family, including Ivan Milat's elderly mother, Margaret.

Despite the neighbours guessing that something big was up, such was the secrecy in police ranks that many of the younger officers who were to take part in the raids were not aware Operation Air–1 was to start until they were briefed at the Goulburn Police Academy at 5 am.

At 7.43 am Margaret Milat answered the determined banging on the door of her weatherboard home in Campbell Hill Road, Guildford. Now aged 75, white-haired and recovering from a recent bout of illness, she lived there alone with her brain-damaged son David, who had not yet got up. Still in her pink dressing gown, there was little she could do to stop the emotion-charged police officers as they flashed a warrant and pushed past her to begin a thorough search of the house.

Detective Sergeant Gae Crea examined a grey metal

locker secured with a padlock. Neither Mrs Milat nor David had a key. But after forcing the cupboard open, Crea found three rifles. One had the name 'Ivan' engraved at the end of the barrel and another was threaded for use with a silencer. The ballistics unit was already convinced that markings on bullets that killed Caroline Clarke showed they had been fired by a gun fitted with a silencer. Sergeant Crea was also aware that Milat had been living with his mother in the Guildford house at the time the seven backpackers had disappeared.

Moving into David Milat's bedroom, Sergeant Crea searched for a particular weapon that had been mentioned by neighbours to police. After a short hunt around, he found what he was looking for: a cavalry-type sword in a sheath. Could this have been the weapon that had decapitated Anja Habschied? It joined the other weapons to be sent off for forensic tests.

Meanwhile in the Southern Highlands, scores of heavily armed police raided homes occupied by Ivan's younger brothers: Walter, in the district of Hilltop; William in Bargo; and two caravans occupied by Richard and his de facto wife, Elizabeth Smith, in remote bushland at Hilltop near the Wombeyan Caves. All homes were within 70 kilometres of one another.

In a photo album found at William's home, Detective Sergeant Royce Gorman found pictures of a four-wheel-drive Nissan vehicle identical to that used in the kidnapping attempt against Paul Onions. Captions on the photos identified the vehicle as 'Mack's truck', and police had identified 'Mack' as one of Ivan's nicknames. The vehicle had a bull-bar on the front and appeared, from the photos, to have white sheepskin seat covers.

Richard Milat's property, covering more than 400 hectares, was so inaccessible that police who had been brought in by mini-van and bus had to set up a base camp at a hobby farm on an adjoining property and walk the rest of the way. They spread out around the two caravans located there, paying particular attention to rubbish areas and places where fires had been lit. As they continued the search of the property — which Richard had purchased on a 50–50 basis with Walter for the purposes of camping, motorbike riding and shooting — police found a sleeping mat and a sleeping bag in a cupboard in a canvas annexe linking the two caravans. They took them away, wondering if they were connected with the missing backpackers.

A hobby farm at Buxton, also in the Southern Highlands and occupied until 1992 by Ivan's brother Alexander and his wife, Joan, was another police target. For much of the day, police in dark-blue overalls or black leather jackets searched all the raided properties from top to bottom, including outhouses. The searches were thorough, officers collecting even old rags, pieces of rope, pieces of plastic. They knew much of it would eventually be discarded — but there might be things among the collection which could be linked to the murdered backpackers.

Aided by sniffer dogs, police paid particular attention to Walter's bushland home and two caravans parked about a kilometre away. With shovels and rakes, officers dug up earth at the side of the house while others scoured the ground with metal detectors. At the back of the house they opened up a locked under-ground workshop, built by Walter — according to neighbours — some three years earlier.

By the end of the day, the police working at Walter's place had taken possession of an arsenal of some fifteen rifles, including an Anschutz without a breach bolt and a pistol, plus two backpacks, pieces of clothing and blankets. They also found a yellow haversack, with Ivan Milat's name on it, in the workshop (or alcove, as police preferred to describe it). Inside the haversack was a single bolt from an Anschutz rifle, wrapped in a piece of red-checked shirt.

Detective Sergeant Michael Plotecki, one of those who

searched Walter's property, was particularly interested in boxes of ammunition which bore the same manufacturer's batch number as an empty box discovered some 160 metres from the body of Gabor Neugebauer.

Walter and Richard Milat faced intense questioning before being released on bail on a number of firearms and drug offences.

On the day of the raids, Ivan's younger brother George was drinking coffee at his kitchen table on a farm at Douglas Park, south-west of Sydney. Out of work and living alone since his divorce, George spent his days wandering around the property, keeping it in good order. Although not a tall man, George, with flecks of grey in his beard and curly hair, had a good physique and a resilience that led him to strut around in shorts, even in winter, among the sheds and car chassis that had found their way onto the property. His legs and arms bore evidence of his numerous visits to the tattooist and he spoke in basic English, but he had won many friends in the neighbourhood for his good nature and open manner.

The phone rang. Outside, his blue heeler dog barked and strained on its long chain. George put the coffee mug down and walked over to the phone. It was the afternoon of 22 May 1994.

'Hello,' said George.

'George,' a voice said. He recognised his oldest sister Olga immediately. 'Those backpacker murders ... they've picked up Ivan. They're blaming it all on him.'

He knew all about the backpacker murders. There wasn't a person in Australia who hadn't heard about the seven bodies found in the Belanglo State Forest, south of his place. His farm was about a third of the way between Liverpool, where most of the travellers had set out for their journey south, and the forest. He'd also realised, from reading the

163

newspapers, that if the two British girls had travelled from Bulli Pass to the Hume Highway, they would have taken a road running a little to the north of where he lived.

Now his sister was telling him that the police had got Ivan. But over the years George had become accustomed to hearing that his brothers had been questioned by the law for one thing or another, and his first reaction was: 'Well, that's tough luck that he should get something like that thrown at him.'

Later, his mother rang. 'Have the police hit your place?'

'No,' said George, 'no-one's been here.' And they hadn't. Of all the Milat properties to the west and south-west of Sydney, George's had remained untouched when police had carried out their series of dawn raids. But why, he asked himself, would the police raid him? He didn't have a lot to do with his brother Ivan nowadays. They'd simply gone their separate ways.

George had put the phone down after his mother rang and, now that he was giving the beer a miss, went off to make himself another cup of coffee. He sat down at the old kitchen table and stared out towards the outhouse, where he kept his skinning knives and a sharp machete that he used in the bush. 'Jeez,' he said. Then he closed his eyes and thought a great deal about his brother Ivan.

'Greta Pearce' (not her real name) was not surprised to read about Ivan Milat's arrest. Twenty-three years earlier, in 1971, she and her friend 'Dianne' (not her real name) were picked up by Milat while they were hitch-hiking on the Hume Highway. He had driven them into a field and threatened to cut their throats if they did not let him have sex with them. He tied up the young women 'like chickens', with a piece of cord, and then raped Dianne in the front seat of his V8 Falcon sedan.

Later, when he stopped at a garage with the young

164

women, one of them was able to raise the alarm. Milat drove off, but was chased and caught by police. He was arrested, but while on bail he fled to New Zealand.

When he eventually returned to Australia three years later, in 1974, he was found not guilty because of a discrepancy in the women's stories.

Greta had always remained convinced that, had she and Dianne not escaped from the car, they would have died later that night. She also knew she would hear the name Milat again in the future, and that it would be in relation to a similar, if not worse, crime.

CHAPTER TWELVE

Police interviewed a woman who had been a neighbour of Ivan Milat and his wife, Karen, in the years when they lived in Sorensen Crescent, Blackett, near Mount Druitt, in Sydney's western suburbs.

Sometimes, when the neighbour walked past the Milats' small brick house on the corner she would see Ivan sitting on the step polishing a gun. When he saw her watching, he would give her a momentary glare as if she had disturbed him while performing a private ritual, then he would pick up the weapon and move around the back. At other times, the neighbour would see him standing in a vest in the garden, biceps bulging as he worked out with weights.

And then there were the secret moments Ivan's wife spent talking with her — times when Karen opened her heart before her husband came home. She talked of the beatings, the sexual domination, the verbal abuse, the total domination of her life. 'I'm so terribly unhappy,' Karen would say. 'If only I could escape. I thought we would be fine together, but it didn't work out that way. He gets on well with everyone, but as far as I'm concerned I'm just a woman to be kicked around and abused.'

This slightly built woman was by now in her early 30s. In the three years they had been married, Karen grew to hate her husband. Sure, Ivan earned good money and he had provided her with a home when she'd been a single mother with a young son years before, when her future looked very bleak. Things hadn't been too good with the natural father of her son, and while she was still pregnant Ivan had started dating her after they were introduced by her second eldest brother in the mid 1970s. She knew nothing about the rape charge of which he had been acquitted.

Ivan had lived with her for a while at her home near Liverpool and then, in 1978, she and her son moved in with him at his mother's home in Campbell Hill Road, Guildford. Karen was full of hope that her life would take a turn for the better. Ivan was more than ten years older than she, but he often joked that there had been twenty years difference between 'his old man' and his mother, and they'd managed pretty well and had raised fourteen children.

Karen had spent her childhood in a weatherboard house in Reilly Street, Lurnea — a five-minute drive along the Hume Highway from the centre of Liverpool — with her mother Elaine, father Ron, who worked as a bus driver, and her three elder brothers. By 1979 the family had broken up: Karen had started a new life with Ivan, and her parents and brothers moved to the Central Coast area of New South Wales.

Life with Ivan at his mother's home was rather cramped, with Richard also in residence and numerous brothers coming and going, but Karen enjoyed Ivan's 'manliness'. He was a good worker and a 'fixer', a man who could lend his hand to anything practical.

'Don't worry,' he had assured Karen. 'We'll find a place of our own soon. And we'll get married. I reckon it's about time we did something about it.'

In the early 1980s they found their dream home in Sydney's western suburbs — a brick house occupying a corner block in Sorensen Crescent. There was nothing about the couple and the young boy that caught the neighbours' attention, apart, perhaps, from the difference in their ages. And Blackett wasn't the kind of place where you had nothing else to do but mind other people's business.

The couple didn't get married until 20 February 1984, but by then Ivan and Karen had slipped easily into the community as a family unit. They were just like everyone else in the neighbourhood, a working-class area where, depending on the ages of their children, most husbands and wives all went out to work, leaving their kids to knock around the streets after school until tea time. If the children were still young, their mothers remained at home, and some went to the school gate to collect their youngsters. Karen was one of those.

Ivan had a good job as an asphalt layer with the Department of Main Roads, but it often meant that he left home early to get to his work site, and he would sometimes be away for weeks at a time, sleeping in motels or in a roadside caravan with his workmates.

On some weekends Ivan and Karen and her son Jason would head south to join Ivan's brothers for a camp-out in the bush. Sometimes they'd take a trailer, with the boy's mini-bike strapped down in the back with a length of blue and yellow rope. Jason also liked to watch his stepfather make model trucks, and would look carefully as Ivan opened up little tins of paint and decorated the models in camouflage colours. It was fun, too, to watch Ivan fiddle around with a police scanner, listening to all the messages from miles around. Sometimes they picked up aircraft and ambulances.

Karen had grown to live with her husband's obsession with guns. He'd told her how he'd caught the bug from his father, who had taught him and his brothers how to shoot. But now Ivan loved watching Wild West movies and videos and fancied himself as something of a modern day cowboy, calling himself 'Texas' or, to amuse Jason on one of their trips to the Southern Highlands, 'Bargo Bill'. One of Ivan's most treasured possessions was a black revolver, given to him by his brother Walter in 1981. Ivan was so impressed with the gun that he bought an engraver to etch the name 'Texas' on each side of the trigger and at the bottom of the butt.

Although she tolerated Ivan's passion for guns, she was uneasy about the weapons nevertheless. She confided to her neighbour: 'He even keeps a loaded pistol in a sock under the front seat of the car. Sometimes he tucks it into his boot and walks around with it, like a cowboy. When we go to the pictures, he sits there with that damned gun tucked in the side of his boot. It scares the life out of me. One of those guns is going to go off one day.'

Sometimes the sound of an engraver would echo through the house in Blackett as Ivan etched his name, initials, or 'Texas' on numerous possessions, including a rifle with telescopic sights and a paintball gun. He sometimes used a special signature when etching his initials — running the I through the centre of the M.

With Jason and Ivan, Karen travelled to numerous places in the Southern Highlands. In 1983 he took her to the Belanglo State Forest four times. She believed it was in a four-wheel-drive they owned, but Milat was later to dispute that, claiming the only vehicle they had at the time was a Mitsubishi Colt. On one trip to the forest, he shocked Karen when, after shooting down a kangaroo, he walked up to it and slit its throat.

'I've fired guns a few times when I've gone down with him to meet his brothers, but to be honest I just can't work up any enthusiasm for them,' Karen told her neighbour at one of their secret meetings, which were increasing in frequency. 'He's getting more and more obsessed. He reads all the gun magazines and talks about weapons all the time, as if there's nothing else that matters in the world.'

169

In the bush he shot at kangaroos, rabbits and wild pigs, and tested his skills on tin cans and bottles.

As the months turned into years in their marriage, Karen grew increasingly disillusioned with her husband. Jason seemed to get on well with Ivan to some extent, but Ivan's interest in her was virtually non-existent. He was violent in his lovemaking, Karen confided to her neighbour as she drank coffee after coffee, but his true passions were his music — he was always playing Slim Dusty's 'Black Smoke Blowing Over 18 Wheels' — his gun, and keeping his body in good shape. He made himself some concrete weights by filling buckets with cement, so each weighed close to 23 kilograms (50 pounds), lifting them with a steel bar that ran across his shoulders.

Karen often thought Ivan was beginning to look more and more like someone from a bygone era — from back in the days of the Wild West — with his blue eyes, his sideburns and moustache, and a pistol in the side of his boot. And it worried her that he was getting Jason interested in guns. Ivan sometimes took the boy shooting in the Southern Highlands and in 1986, when Jason was 10 years old, Ivan bought him a rifle for his birthday.

Karen's dream had turned sour. Instead of finding lifelong happiness, she began to live a life of loneliness and, when he was home, misery under Ivan's iron rule.

'He won't allow me to do anything without his permission,' she told her compassionate neighbour. 'It's really getting me down.'

While Ivan was working, Karen would talk to whatever neighbours would listen to her tales of woe. They listened patiently. As she talked, she always kept an eye on her watch. She did not want to be found away from the house when her husband came home. He would demand to know where she had been, who she had been talking to.

Despite the tales of cruelty and beatings that Karen told

about her husband, the neighbours saw only a clean-living, non-drinking, non-smoking fitness fanatic, who worked out with his weights in the garden and always greeted them with a friendly smile. If he arrived from work looking tired and grubby, it wasn't long before they saw him transformed — showered, changed into casual clothes, and standing in the garden breathing in the evening air.

He was obsessed with his Valiant Charger, and then his red Mitsubishi. Milat's weekends, according to neighbours, were usually fully occupied with vacuuming, washing and polishing the car, sometimes assisted by his young stepson, and with tending to the peach-face parrots and lovebirds he kept at the back of the house. Occasionally, accompanied by one or two motor-enthusiast neighbours, he would take the boy to a car or truck drag-race meeting at Oran Park, 10 kilometres west of the start of the Hume Highway.

But while Ivan indulged in his obsessions, Karen's misery grew. She told neighbours how much she once used to enjoy going out with her husband at weekends, but those trips were now few and far between. The reality was that the bond between her and her son, of whom she was very protective, was the only real love left in that house on the corner of Sorensen Crescent. She wanted to go dancing with Ivan — just go out and rave now and then — but her older, more austere husband did only what he wanted to do. Despite the tension between them, which Karen believed stemmed from their age difference, and the loneliness she endured while he was away, sometimes for a week at a time, Ivan still poured his attention on to the boy.

And he was always ready to lend a helping hand to a neighbour — laying bricks or, on one occasion, helping someone to cut down a big tree. But if he and Karen were invited to a party, he would make only a token appearance, standing around awkwardly because he didn't drink and had given up smoking, and he'd leave with his quietly protesting wife at the earliest opportunity. Despite this behaviour, Ivan appeared, to most of the neighbours, to be the perfect husband.

Only those who heard Karen's tearful stories of life behind the closed door of their home learned about the darker side of their relationship. She told one friend she'd made in the neighbourhood that her husband treated her as if he was a caveman and she was his 'woman': pushing and shoving her around and treating her like a slave.

'He gets his kicks from dominating me,' she told the woman neighbour to whom she was particularly close. 'Whatever I try to do to please him, he says I should have done it another way and then he'll beat me, slap me across the face, punch me on the shoulders. I don't believe there's any way I can please him.'

Ivan and Jason's relationship may have appeared to some to be that of a loving father and son, but the neighbours heard from Karen that Jason had seen how his stepfather treated her, and had come to fear him. It was her son's fear, she believed, that led to him developing asthma.

A particularly cruel incident, which the neighbours virtually lived through with Karen, was the time when Ivan smashed the glass top of the coffee table in the lounge room with one powerful blow of his fist. When she attempted to clean up the broken pieces, he ordered her to leave everything where it was. Each day she had to step around the glass fragments, anxious to clean up the mess, but not daring to. 'He took photographs of the glass on the carpet and showed them to his family to give them the impression that I wasn't looking after him properly,' she told one of her friends.

Unable to take the misery any more, Karen summoned up the courage to tell Ivan that she wanted to take what was hers and get out of his life. He wouldn't hear of it and, although he didn't react violently, he made it clear that the discussion was finished — and he didn't want her to mention it again. But having stated her point, Karen kept up the pressure until Ivan finally offered to give her $4000 as a 'pay off'. On hearing this, Karen's friends told her that Ivan, considering the way he had treated her, would never give her the money.

Finally, on St Valentine's Day, 1987, Karen took things into her own hands. She waited until Ivan was away for a few days, then gathered together everything that she considered hers. She left behind a stereo, a wardrobe, a bookshelf, blankets, pillows and a bedroom suite, but cleaned out everything else and fled from Sorensen Crescent and its miserable memories.

Ivan flew into a rage when he returned from his road working contract and found the house deserted. He set out on a mission to find his runaway wife.

His first task was to track down Karen's mother and stepfather and demand to know his wife's whereabouts. There was a frightening confrontation. Despite Ivan's furious theats, and despite a mysterious fire in their garage, Karen's family courageously concealed her whereabouts — she was a long way away, at a secret address in Queensland.

In time, Ivan accepted that the marriage was over.

The Blackett house was sold, and Ivan and Karen were divorced in July 1989. He then moved back in with his mother and brother David, and was living there when newspaper stories started appearing in early 1990 about two missing backpackers from Melbourne, James Gibson and Deborah Everist.

In early 1994 the police contacted Karen. She had started a new life. She was shocked that the past had come back to haunt her. She had hoped she would never hear the name Ivan Milat again. And now they wanted her help in building up a picture of the man whose behaviour with guns had started to worry her years before.

'We want to ask you what weapons he used to own and as much as you can tell us about his behaviour,' one of the Task Force officers told Karen when he called at her new home.

'What is this all about?' she asked.

'Karen, this has nothing to do with you, but your former husband is under suspicion of being involved in the murders of a number of backpackers. You may even have read about it. They were all killed after you and Ivan were divorced, but you may be able to help us.'

'I don't want to be involved,' she said. 'My life with him is long over. It was all in the past. Please leave me out of it.'

It took a great deal of persuasion and several meetings for Karen finally to agree to give evidence against Ivan Milat.

'You have to understand my fears,' she said. 'Do I need to spell them out to you?'

'We understand your concerns,' she was told. 'You'll be given all the necessary protection.'

'I'm going to need it,' she said.

CHAPTER THIRTEEN

The search of Ivan Milat's home continued on 23 May 1994, the day after the raid.

Detective Senior Constable Andrew Grosse worked with his colleagues to collect numerous items from the house and garage. Apart from the furniture they were prepared to collect just about anything, because at that stage they had only a general idea what items in the house could be linked to the backpacker murders. Any weapons they might find would be of major importance, but they continued to collect even the most obscure items, such as clothing, lengths of window sash cord, and electrical tools with the initials 'IM' engraved on them. Loose and boxed cartridges and empty cartridge cases, trouser belts, a plastic butt plate from a Ruger rifle, bags of all description ... the items were all photographed, their positions where they were found noted, and then dispatched to a room at the Campbelltown Police Station to be assessed.

'Hello, what have we here?' said Grosse when he noticed part of a plastic bag protruding from under the washing machine in the laundry. Pulling it out, he saw it contained a Browning self-loading pistol, a cartridge magazine holding five cartridges, and a brown suede gun pouch.

Police also seized a book entitled *Violent Crimes that*

Rocked a Nation — Unsolved, an instruction booklet for a Ruger 10/22 rifle, and a green water-bottle that was found inside a cardboard box in a bedroom and which was of a type a backpacker might carry. Like all the other items, the water-bottle would be sent off for testing by experts who would look for fingerprints, scratches and any other clues that it might yield.

As the search progressed at his Eagle Vale home, Ivan Milat was led into the nearby Campbelltown Magistrates Court. Hidden from public view under a jacket when he was arrested twenty-four hours earlier, the face of Ivan Robert Marko Milat was now exposed to those who had been able to crowd into the court.

He wore the same clothes as when he had been arrested, a blue-checked shirt and jeans, and his steely blue eyes glanced around the courtroom, pausing on no-one in particular. The public in the packed gallery kept their eyes fixed on the sturdy figure with a large moustache, sideburns and some greying at the sides of his thinning, dark hair. His upper lip protruded slightly.

At the invitation of Magistrate Kevin Flack, Milat sat down and then listened as details of the hold-up of Paul Onions were outlined to the court: how it was alleged that Milat had approached Onions and offered him a lift, how the hitch-hiker was later confronted with a revolver, resulting in his running away and hearing a gunshot as he fled for his life. It was earlier that month, on 5 May, that Onions had been shown thirteen photographs, including one of Milat and, said police prosecutor Senior Sergeant Eddie Billett, Onions had 'positively identified' the defendant as the man who had robbed him.

Sergeant Billett then referred to an alleged conversation that the two men had had before the robbery. Milat had volunteered the information that he was called Bill, that he worked for the roads department at Liverpool, that he was divorced, and was of Yugloslav background. The victim, the sergeant added, had described the vehicle and it had been established that Milat had owned an identical vehicle in the name of William Milat. 'At the time of his apprehension,' Sergeant Billett continued, 'the defendant denied that he used the name of Bill, or owned a motor vehicle at the time of the offence, and denied owning firearms. It can be proved that all these denials are false.'

After his arrest, Milat had hurriedly called in the services of a solicitor — John Marsden, who had defended Milat at his 1974 trial on the rape charge. Marsden was a prominent lawyer with an impressive background, which included serving as President of the Council for Civil Liberties, President of the New South Wales Law Society, and being a member of the New South Wales Anti-Discrimination Board. In 1984 Marsden had lobbied for the decriminalisation of homosexuality, and eight years later he called on the New South Wales state government to decriminalise marijuana. In 1992 he joined the New South Wales Police Board.

The officers who had worked so hard on the backpacker murders were astonished that a lawyer serving on the Police Board was, technically, to act against them by defending the man who had been arrested. At this point, however, no charges had actually been laid against Milat in relation to the seven killings.

Applying for bail, Marsden told the magistrate that Milat had had stability of work and residence for the past twenty years, including living with his wife until the late 1980s, when they were divorced. He had then lived with and cared for his mother, after which he moved to the house at Eagle Vale with his sister.

Referring to the case against his client, Marsden said: 'Two words make it emotive. They are "backpackers" and "Belanglo". But my client is only charged with one incident relating to something that occurred four years ago.'

Bail was refused.

Some time after Ivan Milat had been charged, his younger brother George was cleaning out his modest farmhouse at Douglas Park when two police officers called by. They hadn't come to search — the policemen knew George and they just wanted a chat.

'George,' they asked, 'do you think your brother was capable of committing these murders?'

George thought for a moment and said: 'Everybody's capable of killing somebody else. The question is whether they would actually go ahead and do it.'

And as Ivan prepared to go through the long processes of the court, George wondered whether, in all the years they had spent together, he had really known his older brother. 'You know,' he told a friend, 'I wouldn't like to say with me hand on me heart whether I think he's guilty of this back-packer thing or not. Who am I to judge another person, even if he is me brother? I've heard they've found back-packs. Well, maybe Ivan found them all. His job with the DMR took him along the sides of hundreds of roads where people dump or lose things. I've got backpacks, too, that I've found out in the bush — backpacks and water-bottles. But if he's guilty of this, if he really has done it, they should hang him. Me brother or not, he should hang if he done it.'

The search of the various Milat properties continued, but the police refused to say what they were looking for. Although one of the cadaver-sniffer dogs was back in action, hunting through the rugged bush around Richard Milat's property, the police gave assurances that they were 'not necessarily' looking for more bodies.

Ivan Milat's house was being searched meticulously. Police crawled across the roof, lifting tiles off and probing underneath the guttering. Other officers used torches to peer into brick cavities, and plaster work was torn away to allow for a search behind it.

Consideration was even given to bringing in a machine to excavate the back yard, but after exploratory digging and running metal detectors over the earth, it was decided not to take such drastic measures. The police should have taken that step. Because, for all the searching of the house, inside and out, there was something they did not find. An illegal pistol, so cleverly hidden that only total devastation of the garden would have unearthed it ...

Shirley Soire, a short, dark-haired woman with age lines beginning to creep across her face, listened to the steel door clang shut behind her as, accompanied by a prison officer, she walked along a narrow corridor in Long Bay Jail. As Ivan had been regarded as the 'King' of the Milat clan, so she was the 'Queen'. She had visited her arrested brother several times, but this rendezvous behind bars, the first of months of weekend calls by her or her brother Walter, or by Ivan's girlfriend, Chalinder Hughes, was to be significant. Out of earshot of the prison officer, Shirley listened as her brother asked her to do him an urgent favour.

'I've buried a pistol in the garden,' he said in a voice she could hardly hear. 'It's in a plastic bucket and it's buried near the gully trap [a drain]. I want you to dig it up and get rid of it. I don't care how. Just get rid of it.'

The weapon Milat was so concerned about, a Colt .45 pistol, had not been linked to any of the victims in the forest. Why Milat was so concerned to have it disposed of, risking his sister's getting caught as she dug it up, was to remain a mystery. But Shirley had received her instructions and she promised to carry them out.

In time, she contacted her younger brother, Walter. 'I've got this pistol,' she said. 'I don't know what to do with it — whether to throw it in the river, sell it, or what.'

Walter Milat put the word around. A pistol was for sale. It wasn't long before Walter was contacted. He met a man in Campbelltown, agreed on a price of $800, then went to the house in Eagle Vale and picked up the gun. He met the contact later, took the money and gave the gun to the man. Later that afternoon, he drove back to Cinnabar Street and gave Shirley the money.

When Shirley next saw Ivan in prison, she leaned forward and whispered. 'Don't worry about the pistol. It's all been taken care of.' Ivan Milat nodded with satisfaction. Had the weapon been used in another crime which, had it been found, could pin Milat to the offence? Police would never know the answer unless the weapon could be found and traced back to him.

As the search wound down at Walter's home at Hilltop, extra police moved to the address at Buxton where Alex and his family had lived until moving to Queensland two years earlier. The current occupants were moved out to allow officers complete freedom to search. Wearing gloves and face masks, they paid particular attention to an old well, and used metal sieves to sift through soil excavated from bushland at the rear of the house. It was here that Alex had built a private rifle range, 5 metres high and 15 metres long, and — George Milat was to claim to friends later — it was so impressive that police officers from Mittagong, Picton and Bowral would sometimes call there and fire shots. During the police search, one Buxton resident mentioned that she regularly heard the sound of shots coming from the hobby farm while Alex was living there, but Alex had told his neighbours that he had a bird problem.

The police dug along the sides of the rifle range with trowels, and filled buckets and brown paper bags with thousands of spent cartridges and projectile fragments. The bags and buckets were then carried to teams of officers sitting at trestle tables, where the work of hand-sorting the pieces was being conducted. The police had to dig through nearly 100 tonnes of dirt, but there wasn't a man who was not determined to devote hour upon tedious hour to the task. Every find of any note was recorded in exhibit books and then taken to an incident room at Campbelltown Police Station, or sent off to Sydney for examination by scientific and ballistic experts.

On Tuesday 31 May, Ivan Milat, clean-shaven this time and wearing a light-blue pinstriped business shirt and dark-blue trousers, was driven under tight security from Sydney's Long Bay Jail to appear once again before Magistrate Kevin Flack at Campbelltown Court. Now there was no 'simple' charge of an armed hold-up. Milat was accused of all seven backpacker murders, along with the lesser charge of holding up British tourist Paul Onions, and other offences of possessing seven weapons which were prohibited in Australia. And, for the first time, details of how the young people had died, and of the evidence that police found at the various Milat family homes, allegedly linking Ivan to the murders, were about to be revealed to those who had packed into courtroom number six.

The prosecution case was to be presented by Mr Ian Lloyd, QC, a bespectacled, flamboyant 42-year-old who had already reached the prestigious position of Senior Crown Prosecutor. A former law student from Sydney University, he had moved to Hong Kong in 1980 to take on both private and government legal work, including murder briefs and presenting prosecution evidence in billion-dollar fraud and corruption cases for Hong Kong's Independent Commission Against Corruption. Ian Lloyd had even worked with the Federal Bureau of Investigation during the Independent Commission Against Corruption fraud inquiries, and was so impressive that in 1988 the New South Wales Department of

Public Prosecutions recruited him to prosecute serious fraud cases. A year later he was made a Queen's Counsel. Now Lloyd was about to become embroiled, at least at the committal stage, in one of Australia's worst murder cases.

The extensive police search of the past ten days, he said, had revealed evidence that linked Milat with the murders. Apart from evidence found at Ivan's house in Eagle Vale, investigations at the homes of Richard, Walter and William Milat in New South Wales, and that of Alexander Milat in Queensland, had uncovered property that Ivan Milat had given them — including a backpack similar to the one owned by Simone Schmidl, and a sleeping mat and sleeping bag similar to those owned by Caroline Clarke.

Mr Lloyd added that a blue Hi Sierra daypack, similar to the one that had belonged to Simone Schmidl and which she had been carrying in addition to her brightly coloured backpack, had been found, along with a revolver and ammunition, hidden by Milat in a room under Walter Milat's house at Hilltop after he heard that the police were making inquiries about him. Among the ammunition and rifles that police had found either at Ivan's home or that he had 'concealed' at his brothers' properties were a 12-gauge gun, a crossbow, two Chinese SKS assault rifles, a .44 calibre pistol, three Ruger rifles, two 12-gauge shotguns and a number of air rifles.

'Ammunition boxes similar to the ones found near the Neugebauer murder scene were found at the house. These boxes finished production thirteen years ago. All of the above firearms were moved to the brother's home from Eagle Vale between 1 December 1993 and 22 May 1994,' said Mr Lloyd.

The prosecutor added that police had found the trigger assembly, bolt, magazine, spring mechanism and a 25-shot magazine of a Ruger 10/22 rifle inside a plastic bag in the lounge room wall cavity of Ivan's home. The bolt had been positively identified by ballistics experts as a component of the rifle that fired the .22 calibre cartridges found near the bodies of Caroline Clarke and Gabor Neugebauer. Another rifle part — a Ruger receiver, the casing for the bolt — had been wrapped in plastic and hidden in a boot in the hallway cupboard. A Ruger barrel band had been found in a bedroom opposite Milat's room. A Vau de Hogan-brand tent and a multi-coloured Arno-brand backpack strap found in his garage were similar to property owned by Simone Schmidl, said Mr Lloyd. A bedroom had also yielded a Salewa-brand sleeping bag.

Found at the Queensland home of Alexander Milat was a Salewa-brand backpack similar to Simone Schmidl's. Mr Lloyd said that Ivan had given the backpack to Alexander and his wife some time after Easter 1992.

In Ivan's garage, Mr Lloyd continued, police had also found a bag containing five pieces of rope, each about 1 metre long. These were similar to the bag and rope produced by the man who pulled the gun on Paul Onions, who was being referred to at these proceedings as Witness A.

Throughout Ivan Milat's house, the court heard, police had found black electrical tape and black adjustable ties which, along with the rope, were similar to those found at the murder site of the German couple, Gabor Neugebauer and Anja Habschied. As the court listened silently, and people in the public gallery occasionally glanced at the expressionless man in the dock, Mr Lloyd went on to describe more allegedly incriminating items from the Eagle Vale house.

Two boxes of Eley-brand ammunition discovered in the home were similar to the box found at the German couple's murder scene, he said. A home-made silencer had also been found at the Eagle Vale house, and there were indications that a silencer had been used in the murder of Caroline Clarke. In the kitchen at Eagle Vale, police found an

Olympus camera, which appeared to be the same type that Miss Clarke had owned.

Milat's lawyer, John Marsden, was determined to have his say. At this point he jumped to his feet and protested about the number of times that Mr Lloyd's statement of facts contained the words 'indications', 'similar', and 'the same type'. He asked, for example, how many people owned Olympus cameras, and went on to say that his client denied the charges.

'He has not made a statement to police and the only statement he will be making is a full and complete denial in relation to the circumstantial innuendos and allegations,' said Mr Marsden. 'What I am instructed to ask is that, while my client is clearly not applying for bail, he wants it reported that he is strongly denying these claims and that he is concerned as a member of the community at the hype over this matter.'

But it was what Mr Lloyd had to say next that became the focus of the entire hearing and gripped the courtroom. In graphic detail, he outlined what had happened to the seven victims.

Joanne Lesley Walters, 22, had been gagged by cloth and two other pieces of cloth covered her face. Forensic examinations revealed she had suffered multiple stab wounds to the front and back upper body area. There was evidence she had been sexually assaulted.

Caroline Jane Clarke, 22, had been shot ten times in the head and stabbed once in the lower back. There also were indications that she may have been sexually assaulted. A maroon sweatshirt was wrapped around her head, and the shots had been fired through this head covering. Three shots had entered the right side of the skull towards the rear, two shots had entered the left side towards the rear, three had entered the rear base of the skull, and two had entered the upper forehead. Markings on some of the bullets indicated that a silencer might have been fitted to the firearm.

James Harold Gibson, 19, had suffered multiple stab wounds to the upper front and back part of the body. Knotted pantyhose found at the scene suggested that he or Deborah Everist had been bound.

Deborah Phyllis Everist, 19, had been stabbed only once, but several slicing-type injuries and a fracture were detected on the skull. Her jaw had also been broken.

Simone Loretta Schmidl, 21, suffered multiple stab wounds to her back.

Gabor Kurt Neugebauer, 21, had had a piece of cloth placed inside his mouth, while another piece of cloth had been tied around his head in the form of a gag. He had been shot six times in the head, three bullets entering his skull on the left side and three at the rear base. There was also evidence of strangulation.

Anja Susanne Habschied, 20, had been decapitated and her head remained missing, despite an extensive search. No animal could have carried it away, said Mr Lloyd. The German tourist was also naked from the waist down.

Members of the public who had squeezed into the court gasped as they heard the evidence about the severed head. They stared hard at the man who was sitting in the dock, but many could not see him clearly because he had his back to them. Nevertheless, it was clear from their shocked faces that the revelations by Lloyd had had a great impact on them. Many journalists did not even wait for the rest of the court proceedings. On hearing of the manner in which the backpackers died, particularly Anja Habschied, those with early or running deadlines scurried from the court.

Milat was told he would be remanded in custody and was led out through a side door. A waiting police van took him back along the Hume Highway to Long Bay Jail. In the weeks to come, Milat was to make several more appearances at courts in either Campbelltown or Sydney, with the police announcing on each occasion that their inquiries were continuing and that statements were still being collated.

One of the people contacted was 35-year-old Graham 'Jock' Pittaway, a red-haired New Zealander, who had sent the postcard starting 'Hi Bill' to Milat which had been found in Milat's bedroom drawer. Jock Pittaway had found Milat to be a good friend after meeting him while they were working on the roads in 1981. They had gone shooting on Milat properties in the Southern Highlands and once when Pittaway and his girlfriend Eleanor Shannon were evicted from their flat because he was out of work and down on his luck, Milat had given him money to rent a new place and start over again.

Detectives learned from Pittaway, who was by now living on a sheep farm back in New Zealand, that he had owned a 10/22 Ruger. But he kept it for only four months before selling it in Broken Hill, in outback New South Wales. He had gun licences for Queensland and New South Wales but the last time he had seen his New South Wales licence was in about January 1991, when, because he wasn't planning to use it again, he had cut it up.

Pittaway recalled for police how he had been shooting at Milat properties at Wombeyan Caves and Buxton. At the Buxton property, then owned by Ivan's older brother, Alex, he and Ivan had used a firing range which had been given police approval but they'd also gone shooting for wild goats and kangaroos which they'd use for their own food or for the Milat dogs. When they aimed at wild animals, said Pittaway, they always shot to kill. 'You'd touch a roo's eye with your finger and if it didn't flicker it was dead. If it moved, you'd shoot it again.'

The detectives made their notes. Then they came to the point. 'We're interested in a rifle that was purchased with your New South Wales licence in 1992,' one of the officers told Pittaway, despite his claims that his licence had been cut up. 'Someone went into the Horsley Park Gun Shop in Sydney on 4 April 1992 and bought a Ruger 10/22 rifle with it. Was it you?'

'I don't know anything about it.' he replied. 'It certainly wasn't me.'

'Can you explain how a Ruger 10/22 came to be used with your licence?'

'I can't,' Pittaway insisted.

Because of his close friendship with Milat, Pittaway was asked about Milat's preferences for smoking and drinking. Detectives were thinking of the used cigarettes and sherry bottles found near the death scenes in the forest. Milat used to smoke a long time ago, but in recent years he'd always refuse a proffered cigarette. 'I hate them,' was his usual reply. Once when Ivan had accepted a cigarette he lit it up, then spat it out. As for drinking, he'd only seen Milat take a glass or two of wine at his girlfriend's birthday in 1990.

'What about moustaches?' Pittaway was asked. 'Did Ivan have one?'

'Aw, sometimes he'd grow one, a long style that came down the sides of his mouth, but then he'd shave it off.'

On the roads together, had Milat ever shown an interest in hitch-hikers? Pittaway thought for a while, then recalled an occasion when they had seen a girl thumbing for a lift. 'I told Ivan we ought to pick her up but he just said he wasn't going to stop. "I don't know why people hitch-hike," he said, and I told him I agreed because there were some crazy bastards out there.'

At one of the hearings, solicitor Marsden dramatically announced, without giving a reason, that, at the defendant's request, he would not be representing him any more. In fact, no reason was ever to come to light. The remainder of the hearing saw Milat standing in the dock and arguing that the police had been unable to produce one piece of evidence linking him to the crimes. He also angrily hit out at Lloyd when the prosecutor said that bail was being opposed because in 1971, while facing a charge of raping a hitch-hiker in a forest, Milat fled to New Zealand and was not re-arrested until 1974.

Jumping to his feet, Milat told the court he was unhappy about the alleged rape being mentioned. 'The world now thinks I'm a rapist. He [meaning Lloyd] doesn't say I was found not guilty. It sounds good, all these allegations, it sounds good.'

Lloyd told the magistrate that 'matters were coming to light all the time'. Much of the backpacking gear the police found had been provisionally identified as that which featured in last-known photographs of the travellers when they were in Sydney.

After hearing that his application for bail was being turned down, Milat called out as police led him from the court: 'I think you are framing me up. This is another Chamberlain here.'

This was a reference to Australia's infamous Azaria Chamberlain case, in which Mrs Lindy Chamberlain, the wife of a Seventh Day Adventist Minister, was charged with the murder of her nine-week-old baby Azaria in the desert near Ayers Rock in the 1980s. The police rejected her claim that a dingo — a wild desert dog — had taken the child from the family's holiday tent and, at the end of the case, which relied on circumstantial evidence, Mrs Chamberlain was convicted and sentenced to jail for life. But after nearly four years in prison she was freed and pardoned when a fresh inquiry revealed faults in the Crown case.

Back in Long Bay Jail, Milat, with guidance from the New South Wales Legal Aid Commission, sought out a new lawyer. He claimed, and it was agreed, that he would not be able to meet the enormous costs of his defence. He came to hear of a young man who had built up a reputation for defending people on legal aid and attacking the system that had disadvantaged them.

Queensland-based Andrew Boe had to seek special leave to appear in New South Wales. One of his most prominent cases was the successful appeal of Robyn Kina, freed in 1993 after spending five years in jail for murdering her de facto husband. Boe, who was born in Burma and was a Buddhist, had also been involved in successfully defending a Brisbane woman who dumped her newborn baby in a garbage bin.

As the weeks rolled on towards the start of Ivan Milat's committal hearing, his brothers Walter and Richard had their cases dealt with by the courts. In a joint admission at Campbelltown Local Court on 10 August 1994, both men pleaded guilty to a total of thirteen firearms and drugs charges laid by the Task Force Air police. Richard was found guilty on two charges of being in possession of five prohibited weapons, including a crossbow; one of unlawful possession of a driver's licence in the name of Paul Miller; and one of possession of cannabis leaf.

Walter pleaded guilty to nine charges — seven of which related to the illegal possession of firearms, including a crossbow, a paintball gun and twenty-one different guns and three silencers; cultivating two cannabis plants; and of being in possession of enough cannabis leaf to be deemed a supply amount. Sergeant Eddie Billett said that a police search at Walter's home had revealed two .223 Ruger rifles, two .177 Diana air rifles, a 12-gauge shotgun and a 12-gauge double-barrelled shotgun. A further search in the rafters located two SKS rifles and, in the roof cavity, an assault rifle.

At the end of the hearing, Richard was put on a three-year good behaviour bond and fined $2000; his brother's sentence was deferred. When Walter appeared before the court again on 29 September for sentencing, his lawyer, John Marsden, said his client had 'gone through hell on earth' over the past four months. 'He's a caring father,' said Marsden. 'He's a working man who gets on with his business. It's been hard on him and his health and it has also caused a lot of damage to his wife and children.'

Asking the magistrate to be lenient, Mr Marsden said his client had lost contracts and jobs for his business, and had suffered enormously. 'This person will go through hell for the next four or five years when certain charges will be aired throughout the courts against his brother [Ivan].'

But Magistrate Peter Ashton expressed concern about the charges involving silencers and the number of weapons found. 'Why would someone want to have such an arsenal of weapons?' he asked. 'I can't see many uses for silencers or pistols for anything which is not unlawful.'

Walter was fined $2700 and placed on a $2000 three-year good behaviour bond. Outside the court, he wrapped his arm around his wife Lisa and said: 'I'm really glad this is all over. I'm going home.'

While it was over for Richard and Walter for the time being, Task Force Air officers and other members of the police force were busy sifting through the mass of evidence they had collected from the Belanglo State Forest and the Milat family properties.

As prosecutor Lloyd had already told the magistrate, the bolt found in the wall cavity had been linked to cartridges fired in the forest. The proof had come as the result of diligent work in the firearms and ballistic branch of the Forensic Services Division of the Australian Federal Police by the officer in charge, Detective Superintendent Ian Prior, and his colleague Detective Senior Constable Gerard Dutton. Prior had been handed a collection of empty cartridges along with fired bullets collected from the forest and from the head of Caroline Clarke. Cartridges, used and unused, from Milat properties, had also been passed to him.

Prior and Dutton's task was to look for markings on the fired cartridges from the forest that would positively link them to cartridges and weapons collected from the Milat properties. The experts had been given the Ruger bolt found in the wall cavity at Cinnabar Street and the Anschutz bolt found in a haversack which had Ivan's name on it at Walter's home.

Dutton selected a Ruger 10/22 rifle from the ballistics reference library, a storehouse of equipment for use by forensic experts, and removed the bolt assembly and magazine. He replaced these with the bolt and magazine found at Milat's home in Eagle Vale, and then carried out a test by firing ten Winchester-brand .22 cartridges. When he examined the cartridge cases, Dutton found markings that were similar to those on the empty cartridges found near Caroline Clarke's body. The markings on the test cartridges and the cartridges found in the forest displayed such close characteristics that Dutton was left in little doubt that the bolt assembly found at Ivan Milat's home had fired the cartridges ejected in the forest. Dutton found that certain marks, which were unique to the bolt face and firing pin, consistently appeared on the test cartridges and those found in the forest.

When he stripped down the bolt assembly and examined the breech face, Dutton found that the face disclosed burrs on the metal surface near the ejector aperture and the firing pin aperture. Those marks were repeated on each firing — in ballistic terms, the marks left their signature on each cartridge.

Dutton tried to determine whether the bullets recovered from Caroline Clarke's skull had been fired from those cartridges and he was able to assess that some bullets collected from Alex Milat's property, where the brothers had set up a shooting range, had the same rifling characteristics as the spent bullets found in Caroline Clarke's head. In addition, a fired cartridge case found at Ivan Milat's home was consistent with having been discharged by the same weapon that fired the cartridges found near the young Briton — the same weapon that the Ruger bolt had been attached to.

Similar microscopic and test-firing work was carried out on spent cartridge cases found by police 165 metres from the remains of Gabor Neugebauer. The ballistic experts looked at markings on the cartridge cases and compared them with cartridges fired with the use of the Anschutz rifle bolt. Again, the experts were convinced they had a match. They also found consistencies in spent bullets found in a tree near Neugebauer's body and in test-fired bullets using the Anschutz bolt. But other bullets found near Neugebauer revealed they had been fired by the Ruger bolt. So two separate weapons had been fired at the German couple's death scene. The police had the bolts. But the Ruger barrel was missing. They were, however, certain the Anschutz rifle seized from Walter's alcove — and which had been threaded on the end of the barrel as if for use with a silencer — had been used with the bolt they tested.

In another department of the Forensic Services Division, handwriting expert Sergeant Frederick Mesker turned a green plastic water-bottle over in his hands. He had removed it from a cloth container, which had had a label cut from it by someone and replaced with a piece of tape to give it added strength. Mesker laid the cloth container to one side and stared at the plastic bottle, wondering if it would yield any clues to its owner. To a layman a plastic bottle was hardly going to be of any use in pinning seven murders on someone, but in forensic work it was often evidence that was not immediately obvious that provided the telltale clues. The bottle had been found at Milat's home, but could it have belonged to one of the backpackers? There were no fingerprints on it linking it to any of the travellers, and the cut-off label, if it had contained a name of the owner, had probably been long discarded.

But there was still work that Mesker could do and he hoped it would pay off. He placed the bottle under an infra-red light and, to his growing excitement, noticed something that had not been visible to the naked eye. As he looked more carefully, he could make out letters. Peering closely, he now saw they spelled out SIMI — Simone Schmidl's nickname. The letters, he concluded, had been scratched off the bottle, but enough of an imprint had been left for the infra-red technology to enhance them.

Mesker took photographs, enlarged them, then set about comparing the writing on the bottle with handwriting in letters Simi had written to her parents. Although he had only four letters on the bottle to work with, he was reasonably sure at the end of his comparisons that they had been written by the same hand that had penned the letters to Germany.

Further forensic work was proceeding on two of the backpacks. Detective Senior Constable Lyle van Leeuwen had been given the multicoloured backpack, believed to have been owned by Simi and which was handed to police by Joan Milat in Queensland, to study. With the aid of a photograph of Simi with her backpack, van Leeuwen was able to find nine points of similarity between the article and the one in the picture. Among the matches were sections of the multicoloured side panels where they joined the black material on the rest of the pack. He believed, too, that the label and side straps were the same.

He also looked at a photograph of Simi in her sleeping bag and compared that item with a sleeping bag found in a walk-in wardrobe in the bedroom of Ivan Milat's sister, Shirley Soire, at Cinnabar Street. Looking at the actual article and the photograph, he was able to find no less than twelve points of comparison. Similar matches between items and photographs were achieved with what appeared to be Simi's blue daypack, a tent and a sleeping-bag cover.

The police officer's work was not over. Although the families of all the backpackers would be asked to examine all the seized camping equipment in person, he needed to establish that in essence what the police had found at the Milat homes had been taken from the murdered travellers.

Having completed his examination of some of the camping gear, van Leeuwen looked carefully at a photograph of Milat's girlfriend, Chalinder Hughes, wearing a turquoise and white Benetton top as she posed at the seaside. The picture had been found in a photograph album seized at the house in Cinnabar Street. Laying it to one side, van Leeuwen next looked at a photograph of Caroline Clarke wearing what looked like an identical sweatshirt. In order to satisfy himself, the senior constable concluded there were matches between the turquoise collar, the arm and wrist bands, the V-neck, the turquoise Benetton-brand name across the front, a turquoise band, and a straight bottom hem. It was possible the two tops were not the same — the left wrist band of the top worn by Miss Clarke appeared to be narrower, for example. However van Leeuwen concluded that might be because the band was puckered. In any case, he believed that the similarities he had found outweighed the differences.

At the New South Wales Department of Health's Division of Analytical Laboratories, DNA expert Dr David Kessly peered through a microscope at a piece of bloodstained sash cord which had been found among other pieces in a pillowcase in Ivan Milat's garage. The blood had long dried, but he was confident of being able to make a comparison with blood samples sent from Victoria and overseas. Police had received samples from the parents of all the murdered backpackers but it was from the Clarkes that he was able to make a positive finding. He concluded that the blood on the sash cord could have come from the Clarkes' daughter.

Robert Goetz, who worked in the same laboratories, also concluded that blood on the sash cord could have come from Caroline Clarke.

The two men worked out the odds: of 96,000 couples — a figure that was later to be raised to 118,000 — only Caroline Clarke would have matched the parental blood.

On 7 October 1994 the ballistics expert, Detective Senior Constable Dutton, crawled over the front seats of a Nissan four-wheel-drive — the vehicle previously owned by Ivan Milat before he sold it. It had been 'borrowed' from its current owner and driven to Chatswood Police Station for an inspection. Dutton was extremely interested in a small hole in the passenger seat upright. This appeared to be in line with damage to the passenger door which had been repaired. The hole in the seat and the damage to the door looked for all the world to the police officer to have been caused by a bullet fired by someone sitting in the driver's seat.

The case against Ivan Milat was growing stronger by the day.

CHAPTER FOURTEEN

After being in jail for exactly six months to the day, Ivan Milat's committal hearing finally got under way on 24 October 1994 at the Campbelltown Magistrates Court. From the time of his arrest until then, the prosecution had been awaiting the results of scientific tests, including the meticulous examination of weapons and cartridges. Detectives had also travelled to Britain and Germany to show camping gear, or photographs of it, to the relatives of the dead backpackers to establish identification.

Now it was prosecutor Ian Lloyd's task to convince Magistrate Michael Price that there was a strong enough case against Milat to have him committed for trial, and to answer the murder charges before a jury. Privately, there wasn't a police officer who had worked on the murder inquiry who did not believe they had unearthed enough evidence to send Milat for trial.

Milat was led up to the dock from the holding cells under the 'old' courtroom in the judicial block. He was dressed in a navy-blue sweater, blue shirt, navy trousers and black elastic-sided, ankle-high boots. With his hands gripping the side of the bench seat, he leaned forward and cocked his head slightly to one side as if to better hear what Lloyd was about to outline to the magistrate.

To Lloyd's left was the defence team, led by Queensland barrister Cate Holmes. She was supported by the briefing solicitor, Mr Boe. It was exactly 10 am when prosecutor Lloyd, wearing a suit at this stage of the proceedings (as opposed to the wig and gown he was used to wearing in higher courts), revealed that the last six months had not been wasted — to support the Crown case, there were statements from 300 witnesses, along with hundreds of photographs. And he was quick to make the point that 'whoever killed one of the deceased backpackers killed them all'.

One of Lloyd's first witnesses was Detective Senior Constable Andrew Grosse, who propped a 153-page statement on his lap and used it as a reference to tell the court about the discoveries of the bodies and the results of the post-mortems.

But when Grosse produced the Salewa-brand backpack, taken from Alexander Milat's home in Queensland on 21 May and drew the court's attention to the initials 'IM' written inside the top flap, Milat shouted: 'You put it on there yourself!' His outburst, for which he apologised to the magistrate by saying, 'I'm terribly sorry, Your Honour', came a year to the day after Simi's remains had been found in the forest.

It was indeed an auspicious day. The court adjourned that afternoon, Tuesday 1 November, after the decision a few days earlier by Magistrate Price that it would be beneficial for him to visit the forest and examine the places where the bodies had been found.

The storm clouds rolled in as the magistrate and the prosecution and defence lawyers, accompanied by police officers who would act as guides, headed for the forest of death. With the rain now lashing down, the magistrate, wearing a plastic cloak, jeans and runners, trudged over the forest debris where the victims had spent their last moments.

Cate Holmes, also in jeans and a white raincoat, stared grimly at the various grave sites.

Some of the death sites were still adorned with fading fabric flowers and the dried-out stems of bouquets, left months earlier by relatives who had come to pay their last respects. At the boulder where Joanne Walters' body had been found, a weathered card bore the words: 'No birthday card today, Joanne. Only the love we have always had. Love always.' It was signed by her parents and sister.

Back in the court in the following days, Miss Holmes rose numerous times to challenge the evidence of police witnesses. She succeeded in getting Detective Senior Constable Grosse to agree that although cartridges found in the forest where Caroline Clarke's body had been found appeared to have been fired by the bolt recovered from Milat's home, none of the bullets recovered from the bodies of Caroline Clarke or Gabor Neugebauer could be matched to any particular gun because police had not found a gun barrel. Grosse also found himself under intense questioning by Miss Holmes about the relevance of some of the items seized at the Milat house. He conceded that shotgun cartridges and airgun pellets were not relevant.

Miss Holmes also wondered about the relevance of the driver's licence in the name of Michael Milat. Did it, she wanted to know, show anything other than Ivan Milat being 'a naughty boy' who had a licence in a false name?

'I did consider it relevant that he had a licence in another name,' said Grosse.

There was tension in the court on the morning of Tuesday 8 November when a side door close to the witness box opened and a slightly built, fair-haired man took his seat a short distance from the magistrate. For now, he was to be known only as Witness A. His name was Paul Onions, the British backpacker who in January 1990 had escaped with his life from a man who had called himself Bill and who had pulled a gun on him as they drove along the Hume Highway.

Onions related how, on January 25, he had been offered a lift in a silver-coloured four-wheel-drive by a man who had a big moustache reminiscent of the one worn by Merv Hughes. Bill had told Onions how he worked for the roads at Liverpool, was of Yugoslav descent and now divorced. Onions described Bill's changing demeanour, the man's hatred for Asians and how he had ultimately pulled a gun on him, resulting in Onions fleeing for his life up the highway.

When asked if he could identify his attacker in court, Onions indicated Milat. But because identification was of major importance in the attempted murder charge against Milat — a charge that also linked him to the murders of the other backpackers and gave an indication of how the others might have been taken to the forest — Miss Holmes wondered how Onions could now identify a man without a moustache when the driver who attacked him had one.

'It would be fair to say you cannot recognise him now?' she suggested.

'No, it would not be fair. I have great confidence,' said Onions.

Parents and friends of the backpackers were called to give evidence, but a dramatic interlude was to come on 14 November, when Miss Holmes stood to address Magistrate Michael Price. For once, her bar table was not littered with papers and files. All she had with her was a small black handbag.

'Your Worship,' she said as Milat, sitting behind her in the dock, kept his head down, 'I no longer have instructions to act in this matter and I seek leave to withdraw.'

The magistrate glanced at the ceiling and grimaced. Then he granted permission for her to leave. Ivan Milat had sacked his second lawyer and, as before, the reason was not given. It was now left to his briefing solicitor, Andrew Boe, to handle the case for the time being.

Although five witnesses from overseas were waiting outside the court to give evidence, with another two on their way, the first thing Boe wanted to do was put the case off for at least three weeks so he could brief a new barrister and attend to 'administrative arrangements'. But Mr Price was clearly unwilling to grant a long adjournment, pointing out that it was at the specific request of the defence and at significant community cost that the witnesses had been flown in.

Aware that whatever adjournment the magistrate would grant, it would certainly not be a long one, Boe calmly sat down and waited while the first of the remaining overseas witnesses was led into the court.

The evidence of Mr Axel Dornis was related to the equipment that Simone Schmidl had been carrying with her and which had been found in Milat family homes. The company in Germany of which he was export manager manufactured tents in co-operation with a Taiwanese firm. The tent model which Simi purchased in Germany for her trip to Australia was manufactured between 1989 and 1992 and was sold mainly in Europe. He had searched through his records and could find nothing to show that any of his tents had been sold in Australia.

The cooking equipment that the young German woman bought had been manufactured by Peter Killmann's firm in Essen. When he was called to the witness box he identified the pots and pans police had recovered from their raids as having been made by his company. He, too, was certain that they had never been sold to Australia.

Herbert Schmidl walked confidently through the court to the witness box. A powerfully built bus driver with metal-framed spectacles and a thick moustache, Simi's father glared across the court at Milat, who kept his eyes down. Mr Schmidl recalled how he had gone shopping with Simone for her camping equipment, then looked sadly at photographs of his daughter that prosecutor Lloyd handed to him — farewell shots at Regensburg railway station, photos of her on holiday in New Zealand and Australia, and others of her in Germany. And yes, he could identify a backpack, tent, sleeping bag and other items that he had purchased for Simone.

When shown the initials 'IM' written in marker pen on the multi-coloured backpack that Grosse had produced earlier, he was asked if the bag had had these letters on it when his daughter left Germany.

'No,' said Mr Schmidl. 'Somebody else must have added that. It is not the handwriting of Simone.'

What did he make of the name 'SIMI' that had been enhanced by police on a water-bottle?

'It is the handwriting of Simone. I have no doubt about it,' he said.

Giving his evidence with the help of an interpreter, Mr Schmidl spent two hours in the witness box, recalling how he had helped his daughter choose her various travelling items. When he finally stepped down, he nodded politely at the magistrate, saying he was very glad he had been able to help. But as he reached the dock, he fixed a hard stare at Milat, then suddenly rolled his hand into a fist and thrust it upwards towards the defendant. Neither the accused man nor the magistrate noticed the gesture, and Mr Schmidl continued through the courtroom, head held high, and sat down in the public gallery.

Jeannette Muller, now studying at a university in France, had little trouble identifying the camping items she said belonged to Simi. Dressed in blue shorts, a white blouse and with her brown hair down to her shoulders, Miss Muller recalled the four-month camping holiday she had had with Simi in Australia and New Zealand. They had camped out on numerous occasions and the lilac and pink backpack that had turned up at Alex Milat's Queensland home and which she was now shown in court was, she said, easy to identify.

'It's so distinctive,' Jeannette Muller said, 'it's Simi's backpack.'

Then, shown a tent recovered from Milat's garage, the blue daypack discovered in the alcove at Walter's home and a sleeping bag found in the wardrobe of Ivan's sister at Cinnabar Street, Eagle Vale, she said she could identify them all. Then there was the thick rubber band bearing the name Compact-O-Mat, found around the tent in Milat's garage. That, too, was identical to the one Simi had had. She identified the green water-bottle — with the name Simi scratched out — as belonging to her friend, saying it was just like the one she had bought in New Zealand.

The cooking set, found at Milat's home, was shown to Miss Muller and once more she said it was the one her friend had owned. Simi, she remembered, had even shown her how it worked. 'I mentioned I didn't have a cup with me. She said: "I have a couple; you can use one of mine."'

Andrew Boe was anxious to establish that Miss Muller could not say with 100 per cent certainty that the camping gear she had been shown comprised the self-same items that Simi had travelled with. Miss Muller conceded that the backpack had no distinguishing marks that would separate it from another of the same colour and brand.

There were to be more claims the following day of material belong to a missing backpacker turning up at Ivan Milat's home. Jantina Steegstra, 29, one of the Dutch travellers who had befriended the two British backpackers in 1992, recalled taking a photograph of Caroline wearing a long-sleeved Benetton shirt. Another Dutch student, Resy Arts, 20, entered the court to identify a photograph she had given police showing Caroline holding a camera. Shown an Olympus Trip S camera, found in Milat's kitchen, Miss Arts said it appeared to be the same.

The court became the setting for a bizarre scene when the alleged mass murderer was allowed to leave the dock and approach the bench to ask why a new barrister he wanted to represent him, Mr Terry Martin from Queensland, was not being allowed to do so. He was still keeping Boe as the briefing solicitor, but Boe had explained to him that because of the weight of the case and the certainty that there would be a committal hearing and senior counsel would have to represent him, it was essential a barrister be brought in now. Why, Milat wanted to know, was Mr Price refusing permission for the Queensland barrister to represent him?

'I have given my reasons,' said Mr Price, referring to an earlier ruling that it would be inappropriate for Mr Martin to act until his application to practise in New South Wales had been approved.

'I can't hear anything from there,' said Milat, tossing his head back towards the direction of the dock. 'I can't defend meself … you are just going to railroad me.' Pointing out that he had picked a Queensland legal team because he trusted them — hinting that the New South Wales police may have influenced the state's legal profession in this serious case — Milat added that, without them, 'you may as well send me back down to the cells. I can't defend meself. I'm getting framed here for seven murders.'

Mr Price told him that the Crown would call more witnesses and he would have the chance of cross-examining them.

But Milat responded: 'You're forcing me to defend meself. I'm not capable of doing that. I'm a road worker — don't you read the papers? Till this morning I thought I had a perfectly good legal team to handle that. How about giving me a couple of days' adjournment so I can try to sort something out, please?'

Mr Price was, however, unwilling to grant this request, provoking Milat to respond: 'You're really crushing me … You've got all these charges on me and now you expect me to defend meself.'

It was an angry man who was led back down the stairs to the cells before being taken back to Long Bay Jail.

Detective Sergeant Steve McLennan, one of the central figures in the Task Force Air investigations, paced up and down the arrivals lounge of Sydney airport on the evening of Monday 28 November 1992. He was wearing a check shirt and jeans and melted easily into the crowd waiting to greet passengers from the Qantas jet that had started its journey across the world from Manchester, in northern England.

The detective's eyes lit up when a thin man in his late 50s, accompanied by a smartly dressed woman with neatly permed grey hair, emerged from the customs area and made their way down the sloping walkway. McLennan understood how they would have been feeling: the two arrivals were Ian and Jacqueline Clarke, who had come to give evidence for the Crown against the man accused of murdering their daughter. McLennan greeted them warmly and escorted them through the bustling terminal.

Out in the car park, as the couple loaded their bags into the boot of a police car, a photographer approached, ready to take their picture. McLennan would have nothing of this. Just as the camera was about to fire, the detective, who had a reputation among the media as being friendly and approachable, brought up a thick arm which accidentally smacked the camera back into the photographer's face. He bundled his charges into the car and sped off into the night. This was indeed serious business.

Despite his earlier protests, Milat was to learn that the system was not against him. After Mr Martin's own appeal to the New South Wales Attorney General, he was given leave to represent the accused man and was at the bar table three days later when Ian Clarke, dressed in a beige suit and matching brown suede shoes, walked across the courtroom and took his place in the witness box.

The retired banker remained composed as Prosecutor Lloyd guided him through a statement he had given to the police. In September 1991 Caroline had left England for Australia and had kept in fairly regularly contact, phoning every two to three weeks and also writing. The last contact had been a week or so before Easter, when Caroline had spoken to his wife.

Mr Lloyd showed him a red hairbrush with the word 'England' on it — the court had not yet heard where the brush had been found, although it had been discovered at Richard Milat's caravan home.

Asked to comment on the hairbrush, Mr Clarke replied: 'I can do no more than to say it is similar to one Caroline had, but beyond that, I don't think I can comment.' But he added that she had a similar brush at the time she left for Australia.

Shown a blue and grey sleeping bag found at Richard Milat's, he said Caroline had one similar to it.

Cross-examined by Mr Martin, Caroline's father said she had not been living with the family prior to the trip, but she had made the journey north to the house a month before her 21st birthday party in August 1991, departing the following day. She had then set off for a month in Europe before heading off for Australia.

Mr Clarke told the court he and his wife started to become concerned about Caroline around about the time of his other daughter's birthday on 8 May. Caroline had always remembered her sister's birthday, but this time there had been no word from her.

Mr Clarke said that, around about the end of May, Joanne's father, Ray Walters, had phoned him and his wife to express his own very deep concern that nothing had been heard from his daughter — she had always been so particular in maintaining contact with her family. There was little more he could tell the court.

Jacqueline Clarke, dressed in a green and blue floral-print dress and carrying a navy-blue handbag, followed her husband into the witness box. Shown the red hairbrush, she agreed with her husband; it was very much like the one Caroline had when she left their home.

Pain came into Mrs Clarke's eyes when Mr Lloyd asked her to recall the contents of that last phone call Caroline had made a week to ten days before Easter. 'She had said: "Hello, Mum, everything's fine. We are back from Tasmania and we are going to go fruit-picking again. We're going to the Perth area to go picking melons."' Caroline had not said when she and Joanne planned to leave Sydney nor how they would be travelling. Mrs Clarke's voice trembled as she added: 'She was bright and bubbly and happy and everything seemed fine.'

A short time later Stephen Wright, the Kent stockbroker who had made friends with Caroline and Joanne in Mildura and had travelled to Tasmania with them, was called to give evidence. He recalled how the two girls had remarked how much better it was to get off the train at Casula to start hitch-hiking towards Melbourne.

Mr Lloyd then asked him about the blue tent he had owned. Wright recalled that prior to leaving Tasmania he had swapped tents with the young women. He recalled the accident he had had when he stabbed the canvas with a grape-picking knife he had kept in his back pocket, and he also recalled patching the hole temporarily with a sticky address label.

Mr Lloyd instructed the court usher to pass to Wright a rolled-up blue tent and then asked if he could identify it. He unfurled it and started examining the material. Then he held the tent towards the magistrate. 'Here's the hole I made. It's still here,' he said.

It was a dramatic moment. The public gallery was trans-fixed. The tent had been found by police in a cupboard in the annexe between the two caravans on Richard Milat's property in Vera Street, Hilltop. Now here was Stephen Wright positively identifying it as the one he had given to Caroline and Joanne. To emphasise his certainty, Wright repeated how he had used a sticky label to patch the hole and when he had been shown the tent by police the day before he was due to give his evidence he found the label, which had become detached, still rolled up in the canvas.

'When looking at that tent, do you have any doubt that this is your tent?' asked Mr Lloyd.

'None whatsoever,' said Wright. 'I slept in it for about six weeks. It's in worse condition, but I have absolutely no doubt it is the tent.'

Mr Lloyd wanted to confirm the date that Wright had last seen the two women. He said they had stayed in his room at the Kings Cross backpackers' hostel on the night of 17 April 1992, and they left without paying early on the morning of the 18th. He recalled that date because on the evening of the 18th he had taken an overnight bus to Byron Bay, on the New South Wales north coast, to do some diving. He arrived in Byron Bay on Sunday morning, 19 April.

How could he be sure about the dates?

Revealing his stockbroker's efficiency, Wright said he had carried an electronic organiser with him during his travels and punched in a record of the place and date whenever he arrived at a new destination. From the inside pocket of his double-breasted grey suit jacket, he took out the organiser and told the court that he still had the information, which only he could access through a secret code, recorded on it. He switched the instrument on and confirmed to the court that he had arrived in Sydney from Tasmania on 15 April and that he had indeed arrived at Byron Bay on 19 April.

It was the turn of Pauline Vuletich, the Shetland Islands girl who had travelled to Australia with Joanne, to take the stand. As she took her seat in the witness box she suddenly produced a gilt-framed photograph of Joanne. She was smiling at the camera, her head tilted to her right, her long dark hair hanging loosely down over the side of her face. Pauline had set the picture up so it was facing directly towards Ivan Milat. But the accused man kept his eyes lowered. She did not say whether it was a provocative move or a gesture of remembrance for her murdered friend, but neither the magistrate, the court officials nor the lawyers asked her to remove it.

Pauline told of her travels up to Queensland with Joanne and how she had spent the evening of 17 April in the Studebaker's nightclub with Joanne and Caroline, the last time she had seen them.

Shown an Olympus Trip camera, which had been found in Ivan Milat's home, Pauline noted that it had been made in Malaysia — and that Joanne had bought one exactly the same when they stopped over in Singapore on their way to Australia.

The day on which Caroline and Joanne had last been seen was an important matter for the defence. The prosecution had sought to prove that Milat had not been working when the murder victims had gone missing. Mr Martin asked whether she was certain it was Saturday 18 April that she had called around to the hostel and found that the girls had left. Pauline said she was able to put a fix on the date because they had all gone to the nightclub on the Friday.

The court had already shared the sadness of other bereaved parents remembering their loved ones and now it was the turn of Joanne's father, Ray Walters. Pale faced, the boilerhouse controller from Maesteg, South Wales, was spared a long session in the witness box. He recalled the last time Joanne had called the family home was on Wednesday 15 April 1992. His wife had phoned her back immediately, a practice they had been using while Joanne was in Australia so their daughter could save money. After a few minutes of giving evidence, he stepped down.

Gill Walters, dressed in a grey jacket and a tartan skirt and her face filled with pain, made her way to the witness box. Through her tears, she told the court of that last phone conversation with her daughter.

'She had arrived from Tasmania,' Mrs Walters remembered. 'I asked her what she was doing. She was very, very tired but she was in good form. She was hoping to stay for a few days to get over her tiredness and then starting her travels again.'

That was all she could usefully tell the court. She stood up and walked a short distance to some side benches where the other bereaved parents, Mrs Gibson, Mrs Everist and Mr and Mrs Clarke, were sitting. Her husband took her by one hand and Mrs Everist took the other. Like the Clarkes, Mr and Mrs Walters had travelled across the world to utter just a few words. But they had been compelled by love; no-one was in any doubt of that.

Mr Lloyd asked that the name of the next witness be suppressed. The side door opened and a slim woman with tinted red hair walked through the court, shoulders slightly hunched. She was wearing a blue dress with a white floral pattern and she clutched a white sweater. She wrote her current name and address on a piece of paper and handed it to Magistrate Price. This was Karen, the woman who had spent eleven years with the man now charged with the murder of seven backpackers.

Speaking in a soft voice, she said she had met Ivan Milat in the mid 1970s through her second eldest brother and had started going out with him. She relayed how she had eventually married Milat and told how her former husband looked after all the cars he had owned meticulously.

Asked about his interest in firearms, Karen said: 'He was gun crazy.' She had seen him with a pistol, a revolver and a rifle. Mr Lloyd showed her a black revolver, which she recognised: it had been given to Ivan by Walter in 1981. As she looked at the weapon, she identified the engraved word 'Texas' on each side of the trigger and at the bottom of the butt. She recalled that Ivan used the nicknames Mack (as in Mack trucks), Texas, Joe Spanner and Bargo Bill. In 1981, he had bought an engraver and he used it to put his initials on his possessions. He had even engraved his initials on her Mixmaster.

Shown a camouflage-coloured box in which the revolver had been found, Karen said one of Ivan's hobbies was making model planes and he painted them in those colours. The box was kept either under the bed at the house in Blackett or under the back seat of four-wheel-drive he owned.

Karen was shown a pistol by Mr Lloyd. This was the weapon that had been found by Detective Senior Constable Grosse and his colleagues under the washing machine at the Eagle Vale house. She recognised it as the one Ivan kept in a sock under the front seat of his car or it would be tucked into a sock inside his boot. 'It was loaded all the time,' she said.

Then she was shown a rifle fitted with telescopic sights. Her attention was drawn to an engraving of the word Ivan near where the sights were fitted. Yes, she said, she had seen the weapon at the house in Blackett and the name was Ivan's engraving.

Shown a paintball gun, Karen identified an engraving of the word 'Texas' on the grip and, at the bottom of the grip, the initials IM, with the I running through the centre of the M, similar to the way they had been written on the inside of the backpack police claimed had once been owned by Simone Schmidl. Karen recognised the logo, described by Mr Lloyd as 'distinctive', as the same one that had been engraved on her Mixmaster.

Was she, Mr Lloyd wanted to know, aware of the location of the Belanglo State Forest? Karen said she was — she had been there four times with her former husband in 1983. Accompanied by her son, Ivan had driven her there in a four-wheel-drive vehicle to shoot kangaroos. But there were too many people around, so he decided to drive off. On the second occasion he shot two kangaroos. He had gone up to one, slit its throat and then kicked it to be sure it was dead. Their third visit was for a picnic in a gully and the fourth time they went there was just to drive around.

When Ivan went shooting, he would 'shoot at anything he could find — targets on a tree, cans, anything he could see'. At home, she would see him cleaning and dismantling guns and he had no trouble putting them back together.

Karen spoke of Ivan's pastimes. While driving in the car he liked to listen to cassettes, especially Country and Western music featuring singers like Slim Dusty. He was a very strong man, using a long piece of piping with cement-filled buckets on each end to build up his physique. He also used a bull worker, or chest expander. Her former husband was about 168 centimetres (5 feet 6 inches) tall, with sideburns and pale blue eyes. When she was living with him from 1975 to 1981 he smoked, but then he gave it up. She had never gone backpacking with him and he had not owned any backpacking gear. They had a tent, an orange and green one, which they had used when they went to Walter and Richard Milat's property at Wombeyan Caves because there was no house on the land at the time.

Karen said Ivan would go shooting on a pretty regular basis with members of the family, and as an example she spoke of one shooting group at Wombeyan Caves in 1986. This group consisted of her girlfriend's father, her son, Jason, Richard, Walter, Walter's girlfriend at the time, Lisa (later to become his wife), and the Milat brothers' sister Shirley and her husband, Gerry Soire. On one trip to the

Wombeyan Caves property, Karen recalled, Ivan carried the revolver in a holster, was calling himself 'Tex' and 'mucking around like a cowboy'. He took his stepson, Jason, shooting with him at Wombeyan Caves and bought the boy, who got on well with him, a rifle for his 10th birthday in 1986.

When they camped out at the Wombeyan Caves property, Karen recalled, she slept in their tent with a girlfriend and Ivan and Jason slept in the four-wheel-drive. Shirley and Gerry had their own tent. They would make a fire and Ivan would also use a small wood stove. He did, she recalled, possess pots, pans and cutlery.

As for the end of her marriage, Karen agreed with Mr Martin she had walked out, taking property with her. But she had left behind a stereo, a wardrobe, a bookshelf, blankets, pillows, a bedroom suite and a lot of odds and ends. She said that in March 1987 she had to ring her husband on a legal matter, but that was the last time she had spoken to him. She had never seen him again.

The man who entered the court on the morning of 6 December bore a studious expression behind his steel-framed spectacles and carried a bundle of papers under his arm. His name was Dr Peter Bradhurst, forensic pathologist at the New South Wales Institute of Forensic Medicine, and he had been called to tell the court the results of his post-mortem examinations on the bodies of all seven Belanglo State Forest victims. No-one foresaw, as he took his place in the witness box, the bombshell he would drop — but first, there were the more formal, and grim, aspects of his evidence to be heard.

In order of examination, he went over the injuries that each had suffered, but in all of the cases it was impossible to determine the exact cause of death because of the skeletal or decomposed state of the bodies and the varied injuries they had suffered. He had not been able to say, he told the court, whether it was a stab wound or a gunshot which had been the fatal delivery and he did not know whether there had been other injuries to tissue because there was little or no tissue to examine. 'It was particularly difficult to work with the five bodies [Gibson, Everist, Schmidl, Neugebauer and Habschied] that were skeletonised,' he explained.

Deborah Everist had suffered four superficial cuts into her forehead and the front part of her skull, but the skull had also been fractured on the right side and her lower jaw had been broken. There was evidence on the skeletal remains of a stab wound in one of her lower left ribs. But because there was no flesh to work with, he was not able to say whether there had been other injuries, such as a stab wound between the ribs or to the abdomen or whether her throat had been cut.

Dr Bradhurst was shown a curved cavalry sword, still in its scabbard, which had been seized by police at Milat's mother's home, and a bowie knife, still in its sheath, recovered from Milat's Eagle Vale house. Yes, he said, the stab wound in Deborah's chest could have been caused by one of those weapons. The injuries to her head could have been caused by a blunt instrument, possible a lump of wood or the toe of a boot. In any case, the stab wound and the skull fractures had required 'a severe form of force'.

The pathologist turned to the death of James Gibson. It was a moment his mother, sitting in the court, was dreading, but her presence — the only parent there — revealed her determination to sit through the description of the injuries that had ended her beloved son's life. He had been stabbed seven times in the chest, including one stab wound which penetrated the spine. Because the blade had struck bone, a severe form of force would have been required. Dr Bradhurst agreed that the bowie knife or cavalry sword could have caused the injuries. As for the cause of death, he said the stab wound that went through to the spine would have caused paralysis, and another wound which penetrated the sternum would have gone into the heart. A stab wound to the right would have entered the lungs while another wound on the left may have penetrated the aorta of the heart and the liver. Dr Bradhurst emphasised that he could only assess a cause of death from marks that had been left on bones. It was possible that other stab wounds had gone between the ribs or there might have been strangulation, so he could only surmise on what he had to work with that death was from multiple stab wounds to the chest.

Mrs Gibson had sat with her head lowered, holding hands with a woman counsellor as the pathologist gave his summary. The counsellor looked at her to check she was all right; Peggy Gibson nodded her head and wiped the tears from her eyes.

Simone Schmidl, said the pathologist, had died from stab wounds. He had found two wounds in her spine and six in the chest, four of them on the right side, the other two on the left. There may have been other injuries, but the skeletal remains gave up no other clues. The young traveller's injuries were consistent with the bowie knife or cavalry sword — or a similar type of weapon.

The court had already heard that the skull of Anja Habschied had never been found. But what the pathologist had to say about the nature of her decapitation conjured up a chilling scene in the forest as she met her death. He believed Anja had been kneeling, with her head flexed forward, exposing the area at the back of her neck where the fatal blow had been delivered. The weapon had been brought down with severe force, striking her on the fourth cervical vertebra. Dr Bradhurst stood up and placed his finger on the back of his neck, just above the top part of his collar, to show the court where Anja had been struck.

He considered the cavalry sword or similar type of weapon, such as a machete, could have been used. The blow which severed the spine was a single delivery because the bone had been cleanly cut. But he added it was possible that such a blow might not have been able to cut through all the soft tissue of the neck and further cutting may have been required. Dr Bradhurst could not find any injuries to the bones on the remainder of the body and without a skull to ascertain whether there were any other head injuries, he could only put the cause of death down to decapitation.

In Gabor's case, said Dr Bradhurst, he could have died from one of three causes: from the six .22 calibre gunshot wounds to the head, from strangulation, or from suffocation due to the gag in his mouth. But if strangulation had been the cause of death, what, Mr Lloyd wanted to know, was the degree of force required? The pathologist felt a severe degree had been used because a bone on the right side of the neck had been fractured. He was unable to say whether strangulation was by hand or by a rope but generally manual strangulation tended to give rise to more fractures than a ligature.

Joanne Walters, with fourteen stab wounds in the body, her mouth gagged and the possibility of a cloth ligature being used, could have died from the wounds, strangulation or from suffocation, said Dr Bradhurst, although he tended to think the actual cause was the multiple stabbings. He felt that the stabbings were consistent with the bowie knife, although both the knife and the sword would have been capable of causing the injuries. He conceded it was possible that, with evidence of an untied ligature around the neck, the young woman had been strangled, with the stab injuries being inflicted afterwards.

Dr Bradhurst then referred to the murder of Caroline Clarke, who had been shot ten times in the head with a .22 weapon and stabbed once in the back. The degree of force in the stabbing, he said, was moderate — it had not caused any damage to the bone. But it was consistent with the cavalry sword and the bowie knife.

'Can you,' asked Mr Lloyd, 'give an opinion on whether Miss Clarke had been killed where she lay, particularly as spent bullets were found in the soil beneath where her head was?'

The pathologist said that assuming the gunshot wounds caused the death, she would have died where she had been found.

'In relation to the injuries you saw, are you able to say as a forensic pathologist whether there was one assailant or more than one assailant?' Mr Lloyd asked.

Dr Bradhurst stared at him for a moment from over the top of his spectacles. It was a question that had not been raised before at the hearing.

'In my opinion,' said the forensic expert, 'with each of the pairs of backpackers that were killed there appears to be two different patterns of injury. With Caroline Clarke and Joanne Walters, Caroline Clarke had predominant injuries of gunshot wounds to the head and only one stab wound being apparent. With Joanne Walters, she had multiple stab wounds. Similarly, with Gabor Neugebauer and Anja Habschied, Gabor Neugebauer had gunshot wounds to the head, evidence of strangulation and gagging, whereas Anja Habschied had been decapitated. Further, with James Gibson and Deborah Everist, there were two different patterns of injuries. I would tend to think it more likely that more than one person was involved.

'But on the other hand, it is also my opinion that it would still be possible for one person to have caused the deaths if that person had been able to incapacitate one of the two at the time before dealing with the other. But because there are two different patterns it is more than likely that more than one person was involved, but it is possible for one person to have done it.'

Suddenly the backpacker hearing had been presented with the possibility of a second, mystery killer. The question raised by Mr Lloyd and the pathologist's answer had opened a new area of speculation that no-one had dared raise in the court until now.

Dr Bradhurst had expressed the opinion that the condition of the backpackers' bodies was consistent with death having occurred soon after the last time they were seen alive. But, under cross-examination by Mr Martin, he conceded they could have died two to three months after those dates.

The pathologist's evidence was over. The magistrate thanked him for his attendance and he made his way from the court. He had dropped a bombshell. But whether or not more than one person was involved, the Crown would continue to bring on their witnesses to build up the case against the road worker who sat in the dock.

The short, stocky man who now stepped into the witness box wore a yellow open-neck shirt, and a grey suit that was a size too small for him. He lounged back in the chair and waited for the questioning to begin. But first there was a formality — the suppression of his name. He wrote it down and the piece of paper was passed to the magistrate. Walter Milat was determined to remain as anonymous as possible, and for the purposes of the court he would be referred to as Witness E.

Wally, as his family knew him, described his occupation as a Gyprocker and said that he lived with his wife at Hilltop. Before his brother Ivan and sister Shirley moved into the house at Eagle Vale, which he thought was in 1993, he had helped with the building of the property, putting Gyprock through the place. What then followed was a formality, but Mr Lloyd had to ask the question — when he was doing the Gyprocking, had he noticed any gun parts in the wall cavities? Wally had not.

When he moved to Hilltop some eight or nine years earlier, Wally recalled, Ivan was living at their mother's house in Guildford. What about the property at Wombeyan Caves Road, asked Mr Lloyd? Wally replied that he owned it with his brother Richard, having purchased it about eight years earlier for camping and shooting purposes. He had used it fairly regularly, sometimes once a week, sometimes once a month. He'd been there with his brother Ivan and friends.

Mr Lloyd asked Wally to think back to Christmas 1993. Did he recall an evening when he spoke to Ivan on the phone? Wally thought that the conversation, about the possibility of Ivan storing some guns at the Hilltop property, had taken place in the late afternoon.

'I was under the impression our sister was complaining about them being at her place at Eagle Vale. So I went and picked them up in my truck.'

Wally had driven to Eagle Vale in his white Holden 'one-tonner' with his brother Richard, who did not live far from him. At the Cinnabar Street house, they had a coffee with Ivan, picked up the guns and left. The weapons, Wally said under further questioning, were on the floor of the garage. Ivan had also gone up into a manhole in the garage roof and handed down a couple of boxes of ammunition which, said Wally, he had put in the truck and taken back to Hilltop.

'Have you ever fired a Ruger 10/22 in the Belanglo State Forest?' Mr Lloyd suddenly asked.

'No,' replied the witness.

'Have you ever fired an Anschutz rifle in the Belanglo State Forest?'

'No.'

These questions came just twenty-four hours after pathologist Peter Bradhurst had told the court of his belief that more than one person had carried out the murders. The court was now aware that an Anschutz gun bolt found at Wally's home had been linked to cartridge cases collected 165 metres from the remains of Gabor Neugebauer.

Mr Lloyd's questions were not finished.

'Do you know anything about the deaths of these backpackers in the Belanglo State Forest?'

'No.'

'Have you ever been with your brother Ivan in the Belanglo State Forest when, to your observation, he fired a Ruger 10/22 or an Anschutz?'

'No.'

Had he ever seen Ivan with a Ruger 10/22? Wally said that he had, down on the block of land at Wombeyan Caves. What about seeing Ivan with a hand gun of any description? Yes, said Wally, he had seen Ivan with a black weapon that looked like a cowboy gun. He did not know where he'd got it from.

When asked by Milat's lawyer, Mr Martin, where he was on Boxing Day 1991, when Gabor Neugebauer and Anja Habschied were believed to have disappeared, Wally said he had gone to his mother's place in Guildford and his brother Ivan had also been there. But he couldn't remember whether Ivan was there all day, because he had got drunk.

During the search of his house, Wally said, the police had gone into the roof and brought down rifles that he owned, and he had told them where his revolver was — hidden in a false panel in the wardrobe, placed there because, being a hand-gun and he not having a legitimate reason to own it, it was an illegal weapon.

Walter Milat's evidence was over and he was asked to step down.

The court waited for two minutes before another man, a few years younger, made his way to the witness box. He was dressed in an ill-fitting dark-grey suit and wore a moustache which came down to the sides of his mouth. Like his brother before him, Richard Milat wanted his name suppressed. A plasterer, he had been living at the Wombeyan Caves property in the Hilltop district for a year and before that he had lived at his mother's place in Guildford.

'Do you recall an occasion when your brother Wally rang you up and asked you to go to Ivan's place to pick up some material?' asked Mr Lloyd.

In evidence which was clearly not accurate, Richard replied: 'It was about six months ago, but I couldn't be 100 per cent sure. It was about 8 pm or 9 pm and he called me, and then he came to my place and we went to Cinnabar Street. Ivan was there and we had some coffee and he said he had to move some guns. He said they were up in his roof. We got them from up in the roof area and we loaded them into the truck and took them to Wally's place.'

Richard said that when he went up into the roof he found guns and ammunition, some wrapped in blankets and rags, and there were also boxes of ammunition.

'Did you ever fire a Ruger 10/22 in the Belanglo State Forest?' asked Mr Lloyd.

'No.'

'Have you ever fired an Anschutz rifle in the Belanglo State Forest?'

'No.'

'Were you ever with your brother Ivan when a Ruger or an Anschutz was fired?'

'No'

'Did you kill any people in the Belanglo State Forest?'

'No.'

'Do you know anything about the deaths of any backpackers in the Belanglo State Forest?'

'Only what I read in the paper.'

Richard recalled under further questioning that some weeks after he had helped Wally to move the guns, he went to his mother's home in Guildford and picked up some wardrobes and tools from the garage, as well as Ivan's backpacking gear. Some of the material was in the garage, and the rest was in boxes at the back of the verandah. He took it all to his place.

When shown a blue tent, a blue and yellow sleeping bag and a green bed roll — items that had already been said to belong to the British backpackers — Richard Milat said he could not be sure if he had moved them from the Guildford house. The sleeping roll, he said, was not his; the tent looked like one he used to have; and the sleeping bag was similar to one he had owned in 1984, but he had not seen it since. Asked what brand his sleeping bag was, Richard said he could not be 100 per cent sure. He was asked about the red hairbrush — which Caroline Clarke's parents said could have belonged to their daughter — but denied that the police had taken it from his possession.

On being shown a photograph of a metal locker which was in the Guildford family home when police raided it, Richard told Mr Lloyd that Ivan had a similar locker, 'but I could not be sure this is the one'.

Mr Martin, too, was interested in the camping equipment taken from Guildford. Richard said he'd had a couple of blue tents which he used to keep at his mother's house, in the garage or in his room. And he had acquired a sleeping bag when he was in Adelaide on a visit.

When asked what height he was, Richard put it at around 178 centimetres (5 feet 10 inches). Yes, he was a smoker: had been off and on since he was 20 and he would smoke whatever brand he could get hold of. As for his moustache, he'd had it for three months, but over the years he would grow it, sometimes longer, and then shave it off. Mr Martin's questions about Richard's appearance led people in the public gallery to wonder whether it was Richard who may have picked up Paul Onions.

'Do you go shooting regularly?'

'Yes I did — until I hurt my leg in a motorcycle accident in 1992. I haven't been shooting since then. But I was a regular shooter up until then.'

Richard Milat had kept his answers brief, and had

certainly not volunteered much information. But another Milat family member was yet to come.

Elizabeth Joan Milat, married to Ivan's older brother Alex, had flown down from Queensland. She was shown a multi-coloured backpack — identified as having belonged to Simi Schmidl — and said she assumed it was the one she had handed to detectives when they called at her home. She recalled that Ivan had given it to her before she and her family moved from their home at Buxton, in the Southern Highlands, in late 1992.

'I go backpacking,' she said. 'Ivan knew I go backpacking. He said a friend was going back to New Zealand and they didn't want it and that I could have it.'

Mr Martin wanted to know whether Joan had used the backpack. She said she knew it would have been used at least when they moved from Buxton, but she had not gone on any trips with it.

Joan was asked about the initials 'IM' under the flap of the backpack, and said that when she took possession of the pack there were no initials on it. She was then asked who had written them there.

'I did,' she said. But she did not explain why she had used Ivan's logo and, strangely, she was not asked.

The Crown case was virtually over. It had run for twenty-seven days, 660 exhibits had been presented, including photographs and statements, and 171 witnesses had given evidence. There was one more witness to come, Chief Superintendent Clive Small, who had masterminded the investigation, but Mr Martin felt that the Crown should have called more.

'I know that several people have come forward to report that they had seen some of the missing backpackers some time after the police had pinpointed the last sightings,' he said. 'I would have liked to have had the opportunity to cross-examine these people about the occasions on which they allegedly saw the backpackers.'

The barrister then said he had learned that prosecutor Lloyd had no intention of calling these witnesses because Mr Lloyd had made the decision that their evidence was not reliable. Mr Martin asked the magistrate for a stay of proceedings until the witnesses were produced. The Crown Prosecutor, he said, had as much of a duty to call material witnesses at a committal hearing as he had at a trial.

'My friend is entitled to make this judgment, but it is my submission that he is erroneous in his judgment not to include them in the brief, and that he should call them,' said the defence barrister.

In relation to the British women, Mr Martin mentioned a motorist, Susan Burns, and her passenger Myrna Honeyman, who believed they had picked up the backpackers from Waterfall railway station between 21 April and 23 April 1992 — certainly after Easter.

Miss Burns had been subjected to hypnosis, and a police officer, Sergeant Roger Johnson, could be called to give evidence about what was said under hypnosis, said Mr Martin. While being questioned in that state, said Mr Martin, Miss Burns told the sergeant that the girls' names were Jo and Caroline, they had large backpacks, and she dropped them at the Caltex service station at the top of Bulli Pass. During the journey, the young women told Miss Burns they had caught a train from Kings Cross station and were going to Yass, near Canberra, to do some fruit-picking. One of the girls said she was Welsh — Miss Burns had trouble with the accent — and both were travelling around Australia. The Welsh girl had also mentioned something about going to Western Australia. The hitch-hikers also said that they had been staying at a backpackers' hostel in Kings Cross and had seen a fair bit of Sydney, including the harbour area, The Rocks, Watsons Bay and the Opera House.

Mr Martin raised the possibility of the Britons meeting someone they knew and said that according to Miss Burns' hypnosis recall, the young women had spoken of a man they had met from Western Australia, and added that they had stayed with him at Mona Vale — a beachside suburb north of the city centre — over Easter.

Although Stephen Wright, who had passed them his tent, had told the court that they were going to the Liverpool area, Mr Martin said: 'What, in fact, did they do on the 18th of April? Nobody knows.'

The motorist got the impression that the young women had stayed with their friend over Easter, and as they travelled in the car they mentioned wanting to go to Ayers Rock and on to Darwin. There was also a reference to Jo having worked for a doctor. In addition, the motorist had mentioned Doc Marten's boots and that the Welsh girl had a strong jaw, which was indeed a feature of Miss Walters, said Mr Martin.

Turning to the disappearance of Simone Schmidl, the barrister said that the senior assistant station master at Albury railway station, on the New South Wales–Victorian border, some 500 kilometres south-west of Sydney, was certain it was the German hitch-hiker he had spoken to on the station on 21 January 1991. He remembered a bandage she had on her ankle — Simone had worn a bandage after injuring herself in New Zealand — and recalled her saying that she was going to meet her mother on 23 January at Melbourne airport. She was carrying a blue overnight-type bag and a large backpack, and told him, in a European accent, that she had no money. Mr Martin did not mention it, but Albury is only 100 kilometres from where backpacking gear thought originally to have been Simi's was found.

Mr Martin then mentioned other witnesses who claimed to have seen Simone in Albury or on the highway, on dates which did not fit in with the Crown's scenario.

'All of these are clearly material witnesses, because if these sightings are correct the police theory of these people going missing on certain days and my client being available to do anything to these persons is, in fact, destroyed,' said the barrister.

Mr Lloyd was unimpressed by the submission. 'You have been trawling through the material and selected a few statements, when in fact there's a mountain of evidence against the sightings you've detailed,' said the prosecutor.

He did not intend to call the people that the defence lawyer had nominated but Mr Martin, he said, could call them if he wished. Although the magistrate turned down the application for a stay in proceedings to allow these witnesses to be called by the Crown, he told the defence that they could call them if they wanted to hear their versions in detail from the witness box.

Mr Martin said he would examine the statements again over the coming weekend, and look into whether it would be possible to track down the witnesses and call them in to what were now the final stages of the committal hearing. But on the last day of the committal, Monday 12 December 1994, Mr Martin did not appear. He had not felt it necessary to travel from Brisbane for the last few hours — before what he and his briefing solicitor, Andrew Boe, realised would be the magistrate's decision to send Ivan Milat for trial.

The Crown called their last witness. Chief Superintendent Small told of the increasing suspicion against Ivan Milat, which was sparked off by the incident involving Paul Onions. He also related the surprise of police at finding the 'wealth of evidence' at Milat's Eagle Vale home.

Andrew Boe, taking over from the absent Mr Martin, wanted to know who decided what evidence to include in the case against Ivan Milat and what to discard. Chief Superintendent Small said that he made the final decisions. And in reply to questions about the police witnesses who would be called and those who had been eliminated, Small said 'a jury will at the end of the day make up their minds who to believe'.

Ivan Milat, dressed in a white shirt and dark trousers, stood in the dock and rested his hands on the rail as the magistrate formally committed him for trial in the New Year. The accused man shook his lawyer's hand, smiled, then turned and made his way down the stairs to a police van that would take him back to jail.

Despite all the evidence that had been presented against him, Milat was still, technically, an innocent man. He would remain so unless and until he was proved to be guilty.

CHAPTER FIFTEEN

While Ivan Milat lingered in Sydney's Long Bay Jail awaiting trial, scientists and detectives worked tirelessly building up what they hoped would be a convincing case against him. Fingerprints were checked and re-checked, expert opinions canvassed, weapon parts, cartridges, empty cartridge cases and fired bullets were re-examined under microscopes and endless hours put in calling on potential witnesses. No clue that could be used against the road worker was ignored. And always at the back of detectives' minds was the possibility that more than one killer was involved.

Often the hard work was rewarded with further evidence police believed would lead to Milat being locked away behind bars for the rest of his life. Sometimes, a particular line of investigation appeared to have great potential, but ended up leading nowhere — as was the case when police were looking into every aspect of Joanne Walters' presence in Australia.

They noticed that on the immigration card she presented when she arrived in Australia in 1991 she had written a contact address in Thunderbolt Drive, Raby. Police interest was immediately aroused because the street was located just 1 kilometre west of the Hume Highway and only some 6 kilometres south-west of Casula, where Paul Onions had been picked up. The address was occupied by a Mr and Mrs C. Maggs and police established Joanne had a connection with the Maggs family: her grandfather and Mr Maggs had once lived close to one another in Wales. Police assumed Joanne had written their address on her immigration card because she was going to call on Mr Maggs.

While detectives' interest was aroused by the location of the address, further inquiries uncovered what at first seemed like a startling piece of evidence. The house across the road from the Maggs family had been owned by Ivan Milat's former brother-in-law, Gerhardt Soire, who was once married to Shirley Soire, the joint owner of the property in Eagle Vale where Milat had been living prior to his arrest. And Gerhardt, police established, was a member of the Bowral Pistol Club, whose headquarters is located in the Belanglo State Forest.

Stunned detectives came up with many theories as they continued their investigations into this curious link to Joanne Walters, but they were eventually able to establish conclusively that it had been nothing more than the strangest of coincidences. Joanne had not gone to Thunderbolt Drive, and Gerhardt had moved from the address some two years before Joanne arrived in Australia. But it emphasised to the investigating officers that nothing could be taken at face value. Every fact had to be checked and double-checked, every piece of evidence examined thoroughly and re-examined.

Key witnesses were interviewed again and again. Milat's former wife, Karen, spent more hours with police as they asked her about her former husband's lifestyle while she was with him, both during the time they were living with his mother in Guildford and later in their own home in Blackett. She was shown a green and white striped pillowcase found in the garage of the Eagle Vale house. Yes, she said, she recognised it — it had belonged to Ivan's mother, whom he had gone to live with for a time after they had split up.

The pillowcase was of vital importance to the case against Milat. In it had been found a number of white sash cords that Karen recognised as being the same type her former husband used at times to secure items in the trailer. Detective Senior Constable Grosse had been satisfied to learn from two forensic experts in Britain (Mr John Barr and Ms Valerie Tomlinson, whose opinions had been sought) that one of the sash cords had been stained with a small amount of blood, as had the pillowcase. The DNA in the blood, Grosse learned, would be found in only one in 118,000 people, greater odds than forensic experts had originally thought — and it was consistent with the blood of a child of Mr and Mrs Clarke. In other words, there was an extremely rare chance that the blood was not that of Caroline Clarke.

There was, too, the ballistic evidence which linked bullets found in some of the victims with weapons collected from raids on Milat family properties. Numbers on boxes of cartridges found at the raid of Walter Millat's house also matched those on cartridge boxes found near the bodies of Anja Habschied and Gabor Neugebaur.

Furthermore, torn pieces of a shirt wrapped around the gun parts found in the wall cavity at Milat's home appeared to match up with material used to gag Joanne Walters. Not only was it the same material, but the size of the cuts and tears and the line of the ironing seam in separate pieces appeared to match.

It was not until 26 March 1996, fifteen months after the committal hearing, that the trial of Ivan Milat was able to get under way in Sydney's historic Banco Court, following months of disagreement about the fees his defence team should receive from legal aid. Now, before the trial could begin, a financial battle was waging outside the perimeter of the court after the Legal Aid Commission insisted that Milat, who had $40,000 in his bank account when he was arrested, should contribute $50,000 towards his legal fees.

Through his lawyers, Milat told the Supreme Court that he could not pay the money because it had already been spent on legal fees, flying his Queensland-based legal team to and from Sydney and providing their accommodation. The remainder of his savings, he said, had gone on family-related expenses.

In that case, said the commission, Milat should use his half share of the house in Cinnabar Street — valued at $186,000 and with no mortgage — as security for the $50,000. A Supreme Court judge, Justice Carolyn Simpson, commented that such a move would be unfair on Milat's sister Shirley, who owned the other 50 per cent share of the house.

It was estimated that the trial could cost the commission up to $750,000, on top of the legal aid amounting to $118,000 for his 28-day committal hearing. Matters were finally sorted out when Milat's lawyers were forced to accept a legal aid offer totalling $2106 a day.

Finally, the case was ready to begin. On Tuesday 26 March 1996 Milat was escorted by four prison officers to a seat in the well of the court and to the right of the judge.

Justice David Hunt had been a judge of the New South Wales Supreme Court since 1979, having been called to the bar in 1959. The 61-year-old judge was softly spoken and was to give the impression of an extremely fair man, anxious to clear up legal problems as they arose — even if it meant sending the jury out of the court time and again while such matters were discussed.

Milat wore a charcoal suit. His face showed no sign of strain, despite the packed public gallery and the long queue left waiting outside for what had been described as one of

Australia's biggest murder trials. A section of the public gallery immediately above the defendant's seat had been screened off by tall sheets of glass as a precaution against anyone, driven by the horror of the case, throwing objects or spitting.

Barrister Terry Martin, who had taken up Milat's case towards the end of the committal hearing, would lead the defence team with the support of Queensland barrister Peter Callaghan and the solicitor Andrew Boe, who had been with Milat almost from the start of the legal process.

The prosecution evidence would be presented by Mark Tedeschi, QC, a slightly built man with a reputation as a forceful lawyer and who spent his spare time taking exhibition-quality photographs, some of which were at that moment on display at the public library just along the street from the courthouse. As his junior counsel he had Dan Howard, a tall, dark-haired Englishman.

The jury, selected by both the prosecution and defence teams and consisting of four women and eight men, sat to the left of the judge directly opposite Milat. They had been whittled down from 1000 summonses that had been sent to residents and then from the 250 people who had showed up at the Supreme Court building. More than half dropped out when told how long the trial was expected to last — at least four months — and finally those available were honed down to eighty and then to twelve.

The location of the jury, in two rows of six, enabled them to observe Milat clearly as the case was presented against him and the prosecution witnesses filed in. Mr Tedeschi chose to stand at the left-hand side of the advocate's table so that he was looking directly at the jurors, with Milat just a little behind him and to his right. Within minutes, he was telling how it would be alleged that Ivan Milat killed the backpackers for his own psychological gratification, and he suggested that Milat may not have acted alone.

'The Crown doesn't know how many persons there were in the forest at the time of the alleged murders,' he said in a quiet tone. 'In other words, the Crown isn't able to prove if the accused acted alone or with another or others. The Crown case is, if the accused was alone, then the deaths were caused by an act which he himself did. Alternatively, if there was another person or persons in the forest, the Crown says the accused and that person were acting together in causing those deaths … and so are acts for which the accused was legally responsible.'

In any case, he said, the murders were killings for killing's sake. 'The victims were killed in ferocious and sustained attacks during which vastly more force was used than was necessary to kill.'

Mr Tedeschi outlined the disappearances, the discovery of the bodies, then called his main witness: the British backpacker who had escaped an assailant close to the turn-off to the Belanglo Forest.

Paul Onions' strong Midlands accent filled the court-room as, answering Mr Tedeschi's questions, he recalled the fear that had run through him after he had accepted a lift on the Hume Highway — a free ride which had ended with him running for his life after the driver of a four-wheel-drive vehicle had pulled a revolver on him.

'If you saw that person in the courtroom now, would you be able to identify the man who was the driver of that car?' asked Mr Tedeschi.

'Yes,' said Onions.

'Can you look around the courtroom and say if you see that man?'

Onions looked to his right and gestured with a quick motion of his hand towards Milat. 'It's that guy there,' he said. People in the public gallery stared at the accused man, who showed no emotion and kept his eyes on the hands he had folded on his lap.

Next to appear in the witness box was Mrs Carolynne Milat, the wife of Ivan's younger brother William. She was a woman in her mid to late 40s, with her hair tinted a light brown. It could only have been an uncomfortable time for her as Mr Tedeschi's questions were to prove, but she held her composure as if she had given evidence many times before. She was asked about dates beside photographs in an album that had been seized at her home at Bargo in the Southern Highlands. The photographs showed Ivan and family members on an Easter picnic. But the original dates that had been written in beside the photographs — Easter 1991 — had been changed to read Easter 1992.

'You altered these photographs so that the photographs of 1991 were relabelled to 1992 — did you do that after Ivan Milat's arrest?'

'No,' said Mrs Milat.

Under further intense questioning, Mrs Milat continued to deny she had changed the dates to provide Ivan with an alibi after learning that two British backpackers had disappeared during Easter 1992. She also insisted that Ivan had been at a family gathering at Ivan's mother's home in Guildford on 26 December 1991, the day the two German backpackers were believed to have been murdered after checking out of a Kings Cross budget hotel.

When she was recalled to the witness box the following day, Mr Tedeschi had an ace up his sleeve — he pulled the photographs of the Easter picnic from the album and asked her whose writing was on the back. She said it was Ivan's handwriting. And yes, she conceded, the dates on the back covered the Easter period of 1991. She said, under further questioning, that she could not be positive that the holiday had occurred in 1992.

Milat's former wife, Karen, dressed in a charcoal-grey pinstriped suit and with her brown hair pinned back with a white band, clutched a handkerchief as she was led to the witness box. She told, nervously at first but gaining confidence as she proceeded, of her marriage to Ivan Milat followed by divorce in 1989. She spoke of his strength — how he had made himself a set of weights for training, and how, because of his desire to be fit and healthy, he used to smoke but had later given it up. She recalled that in 1983 she and her husband and her son went to the Belanglo State Forest four times, and on one of those trips Ivan — known to other family members as Joe Spanner, Texas and Bargo Bill — had shot at kangaroos.

'Ivan liked guns. He knew how to handle them and was confident about them.' He owned a pistol, a rifle, a slug gun, and a six-shot revolver that he stored under their bed in a small wooden case. As for the pistol, he kept it loaded and rolled up in a brown and white sock which he would carry under the seat of the car, but sometimes when he went to the pictures he would tuck the weapon into the side of his zippered boots.

In the second week of the trial, Ivan Milat stood and admitted, on legal advice, that camping gear found at his home and the homes of his three brothers, Richard, Walter and Alex, had belonged to some of the backpackers, but the admission was based on evidence that had been confirmed by the police and not on facts known to him. Milat was in fact telling the court that he would not be disputing that the items had belonged to the backpackers. The admissions resulted in little reaction from the court — members of the public, if not the jury, appeared to have already accepted that the camping items belonged to the missing backpackers.

What the jury would be wanting to know, following Milat's admission, was how the belongings had come into his possession or had ended up in the homes of family members. The articles were a tent, tent pegs, sleeping bag cover, sleeping bag and green water-bottle found at his home

— all belonging to Simone Schmidl; a daypack belonging to Simi found in an apple box in an alcove under Walter's home at Wilson Drive, Hilltop; and a backpack belonging to Simone which had been handed to police by Alex's wife, Joan.

Milat also admitted that a sleeping bag, bed roll and tent belonging to Caroline Clarke were found in a garden shed at Richard Milat's home in Vera Street, Hilltop, near Wombeyan Caves, and agreed that a sleeping bag inside a cupboard in the shed of Richard's home belonged to Joanne Walters.

One of Mr Tedeschi's tasks in presenting the case for the Crown was to try to dismiss suggestions that some of the murdered backpackers had been seen in other areas after the time of their deaths allegedly at the hands of Ivan Milat. In the case of Simone Schmidl, who was reported to have been seen at the Albury railway station, on the border of New South Wales and Victoria, on 21 January 1991 — the day after she was believed by police to have been killed — Mr Tedeschi insisted that those who had seen a woman looking like her had been mistaken. To support his claim, he called a former nurse, Linda Chalmers, who told the court it may have been 21 January that she had gone to the station to ask about trains to Melbourne. Miss Chalmers recalled she had been wearing a backpack and had her dark hair tied back with a headband — in a similar style to Miss Schmidl. When she was asked to look at the former assistant station master, Ronald Bennett, who was called into the courtroom, she said he was possibly the man she had spoken to at the station at the time. But later Mr Bennett, prompted by the defence, said that Miss Chalmers was not the woman he had seen on the station.

'It was her hair style, the dreadlocks, that stuck in my mind,' he said of the woman he had seen. He recalled seeing media pictures of Miss Schmidl and was convinced she was the woman he had seen on the station. 'That hair style and her sitting on the platform is a picture in my mind that won't go away,' he told the jury.

Miss Chalmers had been a prosecution witness, but it was the defence that seemed to have scored the points. Mr Tedeschi would, however, continue to insist that other reported sightings, including that of two British women backpackers who had received a lift from two women near Bulli Pass, were false identifications.

Among those called into the court in the opening weeks of the trial were the parents of the murdered backpackers. They recalled the last times they had spoken to their sons or daughters, but to save them distress, Mr Tedeschi led them through their evidence quickly. In the case of Mrs Gill Walters, Joanne's mother, she was so distressed that she had to be led sobbing from the witness box before she could even give her evidence.

Ms Pauline Vuletich, who had arrived in Australia with Joanne in May 1991, was unable to contain her emotions as she passed Milat in the court after finishing her evidence. 'Scum!' she breathed. Milat raised his eyebrows and looked up. It was the first time he had openly shown any semblance of shock in all the months he had sat in court, including the committal hearings.

Anja Habschied's mother, Olga, left the public gallery in tears as she heard pathologist Dr Bradhurst telling how her daughter had died, decapitated with one blow to the back of the neck while her head was flexed onto her upper chest in what he called a 'style of ceremonial execution'. There were no other injuries that he could find, he said, but she had been naked from the waist down. A machete, axe, large knife or sword, capable of being swung with force, would have been used; when he was shown the sword said to have been found at the elderly Mrs Margaret Milat's house, he said that weapon was indeed capable of inflicting such a blow.

Walter Milat, now aged 44 and dressed in a dark blue suit, made his way into the witness box, in no doubt about the kind of questions that would be fired at him. He knew by heart the list of weapons the police had found at his home: numerous guns, including a .303 repeating rifle, an Anschutz rifle, an SKK model assault rifle, an unused Ruger 10/22 rifle, a Chinese SKS self-loading rifle, a repeating shotgun, a .45-calibre single-shot percussion rifle, a .357 magnum revolver, a home-made holster, hunting knife and sheath, two machetes, two bayonets, a quiver and seven arrows, bandoliers for storing ammunition, a large amount of ammunition, including .22 calibre and .357 magnum, twenty-one knives and a sharpening stone. And the separate Anschutz bolt.

As he took his seat in the witness box on that morning of Tuesday 30 April, weapons were on everyone's minds. Just two days earlier a lone gunman had in cold blood murdered thirty-five people in and around the Port Arthur historical site near Hobart, Tasmania, and an outraged nation was demanding urgent changes to gun laws that made it easy for people to get their hands on weapons of destruction. The jury had been instructed at the start of the trial to ignore anything they saw or heard outside the court that could have a bearing on the way they viewed the evidence, but it would have been impossible for any of those eight men and four women to have closed their minds to the carnage that semi-automatic weapons had brought to Port Arthur on that quiet Sunday afternoon at the end of April.

'Did you,' Crown prosecutor Tedeschi asked the Gyprock worker, 'play any part in the deaths of any of the seven backpackers whose bodies were found in the Belanglo State Forest?'

Walter had already been asked this at the magistrates court and had made his denials. Now he replied just as firmly: 'No.'

Had he ever fired at any people in the forest using an Anschutz rifle or been present when anyone else was shooting at any people? To both questions, it was the same firm 'No'.

Neither had he fired a Winchester rifle at any person in the forest or been present when anyone else fired at any person.

Aware that the gun and bolt found at Walter's home could have fired spent cartridges found near the bodies of Anja Habschied and Gabor Neugebauer, Mr Tedeschi persisted, asking Walter if he had fired an Anschutz rifle in the Belanglo forest. This time, Walter conceded that he may have, an admission that caused the heads of some journalists to look up from their notebooks at him.

But after extracting this admission from the witness, Mr Tedeschi appeared to have no confidence in the truth of the reply. Referring to Ivan Milat, he asked Walter: 'Are you trying to help him by providing some explanation for how cartridges from the Anschutz were found in the forest?'

'No,' replied Walter.

Under further questioning, Walter said Ivan had stored 'some gear' including guns and ammunition in an alcove under his house about three months before the police raids. Asked if Ivan had given a reason why he wanted it moved from the house he shared with his sister, Walter said: 'Shirley was upset about them being around the place — that they would be stolen.'

While Walter was strongly defending himself against suggestions that he knew something about the deaths of the backpackers, defence barrister Mr Martin was getting ready to put further pressure on Ivan's brother. It was in Ivan's interests to show that Walter was the man who should have been arrested.

Mr Martin asked Walter about the affair he believed Ivan had had with his first wife fifteen years ago. 'Do you,' asked

Mr Martin, 'have any bitterness as a result of that thought towards Milat?'

'No,' said Walter Milat.

He also denied he had placed an unused Ruger 10/22 rifle and the blue daypack which belonged to Simi Schmidl on top of a stack of Ivan's goods police found under his (Walter's) house. But under further question he said it was 'quite possible' he had been in the Belanglo State Forest in 1989, 1990, 1991 and 1992, the years of the seven murders. It was also 'reasonably possible' he might have been shooting there with the Anschutz rifle that had been found under his house along with items belonging to Ivan. Sometimes, he said, he had borrowed Ivan's Anschutz and he agreed with Mr Martin that he had almost unlimited access and a key to Ivan's house, which he helped build. Yes, he had been in the house alone and it was true he had once left a rifle in his brother's garage. But he made many denials, including that he had placed gun parts in the ceiling of Ivan's home or a rifle part in one of Ivan's boots, which was in his hall cupboard.

And then again, those same, persistent questions about any role he may have had in the backpacker murders.

'What do you say to the suggestion that you killed the persons found in the Belanglo State Forest?'

'I didn't ... I had no part in it.'

Walter conceded that he used to visit the newsagency at Casula where Paul Onions was said by detectives to have been picked up by Ivan. 'Did you attack a backpacker by the name Onions?' Mr Martin wanted to know.

'No,' repeated Walter.

Then the Crown Prosecutor was back on his feet, wanting to know if Walter would lie to protect his brother and sisters if it were a serious enough matter.

'Perhaps yes,' said Walter, possibly silently recalling the earlier family years when the brothers had all grown up together and had gathered as a huge group around the Christmas table. He conceded then that he had already lied to the court when he said an unused Ruger 10/22 found at his home belonged to Ivan. His explanation — having been assured that the evidence would not be used against him — was that he had bought the Ruger with a false gun licence.

Asked by Mr Tedeschi how he got along with Ivan after finding out his brother may have had an affair with his first wife, Walter said: 'I never let that affect our relationship.' In fact, when Ivan divorced Karen, Walter had offered Ivan his support. 'I remember talking to him about it, telling him the only thing he could do was forget about it and time heals it up,' said Walter.

His evidence over, Walter walked from the court — but soon those same questions about the shootings in the forest were to be directed at yet another Milat brother. This time it was Richard, 40, who was asked whether he had any part in the murders.

'Are you in any way responsible for the deaths of any of the seven backpackers whose bodies were found in the Belanglo State Forest?' asked Mr Tedeschi.

'No,' Richard replied, 'I had nothing to do with the deaths.'

'Do you know who is responsible for any of the deaths of the seven backpackers?'

'No.'

He, too, denied being in the forest when the victims were killed. And he had never fired either a Ruger 10/22 rifle or an Anschutz rifle in the forest. Neither had he stabbed anyone there.

He repeated that he had helped Ivan move a load of guns and ammunition from the house in Cinnabar Street, Eagle Vale, to Walter's place 'a couple of months' before Ivan's arrest. 'I remember Ivan saying words similar to "I had a barrel threaded at Readymix [where Ivan was working] and I've got a problem with it. The police might come to investigate it.'" Weapons with the end of the barrel threaded could be assumed by police to have been prepared for use with a silencer — an illegal accessory.

Richard was referred to his property at Wombeyan Caves, Hilltop, where he occupied a caravan and where Elizabeth Smith, the mother of his son, lived in a separate caravan, the two vehicles being connected by a common annexe. Richard told the court that the camping gear — sleeping bags, a blue tent, a bed roll and some tent poles and pegs — found in a cupboard in a toolshed on his property, could belong to him. Yet Ivan had already admitted to the court on his lawyer's advice that the property belonged to the murdered British women. Richard was not challenged on his claim. He went on to recall how he had moved the cupboard from his mother's home in Guildford, where he and Ivan used to live, but he could not be sure whether the camping gear had been in the cupboard when it was at his mother's home.

Elizabeth Smith was called before the court. She wore trousers and a coloured blouse, and her long brown hair, showing a hint of grey, ran over her shoulders. With an occasional nervous giggle, she told how she had lived with Richard 'on and off' for some fifteen years and he had fathered her son, Justin, now aged six. She admitted she had been an alcoholic for four or five years and that she was 'scatter-brained'. When she was living at 'granny Milat's' house with Richard in the early 1990s she had started each day with a 7-ounce glass of brandy from a bottle she stored in 'Bodger's' (David Milat's) room. During the day she also smoked marijuana, drank more brandy and sometimes beer as well. She would often have to sleep off the effects at various times of the day.

Her memory about who had been present for lunch at Christmas, covering the period when Gabor Neugebauer and Anja Habschied had vanished, was hazy. Ivan, she said, 'may have been there, in and out, I am not sure'. On Boxing Day morning, she said, she saw Mack (Ivan) get some mince from the fridge to feed his cat Gizmo, but under questioning she conceded that it was 27 December and not 26 December when she had seen Ivan feed the cat. The garage door was shut on 27 December, she recalled, indicating to her that Ivan's car was there and he was at home. But on Boxing Day, she remembered, the door was open, suggesting he was out. 'I can't recall if it was for part or the whole of the day.'

Pressed by Mr Martin about who was present at granny Milat's home on Christmas Day, Elizabeth Smith agreed with the barrister that Ivan could have been present because he had given her son a water pistol and she remembered the young boy playing with him. 'With the alcohol in me, I could have been off the wall that day,' she told the court. Yes, she admitted, her recollection of events during that Christmas of 1991 would be most unreliable.

While his de facto wife was giving her evidence Richard Milat waited in the court building, having been told he would be recalled. Sometimes, hands thrust into his trouser pockets, he strolled across the road to a coffee lounge, smiling at the photographers. Now it was his turn to be called back into the witness box for what he knew was going to be some intense questioning.

From 1989 to 1993, he recalled, he worked for the industrial company Boral as an unloader, but not under his own name. He was known there as Paul Thomas Miller. On Thursday 25 January 1989, the day Paul Onions was attacked, he had worked from 6.30 in the morning until 2.30 in the afternoon, according to his work records. He worked the same hours on 30 December 1991, the day that Anja Habschied and Gabor Neugebauer had disappeared.

Richard Milat was asked about his property near Wombeyan Caves, which he moved onto in October 1993. Did he burn items there, about 200 metres from his caravan?

Yes, he said with a dismissive shrug, he had burned things, and he did have a slow combustion stove which he used for warming up the general area if he was working outside. Had he burned a backpack on the property?

'Not as far as I know,' he replied. He couldn't be sure what blue nylon item he might have burned there.

He was a gun enthusiast and a regular shooter, getting his ammunition from Walter, who in turn had bought it from his brother Alex. Some of the ammunition was .22 calibre, possibly, he agreed, Eley and Winchester brands. Mr Martin wanted to know why the police had not taken 1000 to 1400 rounds of ammunition he had kept at his property — had it been concealed from them? No, said Richard Milat, it was packed in a box. And if he wanted to borrow Ivan's rifles he would simply ask and Ivan would let him use them, although he could now only recall borrowing Ivan's .243.

Mr Martin turned to Richard Milat's work at Boral, eliciting from him details of a system whereby four men were able to arrange their hours so that two could leave an hour or more early, with the remaining two covering for them. 'So that even if the work records show you worked until 2.30 pm, you could leave at 1.30 pm, depending on how you organised the people who had the shifts?'

'Or even earlier,' volunteered Mr Milat.

He was asked about black electrical tape, the same type found in the Belanglo State Forest near the murder scene of the German couple. Yes, he said, he had used tape over the years for doing electrical work on cars and he had also used black ties as well as ropes. And he had had large knives over the years, but only 'bread-type' knives, kitchen knives. He had had machetes over the years, too. Had he been to the Belanglo State Forest? He had driven past the road leading into it to get to the Bowral Pistol Club, located nearby. But had he ever turned onto the track leading into the forest?

'Maybe on my motorcycle, I may possibly have recently.'

'You say recently — when?' asked Mr Martin.

'It could have been earlier this year or late last year.'

'What were you looking for?'

'Nothing.'

'Had you been into that area prior to your going into the forest earlier this year or late last year?'

'Not as far as I know.'

'What do you mean, "Not as far as I know"?'

'Going to the pistol club, I could not be sure.'

He agreed he had been shooting in forests in various parts of New South Wales with his brother Walter, but he did not think that included the Belanglo State Forest.

Richard Milat continued to answer most of the questions asked of him, but his answers were couched with doubt: he could not be sure, he could not remember, he could not be 100 per cent sure. But he answered with a firm no when asked, once again, if he had killed anyone in the Belanglo State Forest, if he was present when anyone was killed there, or if he had any knowledge relating to the bodies found there. Neither had he told anyone that he had any knowledge about the bodies.

'Have you ever indicated to workmates that you had knowledge of the bodies in the Belanglo State Forest?' asked Mr Martin in a reference to claims that he used to smoke a bong and had said that the bodies of the Germans had not been found yet.

'No.'

During a discussion with a workmate at the time the bodies of the English women were found, did he say: 'There are two Germans out there. They haven't found them yet'?

'I don't recall that,' he said.

'If you did say that, how did you know that there were two Germans that had not been found?'

'I don't know.'

'Did you have knowledge of German backpackers being buried in the Belanglo State Forest before those bodies were found?'

'No.'

Mr Milat was asked if, on another occasion, he had told the same workmate words to the effect: 'There are more bodies out there, they haven't found them all.' Could he conceive of any circumstances in which he would say something like that?

'No.'

Mr Milat admitted that while he was working at Boral, his appearance changed from time to time. He would grow a beard or wear a longer, thicker moustache. And once, before he had started at the firm, he had run a dark rinse through his hair to pose for the photograph on the driving licence he held in the name of Paul Miller — a false licence he obtained because he drove a high-powered motorcycle and he did not want to run the risk of losing his legal licence.

Mr Martin asked Mr Milat about a discussion he had allegedly had with a workmate in the meal room at Boral concerning rape cases in the media. 'Do you recall saying something like: "Stabbing a woman is like cutting a loaf of bread"'?

'I don't remember saying that,' he replied

'Did you say anything like that?'

'Not as far as I know.'

'Is that a thought you do have?'

'No, I have never had that thought.'

Mr Martin brought Mr Milat back to the time of the attempted kidnapping on Paul Onions. He would have been in his mid 30s then, and his height then, as it was now, would have been about 178 centimetres (5 feet 10 inches). He did not have access to a silver-coloured four-wheel-drive, he said, but said it was 'more than likely' he could hire one if he wanted to. Questioned about his views on Asians, Mr Milat agreed that he believed there were too many Asian migrants in Australia, a belief he would have held in 1990. The jury had already heard from Paul Onions how his would-be kidnapper had expressed anti-Asian views.

Then again, those same questions about any role that he might have played in the murders. 'What do you say,' asked Mr Martin, 'to the suggestion that you killed the persons whose bodies were found in the Belanglo State Forest?'

'I would say that's a lie,' said Mr Milat, denying knowledge to further similar questions.

Then it was Mr Tedeschi's turn once more to interrogate Mr Milat on behalf of the Crown. Had somebody told him that, if he answered questions with such phrases as 'I cannot be sure' or 'I can't remember', he could not be charged with perjury? Was he trying to assist Ivan Milat by answering in that way? No, he said, he was not.

Would he lie to protect himself? 'Possibly,' he said. Would he lie to protect his mother? 'I don't know.' A member of his family generally? 'Possibly.' Over a matter that was very serious? 'Possibly.' Was it possible he would lie about anything? 'Anything is possible.'

'Have you deliberately come to court to give your evidence in a way which is designed with the aim in mind to assist your brother, Ivan Milat?'

'No.'

'Is that a lie?'

'No.'

His evidence was over. He was told he could step down. He walked towards the entrance, his eyes flashing once at his elder brother as he stepped past him. Ivan's head remained lowered.

CHAPTER SIXTEEN

Since relating to the police his conversations at work with the man he knew as Paul Miller, Paul Douglas had learned the other man's real name was Richard Milat. Now, sitting in the dock, he told the jury of the comments Milat had made after he had been smoking marijuana through a bong. Douglas told of Milat boasting that he knew there were more bodies in the forest and that they hadn't yet found the Germans. After relating the conversations for the Crown, Douglas now faced defence lawyer Mr Martin.

In addition to smoking marijuana, Mr Martin wanted to know, did Richard Milat also drink alcohol at work? Yes, said Douglas, he thought he drank whisky — it certainly looked and smelled like it.

Douglas agreed that the following year, when there was publicity about the discovery of other bodies in the Belanglo State Forest, he gave significance to the conversations he had had with Richard Milat, and that the police had come to see him in late 1993 in relation to the comments Milat had made about the Germans and stabbing a woman.

Did Milat keep himself fit? Yes, said Douglas, Milat did push-ups at work, 100 or so. Milat had also told him how he had taught himself to use both hands.

Would Milat change his appearance? Yes, said Douglas,

sometimes he would have a beard for a few months, then he would shave it off. The colour of his hair would also change from brown to light brown.

Des Butler, who worked at Boral for six and a half years, first met the man he knew then as Paul Miller in November 1989. He now knew Miller's real name was Richard Milat, he told the court when he took his place in the witness box.

'I saw him every day at work and I became quite friendly with him. We had the occasional drink together and he fixed practically everyone else's car,' he recalled. On one occasion, Milat asked him to go shooting with him; on the way, he was introduced to Walter and Walter's wife, and then Richard, Walter and he set off for the shooting expedition.

At work, Butler said, Milat smoked hashish 'fairly regularly' through a bong. Normally, he would stay quiet for fifteen to twenty minutes at a time, but after he had been smoking 'that stuff' he would talk repeatedly for six to eight hours.

As with Mr Douglas, Butler was questioned about a comment Milat made about the missing backpackers. Only this time, Butler revealed, the comment had been made before the English women's bodies had been found. Butler was working with Milat on the unloader at about 8.30 pm and he noticed that Milat was affected by hash. During his long outbursts of conversation, Milat said:

'I know who killed the Germans.'

'Had he said anything just prior to that to indicate what he was talking about?' asked Mr Tedeschi.

'I have looked back on it and I think there was something about the Germans being missing.'

'Did you reply to that statement?'

'No, because I didn't believe him.'

When the defence lawyer started cross-examining Butler, he wanted to confirm that Milat would change his appearance. Yes, said Butler, he would have a beard for six months and then he would come in to work clean-shaven, before starting on the beard again. 'The difference in his appearance was very significant,' he said.

Part of the Crown's case was to show to the jury that Ivan Milat had the opportunity to commit the crimes because he was not at work or was not present at a family gathering when various murders were carried out.

Mr Tedeschi had attempted to do this when he questioned Mrs Carolynne Milat and challenged her on the dates on photographs.

Now it was the turn of Mrs Lisa Milat — Walter's wife — to step to the witness stand and tell the court what she could remember of Ivan's whereabouts on Boxing Day 1991, when the German couple disappeared.

Lisa Milat could recall her brother-in-law helping a child with a pump-action water pistol. However, she was reminded that she had told police in a statement in May 1994 that she could not remember whether Ivan attended the lunch at his mother's home on that Boxing Day.

Now, though, she said, she remembered the day because Ivan was helping her nephew to use the water pistol, and water was being squirted everywhere. She remembered hoping he would not squirt her.

'It was 1991 because I was holding my baby son, who could not walk yet,' she told the court. To aid her memory, she also recalled Ivan giving her son a toy machine-gun for Christmas.

'Has somebody told you to say the year was 1991?' Mr Tedeschi asked.

'No,' replied Mrs Milat.

She was also asked if she was 'absolutely certain' that photographs of that day were taken before lunch and before she left to visit her own mother. When she said she was, Mr Tedeschi pointed out that the watch on Mrs Milat senior's arm read either 8.20 or 4.40. Lisa Milat was asked if she could explain how the watch indicated the photographs were taken early in the morning or late in the afternoon.

'Maybe the watch was wrong,' Lisa Milat replied. 'She has poor eyesight.'

Mrs Milat also claimed that her statement to police and evidence at the committal hearing about her husband Walter's whereabouts on 18 April 1992 — when the two English women disappeared — were incorrect. To help her memory, she said, she remembered she was due to give birth to her second child at the time and Walter had gone on a camping trip to the Wombeyan Caves.

She admitted she would lie to protect her husband but would not lie to protect Ivan or if Walter asked her to lie to protect Ivan.

The defence would have its turn, but in the meantime, the Crown team continued to call the witnesses it hoped would convince the jury that the man who sat on the bench on the opposite side of the court was guilty of the backpacker murders.

Sergeant Gerard Dutton showed none of the strain of recent weeks as he walked to the witness box, yet he had had one of the most gruesome tasks that could befall any officer in recent weeks — he was the man who was in charge of ballistics examination at the Port Arthur massacre scene. His job entailed moving carefully through the cafe where people had been shot as they sat at their lunch tables and studying where every bullet had embedded itself. Now he was about to tell the court of his taxing job in examining the bullet-riddled bodies of the backpackers.

The ballistics expert said he had no doubt that the Ruger rifle bolt found in the wall cavity at Ivan Milat's home had fired the cartridges found where Caroline Clarke's body had been discovered. He also said that the same bolt was used to fire a number of cartridges found near the bodies of two of the other victims, Anja Habschied and Gabor Neugebauer.

Referring to Caroline Clarke, he said that after her head had been wrapped in a maroon sweatshirt, she had been shot ten times in the skull from a distance of about 2 metres. The bullets entered her head at three different points. But because the spent cartridge cases were found together, the indication was that the person firing the gun had shot from the same spot. This meant that Miss Clarke's body had been moved between shots.

The gun parts found in three locations at Milat's home made up a Ruger 10/22 semi-automatic rifle with a standard ten-shot magazine. Only the barrel, stock and cocking lever were not found. But using the bolt in another rifle, he had been able to test-fire some cartridges. Markings on the cartridges were unique and matched perfectly the markings on the cartridges found near Miss Clarke's body.

The forty-seven cartridge cases found in an area described by the Crown as a 'shooting gallery', 165 metres from the bodies of the two German friends, had also been fired from the same weapon as that used at the Clarke murder scene. Another forty-six spent cartridges found in that area were 'consistent' with having been fired by an Anschutz rifle and bolt — the same weapon, the Crown contended, that belonged to Ivan Milat but which had been found under the home of his brother Walter. Sergeant Dutton was only prepared to use the word 'consistent' because of corrosion on the cartridge cases.

Mr Neugebauer, said the ballistics expert, had not been killed where his body was found because no spent bullets were found in the soil under his head. There were six bullet entry wounds in his skull, but only two bullets were found in the skull at the post-mortem examination.

Sergeant Dutton had one more positive piece of evidence to present: he had been able to link the Ruger rifle bolt to spent cartridges found at a shooting range on a property formerly owned by Alex Milat. The weapon was 'consistent' with having fired cartridges on Walter's and Richard's properties — places that Ivan had gone shooting.

To support the Crown's case that Milat had the opportunity to murder the backpackers, Mr Tedeschi presented a summary of the road worker's work records at the Roads and Traffic Authority.

The records revealed that Milat was either on holidays or days off when the backpackers disappeared. He was on holiday on 30 December 1989, when Deborah Everist and James Gibson vanished. On 25 January 1990, when Paul Onions was attacked, Milat was either on a leave day or accrued day off. On 20 January 1991, when Simone Schmidl disappeared, Milat was not working, and he was not working on Boxing Day 1991, when Anja Habschied and Gabor Neugebauer vanished. Milat was also off work on 18 April 1992, the date Caroline Clarke and Joanne Walters disappeared.

The Crown was convinced that Walter Milat could provide more information to the jury that would help them decide whether Ivan should be convicted of the backpacker murders, and so on Thursday 6 June he was recalled to the witness box. He was asked about the Boxing Day gathering at Campbell Hill Road and who was present. Walter mentioned several family members, including Ivan, and 'lots of kids' but he couldn't remember them all. Asked whether Ivan had left at some stage, Walter replied:

'I couldn't tell you what went on all day, no.'

Cross-examined by Mr Martin, he agreed that he had owned an SKK rifle and so had his brothers Richard and Ivan. When they went shooting together there would sometimes be an interchange of magazines because they were all the same type. Mr Milat was reminded that in his earlier evidence he said he thought Ivan had owned a Ruger rifle. Had he seen Ivan with that Ruger prior to 1988?

'I wouldn't have a clue of the day,' he said.

Was he familiar with a shooter's licence in the name of Chong?

'Norman Chong, yes, I'm familiar with him,' said Mr Milat. And he agreed that he might have purchased ammunition and a 'couple of rifles' with the licence, including a .303, from the Horsley Park gun shop, although he might have used his wife's licence to buy that particular weapon.

Mr Tedeschi wanted to know more about Mr Milat's acquisition of the Norman Chong licence. How had he got hold of it? Mr Milat said he had been working at a bicycle shop in Campbelltown, giving the proprietor a hand in exchange for a few bucks, and Mr Chong was the mechanic there. He saw the licence on the counter and picked it up.

'Did you steal it?' asked Mr Tedeschi.

'Not exactly,' said Mr Milat, who then said that he might have fished it up off the floor, although he couldn't remember the exact circumstances. He did not ask Mr Chong if he could have the licence.

'So did you steal it?'

'Not in that sense, no.'

Mr Milat explained that while he understood the meaning of the word stealing, he did not think he had stolen the licence because it was out of date.

'When you used it to buy ammunition, it had expired?'

'I think so.'

'Is it your understanding that you are supposed to produce a current licence to buy ammunition?'

'Yes.'

'Why did you use someone else's expired licence rather than your own?'

Mr Milat explained that while he did own a licence, he had mislaid it and had reported its loss to the police. He had eventually re-applied for a licence but the application had been returned because at the time there had been a lot of concern about weapons in the wake of shoppers being gunned down by a crazed gunman in what was known as the Strathfield Massacre.

'Did you lend the Chong licence to anyone?'

'I may have loaned it to Ivan.'

'Did you purchase a Winchester pump-action shotgun in December 1987?'

'No.'

'Did you purchase a Winchester pump-action shotgun at any time from the Horsley Park gun shop?'

'No.'

Asked if he had loaned the licence to anyone in December 1987, he replied: 'Possibly to Ivan, but I don't remember the dates.'

He also denied purchasing a .22 rifle from the gun shop with the Chong licence on 5 January 1988. But he again said it was possible that his brother Ivan had the licence at that time.

Asked about the purchase of a Ruger Mini–14 in May 1988 with the Chong licence, Mr Milat said it wasn't him, that it must have been Ivan. Mr Milat said he might have used the licence half a dozen times himself, mainly for the purchase of ammunition, although it was possible he had also bought a Chinese rifle and the .303 with it. He 'wouldn't have a clue' what happened to the licence. He might have given it to Ivan; he didn't know.

The court had finished with Walter for the time being.

Now it was the turn of Richard to be called back to the witness box, this time at the request of the defence. Mr Martin wanted to question him over whether he had grey flecks in his moustache and sidelevers in 1990. Englishman Paul Onions had already told the court that the man who attacked him near the entrance to the Belanglo State Forest had a Merv Hughes-type moustache and had grey flecks in his sidelevers. Mr Milat, who stepped into the witness box wearing a short moustache, said in answer to questions that he 'didn't know' or 'couldn't be sure' whether he had grey in his hair in 1990.

Anxious to remove any suggestion that it was not Ivan Milat who had tried to kidnap Onions, Mr Tedeschi asked: 'Do you agree that your hair is medium brown?'

'I'm not sure,' said Mr Milat to chuckles in the public gallery. They had become accustomed to Richard Milat's uncertain answers.

Mr Tedeschi asked him to stand in front of the jury so they could see for themselves if he had any grey flecks. Mr Tedeschi said he could not see any. Justice David Hunt also said he could see none. Both defence and prosecution agreed that Mr Milat did have medium-brown hair. But Mr Milat also agreed that he had dyed his hair once or twice and may have done so in 1990.

The Onions attack and Ivan Milat's alleged connection with it was put under further scrutiny when a lotteries official provided evidence showing that Milat was a frequent visitor to the Casula newsagent's, from where Onions had been given a lift by the man calling himself Bill. The representative of the New South Wales State Lotteries, Mr Barry Winning (aptly named, the judge was to remark later), told the court that a Mr I. Milat had three player-registration cards in his name and listed the times they had been used at newsagencies. Mr Winning said that between July 1991 and February 1994, cards in Milat's name were used seventeen times at the Casula newsagency.

The Crown case was rapidly drawing to a close. On Tuesday 11 June the judge indicated to the jury that there were only a few matters to be presented and the defence would be ready to present its case.

One matter that had remained unanswered involved the hairs that had been found clutched in Joanne Walters' hand: six of which had been unidentified by the forensic scientist

Dr Robertson in his initial examinations. Dr Robertson had been unable to say whether any of the unidentified hairs had come from Ivan Milat because he had had no examples from the defendant.

Now Mr Tedeschi was ready to hand in Dr Robertson's findings — and they came as a mixture of shock and mystery. The shock was that some hair samples, which had been cut for examination in the forensic laboratory, had been handled by a scientist who had no adequate prior experience in DNA testing and whose work was found to be wanting. The mystery emerged when it was revealed that Dr Robertson had still not been able to clarify the source of the hairs found in Joanne's hand.

Mr Tedeschi stood in front of his desk with a handful of documents. They were the results of the hair tests and also of DNA testing to establish if the British women had been raped. The court had already been told that it would have been virtually impossible to find any evidence of sperm after more than three months, but what Mr Tedeschi had to say still came as a shock.

First, it was the tests of vaginal swab samples that he wanted to deal with. The testing, Mr Tedeschi told the jury, was performed by a scientist who had not been called as a witness and whose inexperience was unknown to police investigators at the time. Every time the scientist carried out a test on the swabs from the two English women he obtained a somewhat different result, although each test did disclose foreign DNA material — in other words DNA that was not from Caroline Clarke or Joanne Walters.

In the end, said Mr Tedeschi, the scientist acknowledged that he was not qualified to do the job, some of his results were transposed onto the wrong samples and his results indicated multiple contamination of the samples. The samples had been contaminated with foreign DNA in the laboratory during the testing and the chemicals in the laboratory had also been contaminated. In addition, equipment had been contaminated from previous DNA testing.

As a further blow to those who had hoped for something positive from the examinations, the scientist also acknowledged that the specimens themselves would have been contaminated while being taken from the bodies or during handling of them prior to the tests being carried out.

Two other very experienced DNA scientists — one from a government DNA laboratory and one from the private sector — had reviewed the testing scientist's results and confirmed the very real possibility of contamination of the samples and other significant errors in the testing procedures and reporting methods.

Mr Tedeschi pointed out that other samples, when tested previously in another laboratory, gave uncontaminated results, but when tested later in the laboratory of the inexperienced scientist they gave contaminated results, suggesting a likely source of contamination in his working area.

'In the end, all that one can say is that the results indicate the likely contamination of the Clarke and Walters vaginal swabs with foreign DNA material,' said Mr Tedeschi, speaking with a slow and deliberate tone. 'The foreign DNA material, whatever its source, is not attributed to any particular person, including Ivan Milat. It is not possible now to know whether there was originally any foreign DNA material in the vaginal swabs.'

Next he turned to the results of the tests into the hair strands found in Joanne Walters' hand — and the outcome was just as disappointing.

The scientist who examined samples of the hair — and it was not revealed whether it was the same scientist involved with the swabs — acknowledged that his testing was flawed both in the methods of testing used in the laboratory and in his reading and recording of the results. Two experienced

DNA scientists later concluded it would be legally unsafe to rely on any of the results.

However, the court heard, Dr Robertson, who had initially carried out tests on hair samples found in Joanne Walters' right hand, was a very experienced forensic scientist and an expert in this area. Using a sample of fifteen head hairs with which to make comparisons, Dr Robertson examined the six hairs that he had previously been unable to make any decision on. These hairs, he said in his report now being presented by Mr Tedeschi, were head hairs which did not appear to be in the range of the known Walters' head hairs. If the samples he had been given to work with were representative, then it was very unlikely that the six hairs in her hand came from Joanne Walters. However, none of the six hairs bore any resemblance to the head hairs of Ivan Milat, a representative sample of which were microscopically examined by Dr Robertson. Neither were they within the range of known head hairs of Caroline Clarke. It was as close as the scientist was prepared to go in identifying the owner of the hairs.

'It's acknowledged by Dr Robertson that it is difficult to draw conclusive opinions from the visual or microscopic comparison of head hairs,' said Mr Tedeschi. Then, without making any further comment or reference to Dr Robertson's belief that it was unlikely the hairs in her hand came from Joanne Walters' head, Mr Tedeschi told the jury that, although the six hairs did not appear to be in the range of her head hairs, the 'reasonable possibility' existed that the hairs were hers.

But a 'reasonable possibility' was not concrete proof of ownership, and the jury may well have decided to accept at that point that ownership would have to remain a frustrating mystery.

Mr Tedeschi called a handful more of witnesses, mostly to tell the court that rags found at Milat properties, and one found in the forest near the bodies of the German couple, had been cut by an industrial machine and had been supplied to the RTA, where Milat was working.

On the morning of Monday 17 June 1996, Detective Sergeant Stephen Leach was called forward. This bearded and solidly built officer, who had dealt with Milat on the morning of his arrest, was the final witness. He told of a number of newspaper articles published in late 1993 telling how police were looking for a Ruger 10/22 rifle. With the police officer's brief evidence over, Mr Tedeschi told Justice Hunt: 'I now formally close the Crown case.'

No sooner was he seated than Mr Martin rose, strode to the left-hand side of the bar table and turned to face the jury. Now, for the first time, the court was going to hear Ivan Milat's defence.

CHAPTER SEVENTEEN

Mr Milat — began Mr Martin — would tell the court that he did not kill any of the backpackers or have any knowledge of the offences, and that he did not attack Paul Onions. He had never owned a Ruger 10/22 rifle and had no knowledge of the gun parts found in the wall cavity at his home or in his boot in a cupboard. In effect, Mr Martin told the jury that his client was going to deny everything that he had been accused of and would not be able to assist in any way in relation to the property owned by the backpackers and which had been found at his home and the homes of his relatives.

At 12.26 pm that day, Ivan Milat, dressed in a navy-blue suit, a blue sweater and black ankle-high boots, stepped into the witness box. He paused before sitting to swear to tell the truth, the whole truth and nothing but the truth. It had been two years since his arrest and more than twelve weeks since the trial began, but now he was going to put forward his case to answer all the accusations that had been levelled against him. The defence did not hesitate with the answers the court was waiting to hear.

'Did you kill any of the persons located in the Belanglo State Forest?' asked Mr Martin.

'No,' said Milat.

'Were you involved in any way in respect of those deaths?'

'No way at all.'

'Do you have any knowledge of those offences?'

'No.'

'Were you involved in any way in the attack on Paul Onions in January 1990?'

'No.'

'Do you have any knowledge of that offence?'

'No.'

He sat with his fists clenched and resting on his thighs. But he opened them occasionally to reveal gnarled hands from years of work on the roads. Were they the hands of a killer, a man who had manhandled young tourists, tied them up, then shot or stabbed them to death? His performance in the witness box now would help the jury to make up their minds.

Guided by his lawyer's questions, Milat said he had never owned a Ruger and had no idea how the gun parts came to be found in a wall cavity or in his boot at the house he shared with his sister Shirley. But he could explain what he was doing with a manual for a Ruger rifle: 'I think Wally left it there. I'm sure it was Wally's.'

He also mentioned Wally's name in respect of the Anschutz rifle, said to have fired cartridges near the bodies of Gabor Neugebauer and Anja Habschied. He had once owned the gun, having bought it in late 1988 or 1989, but after three months had 'sold it to me brother Wally'. His brother had never paid him the $150 he had asked for the weapon.

With Mr Martin continuing to quietly ask questions, Milat said he had kept gun parts in his house, but they were mainly in a drawer in the spare bedroom. He did, however, make the surprise admission that he had buried a .45 calibre pistol inside a bucket in his backyard because it was illegal.

He had also kept a large arsenal of guns and ammunition in the ceiling of the garage, including illegal Chinese SKKs. He estimated that he had between 20,000 and 30,000 rounds of ammunition for the Chinese weapons alone. He had finally moved the weapons, partly from fear of the police discovering the illegal firearms and also because his sister was concerned about the fire risks associated with keeping ammunition in the roof.

Despite the earlier claims by his ex-wife Karen, Milat said he had never been in the Belanglo State Forest. In fact, in 1983, when she claimed they had gone to the forest, he had owned a Mitsubishi Colt car, not a four-wheel-drive. Milat could not explain how equipment belonging to some of the victims, including sleeping bags, backpacks, tents and clothing, found their way into his house and the homes of family members. He had no idea where his girlfriend, Chalinder Hughes, had obtained a Benetton top identical to one belonging to Miss Clarke.

As for the attack on Paul Onions, Milat admitted he had used the name Bill in 1988 when he was working for the road sweeping company. 'This was because I was going through a divorce and my wife was sort of taking me to the cleaners, so I quit my job with the DMR and went and worked under another name.' And although Onions had said his attacker drove a four-wheel-drive with a spare wheel fitted on the back, Milat said he had not put a spare tyre rack on the rear of his vehicle until December 1990 — eleven months after the attack on Onions.

With the main points of his defence established, Milat returned to the witness box at 10 am the following day, having discarded his sweater this time. Mr Martin asked him at the outset about the bullet damage to the door of his vehicle. Milat said it had happened at the end of 1991 at Wombeyan Caves, where he had gone to do some shooting. 'I was pulling the gun out of the car or putting it in and I must have squeezed the trigger. The gun went off. There was no-one else in the car at the time … After it happened I was so upset that it ruined my day.'

'Did you give a backpack to Joan Milat?'

'Yes. I had seen it lying around the garage at Campbell Hill Road and when I heard she was going on a bush-walking trip in Tasmania I asked Richard who owned it. He said "Nobody really" and I said "Can I have it?" and he gave it to me and I took it up to Joan.'

Milat said he thought his brother had told him that the girlfriend of his friend Jock Pittaway didn't want it any more.

'Did you write IM on that backpack?'

'No.'

Mr Martin then asked his client if he had a moustache in 1990, the year that Paul Onions was attacked by a man he described as wearing a Merv Hughes-type of moustache. No, replied Milat, he did not, although he had had moustaches over the years, sometimes growing them down to the chin. He was asked about his racist views, in the light of Paul Onions' comments that the driver who attacked him was anti-Asian. Milat pointed out that not only did he not have anti-Asian views but his girlfriend, Chalinder Hughes, was Indian. And he didn't have any views about whether the British should be in Northern Ireland.

His attention was drawn to cartridge cases, used and unused, found at his home at Eagle Vale. Why did he have unused cartridge cases? Because, he explained, they could be reloaded and fired again. Cartridges of .45 calibre, he said, were his and would be used in his pistol, and the .38-calibre cartridges would fit Wally's .357 revolver and Alex's .38.

'Did you at any stage obtain a shooter's licence in your own name?' asked Mr Martin.

'Yes, I first got one in 1991, I believe.'

He had also used the Chong licence at the Horsley Park

gun shop, where he had been buying weapons and ammunition from 1987 to 1992. He listed as the weapons he had purchased a .22 JW15, a 12-gauge shotgun, a Mini–14 and 'probably another one — I can't place it at the moment'. He had used the Chong licence because he didn't have one of his own at the time because he hadn't got around to obtaining one. He had found the Chong licence in the lounge room at his mother's place.

Mr Martin moved onto vehicle licences, asking Milat why police found a licence at Cinnabar Street in the name of Michael Milat but with his photograph on it. He told the court that his brother was in Queensland when the application arrived at Campbell Hill Road, so he took the form to the Motor Registry office, had his photograph taken 'and that was it'. He had not owned a motor vehicle licence in his own name since 1972. Although the jury was not told this, 1972 was the date he had fled to New Zealand to avoid a rape charge.

Asked about his whereabouts on Boxing Day 1991, when the German couple disappeared, Milat said he had taken his mother to the Rookwood Cemetery at about 9 am — 'I've got my father there, my sister, my uncle and a couple of other relatives' — and they had remained there for a while because it was also his father's birthday. They returned to the Guildford house between 10 am and 11 am and he had stayed home all day. He remembered that others present that day were Wally and his family; Billy and Carolynne and their young son; Paul and Maria and their children 'and that is about all I think turned up'. Also there, because they were living in the house, were his brother David, Richard and Richard's girlfriend, Liz Smith, and their younger son, Justin.

'Do you,' asked Mr Martin, 'have any knowledge of whether Walter or Richard Milat were involved in any of these offences you are charged with?'

'I have no knowledge whatever.'

'Do you have any knowledge of who placed the gun parts in the cupboard in the wall at Cinnabar Street and in your boot in the cupboard?'

'None whatsoever.'

Mr Martin sat down.

It was time for Mr Tedeschi to begin his cross-examination of the man said to be the backpacker murderer. This was to be the first time the prosecution had had the chance of questioning Milat since the court procedure had begun at the Campbelltown Magistrates Court.

Mr Tedeschi's interrogation of the defendant began inauspiciously enough, with questions about Milat's movements on the day before the police raid on his home. Milat confirmed picking up his girlfriend during the day, buying KFC fast food in the evening, going home with Chalinder Hughes, and remaining in for the rest of the night. And when he had entered the hallway, he had left his work boots in the garage before going into the house itself.

Mr Tedeschi wanted to establish at the start if Milat was going to suggest that the police had planted any of the incriminating items, such as Ruger parts, in his home.

'I am not suggesting that,' said Milat.

'Are you suggesting that someone has come into your home and planted the Ruger receiver in your boot in the hall cupboard?'

'That's right.'

'Someone has come into your home and planted that item, which has been linked to the deaths of two of the backpackers, planted the receiver in a boot in the hall cupboard in a place you would be likely to see it?'

'That's right.'

That question and answer was to set the tone for the rest of the day, with the list of 'planted' items growing steadily.

'Someone, you say, has also deposited Ruger parts in your wall cavity?'

'They must have,' said Milat, refuting Mr Tedeschi's suggestion that the parts would be 'very, very hard for anyone to find'.

'Somebody has come into your house, switched off the alarm, gone up into the roof space and dropped them into the wall cavity?'

'That seems to be the only way it could be done.'

Mr Tedeschi asked Milat about the weapons he had in the house, listing SKK rifles, and what he said were a 'whole lot' of illegal weapons, including hand guns, yet he had only hidden a Colt .45 pistol in the back garden. Why only that one?

'Because it's a pistol.'

'But you had the black powder revolver?'

'Yes.'

'You had a .38 pistol?'

'No.'

'Why hide only the Colt .45?'

'I regarded that as the only really illegal gun I had.'

But hadn't he moved a lot of guns to his brother Walter's place because they were illegal? Not just because they were illegal, Milat replied, but for safe keeping.

Mr Tedeschi asked him again why he hid the Colt in the garden and not in the roof. Milat said that anyone could have found it in the roof.

What of the Browning pistol found under the washing machine — had he put it there? No, he said, he had not, claiming he had not seen it since 1987 when he had split up with his wife, Karen. So, said Mr Tedeschi, mock surprise in his voice, was he suggesting that someone had come into his house and placed the Browning pistol, which had nothing to do with the Belanglo State Forest murders, under the washing machine?

'Something like that, yes.'

Occasionally sipping on a glass of water, Milat said he

imagined it was just 'sheer coincidence' that the gun parts that had been found in the house were painted with the same kind of camouflage paint with which he had painted his own guns.

As for a single fired cartridge case found in bedroom four and said to have been fired by the Ruger bolt found in the wall cavity, was Milat suggesting that someone had come into his house and put it there?

'I have no idea. I didn't put it there. Somebody must have planted it there.'

Mr Tedeschi asked about a book called *Silent Fire, 10/22*, which detailed how to convert a Ruger 10/22 into a machine-gun — from a semi-automatic into a fully automatic. It gave precise instruction on where to put the holes and how to connect different parts and dealt with no other weapon in the world except a Ruger 10/22. The book, said Mr Tedeschi, had Milat's fingerprints on it. The road worker said he imagined his fingerprints were on every page — he had bought it at one of the gun shows sometime around 1990. So in 1990, he was interested enough in the conversion of a Ruger 10/22 to buy a publication detailing how to convert one into a full automatic?

'I didn't buy it to convert anything,' replied Milat. 'I bought it because I was interested in how it was done.'

'You were interested in how a Ruger 10/22 was done?'

'Yes.'

'And it was because you had a Ruger 10/22?'

'No I did not.'

Admitting he also had a manual for a Ruger 10/22 in his home, Milat was asked if he agreed that a fifty-shot Ramline magazine that police had found in the house would be better than a standard ten-shot magazine that comes with a Ruger rifle. Milat said he didn't know, but after intense questioning, he said: 'If you start thinking about it, you would think like that.'

'Why on earth would you have a manual for a Ruger 10/22 rifle if you didn't have a Ruger rifle? Who gave you this manual?'

'I assume Wally did.'

'Why on earth would Wally give you one if you didn't have a Ruger? And why would you write the date of purchase on it?' (A date had been found written on the publication.)

'I can't answer that,' said Milat. 'I've got the book, but I haven't got the gun.'

Turning back to the Browning pistol, Mr Tedeschi asked if it was under the driving seat of the Holden Jackaroo when the police came and if he had tried to hide it under the washing machine.

'I never went to the car that morning,' said Milat.

'I suggest you went to the car and opened and closed it.'

'I did not.'

Mr Tedeschi reminded him that no barrel for a .22 Ruger was found at his home — so was Milat saying that someone came to his home to plant incriminating items, but did not plant the most important part of a weapon when it came to tracing bullets: the barrel?

No, said Milat, he wasn't saying it.

He was aware that in 1994 the police were looking for a Ruger because it was general knowledge, and he knew that police would be able to link a weapon to the murders if they could find the gun involved. But he denied he had got rid of the barrel of the Ruger 10/22 because he had heard that police had found ballistic material in the forest. He denied hiding the Ruger parts in the wall cavity after thinking it would be highly unlikely anyone would find them there, and he also denied that, when the police rang him on the morning of the raid, he hurriedly hid the Ruger receiver in his boot.

Mr Tedeschi suggested to Milat that the reason he moved weapons from his home at Cinnabar Street to Walter's place had nothing to do with security, because, he claimed, they would have been far less secure there, access to the storage alcove being through an outside door.

Next, Mr Tedeschi turned to the Anschutz and wanted to know about the bolt that was found with some of Milat's gear under Walter's home — a bolt that was connected to the weapon that fired cartridges found near the bodies of Gabor Neugebauer and Anja Habschied. How did the bolt, found in a yellow haversack in the alcove, come to be wrapped in a piece of red-check shirt that had an identical pattern to a piece of shirt discovered on a bed in the spare room in the Cinnabar Street house — could he give an explanation?

'I can't give any,' he replied.

The Hi Sierra daypack belonging to Simone Schmidl was brought to Milat's attention. The accused man said he could not explain how it had ended up with his belongings at Walter's home, even though it was found to contain two camouflaged gun magazines belonging to Milat's SKK rifles. The last time he had seen the magazines, they were in a box — he didn't put them in the daypack. Milat agreed that four cartridge clips found in the daypack were 'the same type' as cartridge clips found in his Jackaroo.

When it was suggested he had moved the daypack from Cinnabar Street where he had been keeping it, Milat said he had not, adding: 'Obviously, somebody is trying to make me look really bad.'

Agreeing with Mr Tedeschi's facetious suggestion that someone had planted the daypack under Wally's house, Milat was then told: 'That's manifestly absurd.'

'I don't think so,' came the reply.

Milat was asked yet again to explain how the Anschutz bolt, linked to the death scenes in the forest and wrapped in material from his home, ended up in a haversack that had his name on it. He said it was not his haversack and suggested that someone had written in his name.

Cartridges in the daypack were copper-tipped, the same as copper-tipped cartridges found in Cinnabar Street — 'Amazing coincidences, aren't they, Mr Milat, don't you agree?'

'Yes, I suppose so.'

Simone Schmidl's green water-bottle, the jury was reminded, was found in a box of model aircraft belonging to Milat in the fourth bedroom at Cinnabar Street. Was Milat now saying it had been planted in his home? Yes, he said.

He was asked about the Indonesian money found in his bedroom. He said he had no explanation how it got there.

'You are not suggesting that the police have loaded you up with it?'

'I am not suggesting that at all.'

When asked if 'the person' who had come into his home and put the water-bottle and the Ruger parts there had also planted the Indonesian money, Milat, his voice raised, said to the prosecutor: 'Are you mystified, Mr Tedeschi? Because I am.'

'Did you take that Indonesian currency from Gabor Neugebauer and Anja Habschied?'

'I have taken nothing from them. I have never met them. I wouldn't know who they are.'

What of a 1989 English 20-pence coin found in his car? He said Chalinder's sister, who lived in Dubai but who travelled to England, sometimes came to Australia to visit them.

'She has been in your car?'

'She may have.'

'She was tipping you with 20-pence coins?'

'No.'

'Did you steal it from some backpackers?'

'Definitely not.'

'Did you get it from Caroline Clarke, Joanne Walters or Paul Onions?'

'No.'

Milat was then questioned about a green surgical glove found in the console of his Jackaroo and asked what use he thought someone committing a crime might have for a glove. He finally conceded after several questions that a glove would not leave any fingerprints.

'I ask you if you wore it at any of the scenes of the crimes in the Belanglo State forest in order to prevent fingerprints being left?'

'I wore no glove — I never saw it before.'

'You were going to say ——'

'I was going to say I wore no gloves before.'

'You were going to say you wore no gloves in the forest; is that what you were going to say?'

'No, I was going to say I wore no gloves before.'

Mr Tedeschi concluded his questioning for the day. The court was left in no doubt that he had many more questions he wanted to ask Ivan Milat.

CHAPTER EIGHTEEN

A vital part of the Crown's case was the blood, said to be from a child of Mr and Mrs Clarke, found on a piece of sash cord — sash cord that was found in a green and white pillowcase in Milat's garage. The piece of cord was among five pieces in the pillowcase; the five pieces matched a single length of sash cord found on a shelf and which Milat had not disputed was his. The sash cords, consisting of twelve outer strands and a single core of six inner strands, also matched pieces that helped make up a leash device found at the Gabor Neugebauer death scene.

'Have you,' Mr Tedeschi asked Milat at the start of the accused man's third day in the witness box, 'any explanation as to how these five pieces of sash cord in the pillowcase came to be in your garage?'

'No explanation at all. I have never seen it there.' Milat added that he 'wouldn't have a clue' whether the pillowcase had belonged to his mother. And he denied a suggestion that he had used such cords during the course of the murder of Caroline Clarke. He also denied taking the sash cords from his mother's home to his new residence at Cinnabar Street. He also refuted a suggestion that he had produced the sash cords during the attack on Paul Onions.

Continuing his line of questioning concerning the leash

found at the Neugebauer murder scene, Mr Tedeschi showed Milat four black plastic ties found at his home. Milat said he had got them from the RTA or Readymix and would use them to tie up wiring and so on. Those ties, said Mr Tedeschi, were manufactured by a particular machine in a certain factory in Taiwan and he reminded Milat that black plastic ties of the same type were used to make up the leash device.

Milat said he had no explanation as to how the same black plastic ties in his garage were found in the forest. 'Well,' he said, examining a cluster of ties, 'I know I got these from work. I don't know where the ones in the bush came from.'

'I suggest to you that you were at the Habschied–Neugebauer death scene and were involved in these deaths,' said Mr Tedeschi.

'I was not.'

'And that you left the leash device in the forest, never thinking it could ever be traced to you.'

'No.'

For most of the time as the Crown prosecutor fired his questions — and accusations — at Milat, the defendant sat with his fists clenched against his legs. His face was tight, his eyes blinking rapidly at times. In the public gallery above the well of the courtroom there was a stony silence, all eyes fixed on the man in the navy suit in the witness box, even when Mr Tedeschi, who had his back to the public area, was speaking.

Mr Tedeschi moved on to the subject of a blue tent found in Milat's garage at Cinnabar Street, a tent that had been identified as belonging to Simone Schmidl. Milat said he had no idea how it got there. And what of the yellow and purple Compact-O-Mat band found wrapped around the tent — an identical band to the one found around the head of Simone Schmidl's body? Had Milat any explanation? No, he said, he had no idea how a similar band got into his garage.

The Olympus Trip camera, found by police in a kitchen drawer at Cinnabar Street and identified as being similar to one owned by Caroline Clarke, was produced by the prosecutor. Where had Milat used it? All over the place, he replied. Had he used the camera to take two photographs of Chalinder Hughes in which she is seen wearing the Benetton top similar to one owned by Miss Clarke?

'I wouldn't know,' said Milat. He could have used other cameras since April 1992. This particular one, he assumed, belonged to his sister Shirley. He was reminded that this particular model of camera was manufactured in Malaysia and then sent to the United Kingdom for sale. There were photographs of Caroline Clarke with an identical camera. Did he take it from her? No, he said, he did not. But he agreed he 'could have' taken photographs with that particular camera when he went away to the country town of Yass to do some road work in late April 1992 — shortly after the British women disappeared. But he suspected he had used his own camera at the time, although he told Mr Tedeschi he didn't know what make it was. 'It didn't look like this,' he said, tapping the top of the Olympus that had been placed in front of him on the witness box.

Mr Tedeschi's list of questions seemed endless, but Milat was prepared for them, sitting in that same position, fists clenched, perched slightly forward in his seat, just as he had been when he first sat in the box, and staring expectantly at the prosecutor. His eyes rarely left Mr Tedeschi's face and certainly never looked up to the public gallery.

In a walk-in wardrobe in his sister Shirley's bedroom, the jury was reminded, police had found two sleeping bags: one, a Salewa brand, identified as belonging to Simone Schmidl, the other said to be the one that Deborah Everist had borrowed from her brother for her trip. Milat said he had no idea how they got there, and denied that he had been involved in the deaths of the two young women. He looked at a photograph of himself on a camping trip and carrying a green sleeping bag with a black zip surround, just like the Everist bag, but said he had no idea whose it was. He supposed he would have been carrying it for somebody.

Another bag in the garage contained a multi-coloured Arno-brand strap, formerly owned by Simone Schmidl, mixed in with a number of brown leather rifle straps owned by Milat. But Milat said he had no idea how the Arno strap got there.

The pieces of rag that the police had found in garages at Cinnabar Street and at Milat's mother's home in Campbell Hill Road, Guildford, were the subject of Mr Tedeschi's next round of questions. He pointed out that pieces of cloth from around the Ruger bolt, from around a rifle bolt in a locker at Guildford, and from around the face of Joanne Walters, had all been cut or torn from shirts or blouses in about the same way. And he suggested that all the rags, as well as cloth found at the murder scene of the German couple, had come from one of the homes Milat had lived at. Milat said he would have no idea about that.

Milat's attention was drawn to a photograph of his Harley Davidson motorbike with a revolver in a holster hanging on the bike and an SKK semi-automatic resting against it, along with ammunition on the bike and on the ground. There was also a shotgun and shotgun ammunition. Milat said it had been taken at Guildford, and he had also taken a second photograph of the bike which this time included a Colt pistol in what appeared to be the same holster that had contained the revolver, but he couldn't say which camera he had used. A cartridge found in the Jackaroo and a cartridge adaptor found in Simone Schmidl's daypack would fit a .45 Colt revolver, Milat agreed. Whose Colt was it?

'I assume it was Richard's. I have seen him with it.'

Why was it with his, Milat's, weapons on the bike? Why would Richard put his Colt in Milat's holster on the Harley Davidson?

'He just wanted a photo of it,' said Milat.

'I suggest to you,' said Mr Tedeschi, 'that that Colt .45 revolver was yours and that the cartridge adaptors in your car and in the daypack were for use in that revolver.'

'I have no idea.'

Having questioned Milat about one revolver, he then asked him whether he had ever told a workmate that he had a six-shot .38 revolver. In a drawer at his home police had found some .38 cartridge cases which would have been suitable for use in a .38 six-shot. In the fourth bedroom, the spare room, were some fired .38 cartridge cases along with some copper-tipped cartridges in a cardboard box.

'I suggest to you that during your attempted abduction of Mr Onions you used copper-tipped bullets,' said Mr Tedeschi.

'I never attempted to abduct anyone.'

From the back of the court, a police officer stepped forward carrying an Anschutz rifle, fitted with telescopic sights. It was handed to Milat who was then asked to try to fit a barrel cap onto the end — a barrel cap that had been found in the console of his Jackaroo.

Milat said he could not imagine why the cap would be in his car, but he went ahead with the request to screw it onto the rifle. It fitted, he said.

Whether it was Mr Tedeschi's ploy to show the jury what Ivan Milat looked like with a weapon in his hand — conjuring up, perhaps, an image of him in the Belanglo Forest — was not revealed, but the prosecutor was now ready to send several guns to the man in the witness box. First, though, came a home-made silencer, the one that had been found in the garage at Cinnabar Street. Made from piping to fit a .22 rifle, Milat supposed under questioning that it would fit any weapon of that calibre.

Next to be sent to him via a court officer was Milat's JW15 rifle, found in the Guildford locker. He obliged when Mr Tedeschi asked him to screw the silencer onto the end. He had threaded the weapon, he explained, at work with one of the fitters. Who was the fitter? Milat said he couldn't remember exactly, but he was 'a guy called Tony and he only had one eye'.

With the silencer fitted and Milat holding the JW15 on his lap in the witness box, Mr Tedeschi asked how the size of the barrel compared with a Ruger 10/22.

'I have no idea,' said Milat. 'I would imagine it would be something similar.'

But if someone had access to the same pipe threader that Milat had used at work, it would be possible to thread a Ruger 10/22? The sight, Milat imagined, would get in the way, but if the sight was cut off, he supposed it could be done to a Ruger 10/22.

Ivan Milat was questioned about a Winchester 30/30 rifle that had been found in Walter's alcove. Wrapped up with it in the same red blanket material was the Anschutz rifle said to have been used for murder in the forest. The Winchester, said Milat, was not his and he had not put it in the alcove. He denied he had put the two rifles there together when he, Wally and Richard moved the weapons from Cinnabar Street. He believed Wally had done that.

When Mr Tedeschi suggested he had used the Anschutz at the Neugebauer–Habschied death scene, Milat retorted, with anger in his voice: 'You are wrong again.'

The faces of the jury gave nothing away as they listened to Milat's defence. Now and again one of them would open a thick yellow folder containing photographs and other tendered documents and look something up in relation to the questions being asked. Sometimes, when a legal point had to be raised, Justice Hunt would ask them to leave the court — he did not want them to hear points of law that the prosecution or defence wanted to discuss, such as whether certain evidence would be admissible.

'Mr Milat,' began Mr Tedeschi after the lunch break on Wednesday 19 June, 'you have said that in January 1990 you did not have a moustache, but you have said that over the last few years you have kept it on all the time?'

'Yes,' said Milat, 'I believe I didn't have it on at the time.'

Guided by Mr Tedeschi's questions, Milat conceded that on 12 January 1990 he had been part of a road profiling team which had been called to the scene of a double-fatal accident involving two articulated trucks on the Great Western Highway at Hazelbrook, in the foothills of the Blue Mountains, west of Sydney. Milat was replacing damaged asphalt behind a machine called a rotor mill, a common job after road surfaces have been damaged in accidents. Mr Tedeschi asked Milat to look at a photograph that had been taken at the scene of the repair work being done.

'It shows you in your work gear?'

'That's right.'

'Machinery in the background?'

'That's right.'

'Seeing that photograph, would you tell the jury: have you got a moustache?'

Milat, his glasses perched on the end of his nose, stared at the photograph for several seconds, his expression fixed. Then he simply said: 'Yes.'

'And there are white flecks at the bottom of the moustache, near the chin?'

'You are saying this, I am not. I can't see it.' He took off the spectacles he always put on to look at documents and photographs. 'These are just ordinary reading glasses, they are not microscopic.'

He was immediately handed a magnifying glass. Then, as

the defendant looked more closely at the photograph, Mr Tedeschi said: 'You agree there are white flecks on the sidelevers?'

Without hesitation or further comment, Milat said: 'Yes,' and continued staring at Mr Tedeschi, awaiting the next question.

That question concerned a shooter's licence in the name of Chong — the one that Walter Milat had already admitted 'finding' at the bicycle shop he once worked at in Campbelltown. Mr Tedeschi wanted to know which weapons Milat had purchased with the licence. Milat described a .22 JW15 and a 12-gauge Winchester pump-action shotgun. He agreed he had probably purchased the shotgun on 12 December 1987 and a Ruger Mini–14, which had no connection with the forest deaths, on 25 May 1988. He said he believed he had purchased 'four or five' other guns, including a second Ruger Mini–14 and a Baikal shotgun.

Milat said he had first got hold of the Chong licence in 1987. He did not have a shooter's licence in his own name and did not obtain one legally until about 1992.

Asked why he had not got a licence in his own name in 1987 instead of using the other man's, he replied: 'I have often wondered that myself. I just couldn't be bothered.'

'So you were prepared to break the law rather than get a licence in your own name?'

'Yes.'

Milat said he did not know what had happened to Mr Chong and could not say whether he was still in Australia. He had certainly never given any thought to the fact that he might return one day asking about his licence.

'The benefit of the Chong licence was that there was no reference to you or your address?'

'That's right.'

'So nobody could trace a weapon bought from the Horsley Park gun shop by you using that licence?'

'I suppose so.'

But he strongly denied using the licence to purchase an 'untraceable' Ruger 10/22 rifle, parts of which were found in his wall cavity.

Having finished with shooter's licences, Mr Tedeschi questioned Milat about driving licences. Milat agreed, as he had when questioned by his own counsel, Mr Martin, that he had a licence to drive a car and a motorcycle in the name of Michael Milat. He had first obtained a licence with his own photograph in 1991 or 1992. Prior to that, going back to 1988, he 'might have had' a motorcycle licence, but he wasn't really sure. He conceded he had not had a licence to drive a Mitsubishi Colt he had once owned in the mid 1980s, although at the time he was entitled to apply for a driver's licence in his own name. He could give no reason why he had not applied for one. When he sold that vehicle in 1987 he had started using Michael Milat's name, even though he was entitled to apply for a licence in his own name. Again, he said he could give no reason why he had not.

He had been using Michael Milat's licence when he owned the Nissan and continued using it until 1994. Driving around with no licence, he said, was 'not what I preferred'. He just couldn't work himself up to getting one, he said, even though he knew it was illegal to drive without a licence or without one in his name.

Milat denied knowing whether his brother Wally had bought a Ruger 10/22 rifle in 1992 with a licence belonging to Milat's friend Jock Pittaway. He agreed, though, that he had stored at Walter's home Winchester and Eley ammunition, as well as Eley ammunition at his home in Cinnabar Street.

Could he explain, asked Mr Tedeschi, how ammunition boxes with the same, or similar, numbers as the boxes he owned were found in the Belanglo State Forest, near the bodies of the German couple? Winchester Winner and Eley ammunition was found in Wally's alcove, and Eley ammunition was found in a box in the fourth bedroom at Cinnabar Street. What was the explanation for the same batch numbers being found in the forest?

'I have no explanation,' said Milat, adding that he accepted what Mr Tedeschi was saying.

The prosecutor was not going to let go. The Eley ammunition was manufactured on the same day as the box found in the forest, or, because the date was difficult to read, three days later. The Winchester Winner ammunition found at Wally's place at Wilson Drive, Hilltop, had the same batch number as the ammunition found near the scene of the German couple's murders.

'What has it got to do with me?' asked Milat.

'I suggest you were at Area A [the site of the so-called 'shooting gallery' near the Germans' death scene] and you were involved in the deaths of Anja Habschied and Gabor Neugebauer and you either alone or with another or other persons left these ammunition boxes in the forest thinking you would be unable to be traced to it.'

'You are wrong. I wasn't there. I was at 55 Campbell Hill Road on that day, the 26th.'

Mr Tedeschi moved on to the bullet damage in the door of the Nissan. He suggested that Milat had asked a neighbour to repair it because the bullet had been fired, not when he was putting a gun in or out of the vehicle at Wombeyan Caves, but during a struggle as he was abducting Gabor Neugebauer and Anja Habschied. Milat said that Mr Tedeschi was wrong: when the gun went off, he said, he was alone — there was 'no-one with us', he said. Mr Tedeschi did not challenge him on the use of the word 'us' when he said he was alone. After the bullet had hit the door he had driven home, calling at Wally's on the way, when he told him the gun had gone off 'and hit me door'.

'How long after Boxing Day was it?'

'I believe it was the 29th.'

Mr Tedeschi was interested to know where Milat had gone over the next few days because his log book revealed that he had travelled either 1400 kilometres or nearly 2000 kilometres [there was a discrepancy in the figures in his log book] in just sixteen days. Milat said he was on holidays and could have gone anywhere, including visiting his brother's home.

'You don't think you were on an extended hunting trip?'

'No.'

Mr Tedeschi suggested that the camping gear belonging to Caroline Clarke found at his brother Richard's place had been first brought to Guildford by Milat. Caroline Clarke's tent was found with Milat's own green tent, and Mr Tedeschi suggested that Richard moved not only the green tent but the other camping equipment from Cinnabar Street to Guildford, before moving some of it to the bush block at Hilltop. 'No,' said Milat, 'you are wrong.'

Mr Tedeschi suggested that, in the same cupboard at Richard's place that Milat's tent was found were also found Caroline Clarke's blue three-man tent, sleeping mat and her blue and orange sleeping bag. Also in the cupboard was Joanne Walters' sleeping bag. Milat again denied he had taken that equipment to Guildford before it was moved to Hilltop. Found at Guildford, too, Mr Tedeschi said, was a yellow grandfather T-shirt identified as Simone Schmidl's. Also found there was Paul Onions' Next-brand shirt, discovered in a red plastic box on the floor, a box that also contained a blue check shirt that had been identified as Milat's. Milat, however, only conceded that he 'owned shirts like that one'.

As for the Salewa backpack identified as belonging to Simone Schmidl, had his sister-in-law Joan in Queensland asked him for one? Milat said she had not, but she would have told him about the walking trip she planned to do in Tasmania.

Mr Tedeschi had more suggestions to put to Ivan Milat. He put it to the accused man that when he had moved firearms from his home in Cinnabar Street he had also moved the Hi Sierra daypack, having taken it from Simone Schmidl. Milat again denied it.

Time had run out for the afternoon. Milat took a sip of water and then stood as the judge made his way from the court. The feeling in the public gallery was that so far Ivan Milat had not convinced anyone of his innocence. His failure to explain how any of the backpackers' equipment came to be associated with him had not helped his case, it seemed. Nevertheless, Milat had a faint smile as he stepped down.

At the bar table, Mark Tedeschi packed up his papers. He was smiling faintly, too.

CHAPTER NINETEEN

Back in their rooms at the end of each day's hearing, lawyers for the Crown and the defence went over the evidence, poring through transcripts of the proceedings that had already been delivered to them. It often meant working late into the evening, looking for points that would need to be followed up in further evidence or facts that needed to be emphasised. Sometimes the Crown asked police to check out aspects of the evidence that had been given that day in case it could enhance the prosecution's case against Ivan Milat.

It was obvious that Mr Tedeschi believed the defendant had more he could tell the jury about the ownership of the Winchester 30/30 rifle, the one that had been found wrapped up with the Anschutz connected with the killing. By linking Milat to the Winchester, he believed he could convince the court that the accused man also owned the Anschutz. He began his questioning on the morning of Thursday 20 June by reminding Milat that on the day before he had been asked about the two weapons and that he had said he did not put either weapon in the red blanket material in Wally's alcove and that he had never owned a Winchester 30/30.

'Have you ever used one?'

'Yes,' said Milat, adding that he had had such guns at his

home in Cinnabar Street, had 'played around' with one and fired one.

'I suggest to you that the Winchester in the blanket is yours.'

'No, it is not.'

Mr Tedeschi then sent up to the witness box Milat's photograph album, seized by police. On the cover was a black and white photocopy of Milat in a cowboy outfit, with a holster containing a revolver slung around his hips and a Texas Star badge pinned to his chest. Inside were photos of Milat in the same cowboy outfit, holding a Winchester 30/30 rifle in his lounge room or sitting next to one. In some of the pictures red boxes of Winchester 30/30 ammunition could be seen.

Next, Mr Tedeschi sent a Winchester 30/30 up to the witness box, the weapon that had been found at Wally's home. Asked if it was the same gun he was seen holding in the photograph, Milat said he didn't think so.

Milat said he had moved guns, ammunition and other items from Cinnabar Street to Wally's Hilltop alcove either before or after Christmas 1993. Had the photographs of him with the Winchester been taken before or after the move?

'I'm not sure,' said Milat. 'I think they were taken just before the move of the guns to the alcove, from what I can recall.'

Mr Tedeschi told Milat that the date 16 January was written on the back of the photographs. Did that suggest to Milat that the weapons were in fact moved before the photographs were taken? Milat was unable to help the court on that matter.

He was reminded he had given evidence that he had moved the guns after he had heard from some of his workmates that the police had been asking questions about his guns. If the workmates were in fact spoken to in January 1994, did that help Milat work out that the weapons were moved to the alcove after 16 January? Yes, said Milat, he had already said they were moved after the photos were taken.

'These pictures show you with a Winchester, and found in the alcove was a Winchester. I am suggesting that the Winchester found in the alcove is the same as the one shown with you in the cowboy outfit,' said the Crown prosecutor.

'I don't think so.'

'Who took these photographs?'

'One of my brothers, Richard.'

'Did you take photos of Richard at the same time?'

'I could have.'

'Why were these photos taken?'

'I was trying to make up some cowboy pictures to put in my album.'

Mr Tedeschi continued to press Milat about the ownership of the Winchester 30/30 and Milat continued to deny it, although he conceded that the Winchester ammunition was his — because it was expensive, he kept a quantity of it for use when he borrowed a Winchester owned by his brother. Mr Tedeschi said that when police searched the Cinnabar Street home there was no sign of any Winchester 30/30 ammunition, but at Walter's place, in the blue Hi Sierra daypack, ammunition of that type had been found.

'Do you have any explanation why, on 16 January 1994, you are shown with a Winchester 30/30 and Winchester ammunition, and, by 22 May 1994, there is no Winchester at your home but in the alcove there is and there is ammunition in the Hi Sierra?'

'No explanation.'

'Do you accept that the explanation is that you placed the Winchester in the alcove and you placed the ammunition in the daypack and put it in the alcove?'

'No.'

'That's the logical explanation, isn't it?'

'Not to me it isn't.'

Milat told the prosecutor that when the photographs were taken he owned 'six or seven' rifles, but again denied he had wrapped the Winchester up with the Anschutz.

Referred back to the time of his arrest, Milat recalled how his niece, Deborah, had told him of the police visit to her and how his brother William had phoned early in the morning to say the police had called on him and were making inquiries about one of his, Ivan's, vehicles.

Mr Tedeschi told Milat that when the police rang his home on the morning of the raid his first thought was about his car and the Browning pistol he kept under the front seat. He had, suggested Mr Tedeschi, taken the Browning out from the vehicle and 'in an act of desperation' attempted to hide it under the washing machine in the laundry. Milat uttered an emphatic 'No!' He denied ever going into the garage that morning, did not think his girlfriend, Chalinder, had gone in there either, and said he could give no explanation why two police officers heard a door opening into the garage from the house and the sound of a car door opening and closing.

Mr Tedeschi was reaching the end of his cross-examination. He had asked searching questions and received few enlightening answers from the defendant. Milat's replies had consisted of a string of denials or claims that he could offer no explanation for items that appeared to link him to the murders being in his home or the homes of relatives.

There were a few more matters Mr Tedeschi wanted to put to Milat before his cross-examination was over. First there was the detailed description given by Paul Onions.

'In January 1990,' Mr Tedeschi began, 'you were in your 40s?'

'Forty-five.' Milat took another sip of water before clenching his fists against his legs again.

'In January 1990 did you have a Merv Hughes moustache with grey at the bottom?'

'I never had a Merv Hughes moustache ... I watch the cricket and my idea of the Merv Hughes moustache ... it sweeps back a bit.'

'Did you have sidelevers with grey flecks and dark hair?'

'Yes.'

'A dark complexion ... olive complexion?'

'It was pretty ordinary.'

'You sometimes squint your eyes?'

'I am not sure. Am I squinting them now?'

'You are not outside now. Has anyone told you you hold your mouth in a grin?'

'No.'

'In something of a grin?'

'Every time I open my mouth you can see my top teeth.'

The questioning went on along these lines. Onions and Milat were of similar heights, the court heard, with the Englishman standing at 168 centimetres (5 feet 6 inches) and Milat at 171 centimetres (5 feet 7 and three-eighths inches). Milat agreed that when he was working he wore T-shirts and shorts, and that in 1990 he was as strong as a 45-year-old bloke could be. He had used the name Bill, he was working on the roads, he was divorced and his father was from Yugoslavia.

'Do you agree that all of these features fit you?'

'Yes.'

But there was more. Milat agreed he had a two-door four-wheel-drive, either a Nissan or a Toyota as described by Onions, that it was silver and white with a bull-bar and running boards, it was fitted with sheepskin seat covers, he kept it clean and stored cassettes between the two front seats. There was also a red or crimson stripe along the side, although, Milat pointed out, the predominant colour was blue.

'Do you know of any other person in this world who has all of these features that I have just mentioned, including features of their car?' asked Mr Tedeschi.

'No,' replied Milat, his face expressionless.

Milat agreed with Mr Tedeschi that when he was living at his mother's home in Guildford he had priority use of the garage above anyone else living or staying there. He said he had no idea how Paul Onions' Next-brand shirt and Miss Schmidl's grandfather T-shirt had got into the garage.

'You have told the court that a number of items at your home in Cinnabar Street and among your property in the alcove had been planted there by someone else. Do you think someone was trying to incriminate you?'

'Most definitely.'

'Do you think they were trying to incriminate you by placing the Next shirt and the yellow grandfather T-shirt in the garage?'

'I have no idea.'

'Do you think they did a rather poor job by placing it in the garage?' Again, Milat said he couldn't help with an answer.

In response to prompts by the Crown lawyer, Ivan Milat told the court that his sister Shirley had visited him regularly since he had been in jail awaiting his trial. Having learned after his arrest that the Olympus camera he said she had given to him was strongly suspected as being the property of Caroline Clarke, had he discussed the camera with her during her visits? He replied that he didn't know.

'Well, Mr Milat, here is a camera you have found out belonged to one of the murdered backpackers [and which was] found in your home and it was Shirley who gave it to you the first time you used it. Have you ever said to Shirley: "Where on earth did you get this camera from?"'

'No.'

'Mr Milat, you have been charged with some very serious offences. Here is an item that has been linked to one of the backpackers and which has been found in your home and you tell us that it was Shirley your sister who gave it to you the first time you used it. Why on earth didn't you say to Shirley: "For heaven's sake, who did you get that camera from?"'

'I probably did ask her. I didn't make a big deal of it. If you had asked me three months ago to describe this camera I wouldn't have been able to.'

Asked if he had not thought it was an important matter to find an answer to, he replied that he had been told by his lawyers not to discuss the case with anybody.

Was it his habit to keep a pistol or revolver in his car? No, he said, he wouldn't say it was a regular habit. Mr Tedeschi suggested he had one in the vehicle on 25 January 1990, which Milat denied. What of the .45 pistol he had hidden in a plastic bucket in the back garden — did Shirley know about it?

'I wouldn't think so, no.'

After his arrest, he admitted that he had had a conversation with Shirley and Wally during a jail visit and he had asked Shirley to get rid of the weapon. Asked if he realised that the gun was possible evidence in the case, Milat said he wouldn't have believed so. He imagined the police had all his firearms, he replied, when asked if he knew that the police wanted to get their hands on all his guns. But he knew, went on Mr Tedeschi, that the police had not found them all because there was this pistol in the back garden.

'I didn't know they were looking for a pistol.'

He agreed that he had arranged with Wally and Shirley to dispose of the hand gun buried in the back garden — to dig it up and get rid of it. Later he heard from Shirley that it had been 'taken care of'.

'She knew what you were charged with and she had proceeded in getting rid of it?'

'I assume so, yes.'

'And your brother Walter proceeded in finding a buyer for the gun?'

'I assume so.'

'This was the time when you had been charged with very serious offences and your brother and sister were prepared to assist you to get rid of this firearm buried in your back garden, is that right?'

'Yes.'

Why did he have a silencer?

'To see if it worked. Just to have one to see how they go. When we are down the block shooting near the river there are always other people in hearing distance.'

Did he have any photographs of himself on Boxing Day 1991 at Guildford?

'I don't know. There could have been some taken; I never posed for any. I was just hanging around the place there. I cannot recall any of meself, no.'

Mr Tedeschi asked Milat if he recalled his brother Walter asking him when they were at Richard's block at Hilltop, near Wombeyan Caves, if he could buy his, Ivan's, Ruger 10/22.

Milat said: 'That has got me beat — I have never owned a Ruger.'

'But he has said he wanted to buy your Ruger 10/22.'

'I would say he is lying. I think he might have been mistaken. I think he thought the Ruger I had was mine.'

Mr Tedeschi put it to Milat that Walter had bought a Ruger 10/22 — the unused one the police had found at Walter's home — with money that he had given him and he had used the Pittaway licence at the gun shop. Walter had later told Milat he had left the gun at Cinnabar Street. No, said Milat, he had never been told that personally.

'What do you say to the suggestion that you have been to visit the Belanglo State Forest with Karen?'

'I could say a lot of things, but I will just say she is wrong.'

He denied he had kept a Browning under the front seat

of his car when he was married to Karen and he also disagreed he had ever told his former workmate at the DMR, Anthony Sara, that he owned a six-shot revolver similar to one used by the department's security officers.

Mr Tedeschi had one task left: to formally put to Milat that he had perpetrated all the crimes of which he had been accused. The court was totally silent as the QC began with the claim that, after the attempted abduction of Paul Onions, Milat had kept the backpacker's property, including the Next-brand shirt, a shirt he had taken back to Guildford.

'I never brought anything back to Guildford.'

'I suggest to you that around that time you had no licence to drive, or a licence in a false name.'

'You're right there. I had no licence.'

'And the reason was so that you could not be traced while you were driving.'

'That was not the reason at all.'

'I suggest to you that in relation to the murders of Deborah Everist and James Gibson that you murdered them alone or in company.'

'I never did.'

'I suggest to you that you disposed of Mr Gibson's property in the Galston Gorge.'

'I never did.'

'And preparing to dispose of it, you cut out the name and address on the flap of the bag.'

'I have never seen his gear.'

'I suggest to you that you took Deborah Everist's property and that is how Deborah Everist's sleeping bag came to be in your home.'

'I never took nothing of hers and I know nothing of her stuff at our place.'

'I suggest to you that in relation to Simone Schmidl, you killed her either alone or in company.'

'I never did.'

'I suggest to you that you took her property and that is how it came to be in your home.'

'I know nothing about her property in my home.'

'And you took the cook set found in your kitchen.'

'I know nothing about the cook set in the kitchen.'

'And you gave the backpack to your sister-in-law Joan, knowing that the real owner was deceased.'

'I had no idea that she owned that backpack.'

The questions and answers continued in that tone. By now, it would not have been difficult for the jury to anticipate the answers that Milat had yet to give.

'Concerning the murders of Anja Habschied and Gabor Neugebauer, I suggest you killed them alone or in company.'

'I know nothing about the deaths of those people.'

'And that you used or someone with you used a Ruger 10/22, and the Anschutz found in the alcove, at that scene or nearby.'

'I don't know nothing about what you are talking about.'

'——the Ruger used by you or the person with you, parts of which were found in your wall cavity. And you made and used at that scene in the forest of the deaths of Anja Habschied and Gabor Neugebauer a leash device consisting of sash cord, tape and a black plastic tie and you used a Telecom rope of yours … you used rags in a gag or blindfold.'

'Wrong.'

'And that you and the person with you left the empty box of ammunition at the scene.'

'I never did nothing like that at all.'

'In relation to Caroline Clarke and Joanne Walters, I suggest you killed them, murdered them alone or in company.'

'Wrong again.'

'And at that scene you or someone with you used the

same Ruger to murder Caroline Clarke. And you brought rags to use as a gag or blindfold on Joanne Walters.'

'I never did.'

'That you gave the Benetton top of Caroline Clarke to your girlfriend, Chalinder Hughes.'

'No.'

'And that during the shooting of Caroline Clarke you used a silencer.'

'I have no idea of what you are talking about.'

Throughout the serious accusations thrown at him, Milat remained motionless, his hands still clenched against his legs. Blinking rapidly at times, his eyes remained fixed on the prosecutor.

'I suggest you hid the Ruger parts in the wall cavity at your home. I suggest on the morning of your arrest, you attempted to hide the receiver of the Ruger and the pistol.'

'I never did.'

'I suggest further that you used ropes and your sash cords both in the attack on Mr Onions and in the abduction of Caroline Clarke and Joanne Walters.'

'I don't know nothing about these things.'

'And the property that was found both at your home and at the home of your brother Richard that belonged to Caroline Clarke and Joanne Walters came to be in these places because of your involvement in their deaths.'

'No.'

'And that you were responsible for all of the items of camping equipment from the deceased backpackers being found in the locations they were found by the police.'

'No.'

The cross-examination was over. Mr Tedeschi sat down. The public continued to stare at the man in the witness box. But, with legal argument to follow the next day, it would be another four days before Milat's lawyer Terry Martin would be able to try to repair some of the damage that Milat had caused to his own defence by offering no plausible explanations for the circumstantial evidence that had been laid at his feet.

CHAPTER TWENTY

Perhaps it was the keen amateur photographer in him that led to Mark Tedeschi, QC, paying so much attention to the snapshots that police had collected during the course of their widespread inquiries. Although the exhibition containing some of his works further along Macquarie Street had failed to outlive the duration of the trial, Mr Tedeschi had had plenty of other images to ponder over — and he had used them to his advantage.

He had picked up the changes that Carolynne Milat had made to the dates on the back of photographs of a visit to the country by the Milat family, and which she had claimed gave Ivan an alibi for the time the British backpackers disappeared over Easter 1992. Mr Tedeschi's photographer's eye had scrutinised the picture of Ivan Milat dressed up as a cowboy with a Winchester rifle beside him. And he had studied the picture of Milat as a road ganger in January 1990 in which he could be seen sporting a bushy moustache. Now the QC and amateur photographer sat quietly waiting for the defence to call its next witness. On the table in front of him were two photographs ...

Chalinder Hughes, dressed in a cream suit and brown shoes with low heels, walked confidently through the well of the court to the witness box, fast enough to create a breeze and lift a few strands of her dark hair from her shoulders. It was Monday 24 June, and the following day the trial would have been running for exactly three months. In the public gallery upstairs, the rows of onlookers — many of whom had queued for seats as early as 6 am — watched as she swept her skirt forward and sat down.

Miss Hughes stated that she was an administrative official in a government office. She gazed from behind large round glasses at Mr Martin, who had called her, and, in answer to his question, said that on the morning of the raid at Cinnabar Street, she did not see Ivan go into the garage and she could not recall going in there herself. She was asked about the photographs of herself wearing the turquoise and white Benetton top beside the sea and she said it had been taken at the beginning of 1994 when she and Ivan had gone out for the day.

How had she come to wear it? 'I found it in the ironing room, one of the bedrooms at Cinnabar Street, where all the ironing is kept. I just put it on because the house was cold and when we went down to the beach I was wearing it. The only time I ever wore it was at the beach that day. After that, I put it in the laundry room and have had nothing to do with it since that time.'

'Did Ivan Milat give that article of clothing to you?'

'No, he never gave me anything like that.'

It was now Mr Tedeschi's turn to ask questions of the woman who had met Ivan Milat some two years before his arrest and had started a relationship with him, visiting him at his mother's home in Guildford before he moved to Cinnabar Street at Easter 1993 or around the middle of that year. Armed with the two photographs, Mr Tedeschi walked over to the witness box and showed them to Miss Hughes. He pointed out the sea that could be seen behind her, even remarking that a wave was breaking in one. He asked her again if she was certain it had been taken in 1994. Yes, she said, because she had gone to the seaside with him about six months after he had moved into Cinnabar Street.

Referring to the Benetton top, he asked: 'Are you sure it wasn't at Guildford when you saw it?'

'I only saw it at Cinnabar Street,' Miss Hughes replied.

Mr Tedeschi turned over one of the pictures. The date on the back, he told her, was 1992 — the year the British women had been murdered.

'Do you think it might have been 1992 when the photograph was taken?'

'I'm not sure of the date. It could have been the end of 1992.'

'But for the whole of 1992, Ivan, Miss Hughes, was living at Guildford.'

'I could be wrong [about the date]. I never was sure.'

Miss Hughes repeated several times that she could have been wrong about the date and then said she thought the picture was taken at the beginning of 1993. Mr Tedeschi pointed out yet again that Ivan Milat was even then still living at Guildford, so she could not have seen the garment at Cinnabar Street at that early time.

It was to the Crown's advantage to show that Miss Hughes was wearing the top in the year that the backpackers had disappeared and also to expose flaws in her evidence. Mr Tedeschi also wanted to eliminate any suggestion that the sweatshirt could have been Shirley Soire's, so that Miss Hughes could not say she thought it was Shirley's.

She conceded she was wrong about the date but said she had 'nothing to hide'.

'I suggest to you,' said Mr Tedeschi, 'that it was while he was living at Guildford that you wore this green and white top.'

'Definitely not, Mr Tedeschi, and I don't like to be intimidated. This is very hard for me. My conscience is very clear. Enough people's lives have been destroyed by this. I have come here to tell the truth and that's all. I am sure of where I got that top.'

'I suggest to you that Ivan Milat provided you with that green and white Benetton top,' Mr Tedeschi insisted.

'Definitely not, he didn't know anything about it.' She assumed, she said, that it was Shirley's when she had found it at Cinnabar Street. When she returned from the day at the beach, she said, she had put it in the laundry room at Cinnabar Street because it had a coffee stain on it.

She refuted a suggestion that she had refused to speak to police after Milat's arrest because she was fearful of incriminating him. 'That's totally wrong,' she protested. 'I want the truth to come out and I don't think it is coming out. I'm very angry about that inside.'

Whether the truth had in fact come out in her testimony was soon to be examined by the Crown Prosecutor, Mr Tedeschi. After a few day's break, the court was ready to hear his summing up.

On the morning of Wednesday 4 July, and in the fifteenth week of the trial, he moved his lectern to the end of the bar table and gave the jury a big smile, telling them that they would no doubt be relieved that the long drawn out hearing was in its closing stages, and that he did not intend to go over all the evidence point by point. He was going to proceed, he said, on the assumption that the jury had come to the conclusion, based on all the descriptions by Paul Onions that fitted Milat and his vehicle, that the accused man was guilty of the attack on Onions.

Along with all the features that fitted in with the details given by Onions, the Englishman's later identification of Milat 'is the icing on the cake'.

Mr Tedeschi briefly went over articles found in the forest and which could be linked directly to Milat, including the leash device found at the Neugebauer–Habschied death scene. The sash cord, the leather strap and the plastic ties that made up the leash could all be traced back to Milat.

'It is almost as if the accused left a fingerprint in the forest,' said the prosecutor. He went on to say that Milat and whoever else was responsible for the deaths did not dream 'in their wildest dreams that any of these items could ever be linked back to him or them. But in fact these items can be linked and they can be linked back to the accused.'

Mr Tedeschi said that the evidence strongly suggested the 'very real possibility' of more than one person being involved in the murders. He cited the use of two guns at the Neugebauer–Habschied scene and the difficulty one person would have in handling backpackers who travelled in pairs.

However, Mr Tedeschi was not going to allow the jury to consider that it was someone other than Milat who had tried to abduct Onions. Anticipating that the defence barrister, Mr Martin, might say in his closing address that the Crown had failed to give Onions the chance of looking at one of the other Milat brothers such as Walter or Richard, Mr Tedeschi urged the jury: 'Do not be seduced by that argument.' Onions had made his identification; there was no need to bring a string of other people through the court.

The prosecutor also anticipated that the defence would say that if Milat really did commit the murders, why would he keep rifle parts and the murdered travellers' backpacker gear in the house when he knew, before his arrest, that police were making inquiries about him?

'Well, ladies and gentlemen, the answer is this: this accused never dreamed that there would be the blitzkrieg that took place on 22 May 1994. Ladies and gentlemen, this is a man who had the utter arrogance to fire a shot during the attempted abduction of Mr Onions on the Hume Highway with cars whizzing by — that was the level of his confidence — he was prepared to do that, and he got away with it. Nothing happened. Nobody came knocking at his door a few days later.' Mr Tedeschi paused, but there was more to come about the mind of Ivan Milat.

'Indeed,' he continued, 'the very abduction of the back-packers, taking them in a vehicle along a road where, for all he knew, forestry officers might come along during the time that the backpackers must have been alive in the forest ... there was always the possibility that someone would drive along those fire trails and come upon the scene.

'So the incredible arrogance and the unbelievable self-confidence that the murderer had is exactly the kind of arrogance and self-confidence that led the accused to think that no-one was going to come to his house and come straight in and search it.'

Mr Tedeschi turned his attention to Milat's defence and his failure to call his sister Shirley Soire. It was a matter the prosecutor felt compelled to dwell on, saying that her failure to give evidence was a 'major defect' in the defence case. She was the person closest to Milat because she shared the same house in Cinnabar Street, Eagle Vale, and was therefore the person best placed to give evidence about incriminating items found in the house — articles the defendant claimed had been planted. If Milat's girlfriend, Chalinder Hughes, was telling the truth when she said she found the Benetton top in the ironing pile at the house, then Mrs Soire was the one person who would be able to give evidence about it. Miss Hughes, he reminded the jury, 'really had no explanation' when shown the date on the back of the photograph which put a question mark on her evidence.

Continuing his attack on the failure of Mrs Soire to appear, Mr Tedeschi said: 'This is the Shirley Soire who has been good enough to bring witnesses to court, like her brother Walter, but she's not good enough to walk through those double doors, come into the witness box and take an oath to tell the truth.'

He wondered why she was not called by the defence to

give evidence about how the two sleeping bags belonging to Simone Schmidl and Deborah Everist came to be in her wardrobe. He also asked why she was not called to give evidence about the camera belonging to Miss Clarke that was found in her kitchen; about how Miss Schmidl's cooking set ended up in the kitchen; and about how Miss Schmidl's tent was found in the garage.

'We don't even know whether Shirley would have been able to say something about the Ruger parts in the wall cavity,' said the prosecutor. And, he claimed, Mrs Soire had not been called because her evidence 'would not have assisted the defence case'.

Yet, he went on, this was the same Shirley Soire who had gone into the garden and dug up Milat's Colt pistol, which had been hidden in a buried bucket, and who had got her brother Walter to sell it at the time when Ivan Milat was charged with the backpackers' murders.

'Would you expect the Crown to call someone who has disposed of evidence like that? Of course not. You would not expect her to be co-operative with the Crown,' said Mr Tedeschi.

On the morning of Friday 4 July, Mr Tedeschi concluded his address. His job, in the main, was over. It was the defence lawyer's turn.

Mr Martin conceded at the outset that his client, Ivan Robert Marko Milat, was facing 'the worst possible charges imaginable in Australian history'. As Mr Martin's gaze moved to each of the eight men and four women in the jury, he said: 'You twelve people have currently got the worst job in Australia. I am putting you under pressure, the Crown's putting you under pressure, the community's putting you under pressure.'

His voice rising to almost a shout, Mr Martin implored the jury to consider carefully if they had 'lingering doubts' about the guilt of Ivan Milat. He conceded: 'Whichever way you look at it, it is absolutely irrefutable that whoever has committed these eight offences must be either within the Milat family or so very closely associated with it, it doesn't much matter. Blind Freddy can see that. There can be absolutely no doubt.

'The question is, who is it within the Milat family who has committed these eight offences? The question is, do you have a reasonable doubt that it was Ivan Milat as opposed to someone else in the family? If, for whatever reason, you have a doubt that lingers with you, you must give the benefit of the doubt to the accused.'

While admitting that gear belonging to the seven victims and to Paul Onions was found at Milat's home and those of his brothers Richard and Walter and at their mother's house in Guildford, Mr Martin devoted several hours to casting doubt on the Englishman's evidence. He questioned the process in which Paul Onions identified his attacker from the video he was shown of thirteen photographs, asking: 'What if Mr Onions has wrongly identified Ivan Milat because of family resemblance to Richard Milat?' He asked the jury to note that the video did not show any other members of the Milat family, 'notably Richard Milat'. There could be no doubt that at least some members of the Milat family were suspects in the Belanglo forest murders and that Richard Milat must have been a suspect.

'Why is his face not on the video? Members of the jury, it could not be, could it, that Mr Onions has noted a family resemblance in Ivan Milat, and that has triggered a memory? It could not be, could it, that Richard Milat was Mr Onions' attacker? Could it?'

Once Paul Onions had seen Ivan Milat on the video, said Mr Martin, his recall would have been contaminated by that image. 'It is all over, the damage is done. It is irretrievable because the police never put on the photo board a photo of Richard Milat or any of his family.'

The Englishman, said Mr Martin, and Mrs Berry, the woman who had rescued him on the Hume Highway, had told police that the attacker's four-wheel-drive had a spare-wheel rack on the back, but, said the defence barrister, Ivan Milat did not have a spare wheel fitted to the rear of his vehicle until nearly twelve months after the incident. Onions and Mrs Berry had not been wrong — the vehicle used by the attacker had a spare wheel on the back of it, said Mr Martin. There could be no other explanation for two witnesses saying the same thing. And he followed on that argument by claiming that the vehicle used in the attack was not Ivan Milat's.

Examining the description Onions had given of his attacker, Mr Martin reminded the jury he had said he was strong and solid, in his mid 30s, 183 centimetres (6 feet) tall, with dark hair, and a Merv Hughes-type moustache only thinner. Ivan Milat was 45 at the time of the attack and, although he had dark hair, he was 171 centimetres (5 feet 7 and three-eighths inches) tall. His moustache was a 'drooping Mexican' style, not a Merv Hughes-type. Richard Milat, on the other hand, had been 35 in January 1990, was solid and strong, had dark hair, was 178 centimetres (5 feet 10 inches) tall, and frequently had a moustache.

Referring to Onions' comments that his attacker told him his name was Bill, that he worked on the roads, was divorced, and had a Yugoslav background, Mr Martin said: 'Anyone in the Milat family or close to the family is going to know those basic details. Did Richard Milat know the basic particulars of Ivan Milat? Of course he did.'

It was a myth, said the defence barrister, that Richard Milat could not have committed the Onions attack and another of the offences because his work records showed he worked on those days. His workmates had given evidence that they could get off work early and make an arrangement with someone else to clock-off for them. And while Richard

Milat did not have a four-wheel-drive, 'he could have hired, borrowed or stolen' one.

Mr Martin was not going to let go of the 'other man' proposition throughout the remainder of his address, which continued for a further two days. Richard Milat, he said, had not come under the degree of scrutiny he should have received from investigating officers. He emphasised that Richard, as well as Ivan, had lived at their mother's home, which was the focal point of articles belonging to the backpackers.

But, he said, it was not his client who had taken the gear to the Eagle Vale home and he did not know of its existence there. While some of the items had been planted to incriminate Ivan, it was definitely true that other articles had not been planted. It was highly suspicious that Simone Schmidl's water-bottle was found in the spare bedroom and near it a single spent cartridge case said to be consistent with being fired by the Ruger bolt. For the cartridge case to have been found so near the water-bottle was 'almost too good to be true'.

'Members of the jury,' said Mr Martin, 'there are certain mysteries that will never, ever be resolved.' But, he contended, Richard or Walter Milat would not give 'two hoots' about planting evidence if they were the savage murderers. He wanted to make it clear that the defence was not limiting itself to saying that it was only Richard who could have been the killer.

'The submission I make to you is this: why is it not reasonably possible that Richard Milat, either alone or in company with someone other than Ivan Milat, killed all seven persons. If there were more than one, it could well be Richard Milat with Walter Milat, or Richard with a friend of Richard's — or any combination.'

The defence lawyer reminded the jury that members of the Milat family had told them Ivan was with them on

Boxing Day 1991, when Gabor Neugebauer and Anja Hanschied disappeared. If the jury then felt that Ivan had an alibi for those murders, then he had to be acquitted of all seven because the Crown case had been that the murders were serial killings.

Turning to Walter Milat's evidence, Mr Martin said Ivan's younger brother had 'lied through his teeth' to the court. He had distanced himself from everything sinister and had not been at all helpful to Ivan Milat. That could be because Walter had thought Ivan had had an affair with his former wife, or because Richard and Walter were very close and went shooting together.

Another reason for Walter and Richard supporting each other could be seen in the fact that they had moved into the same area together and Richard borrowed Walter's rifles in preference to Ivan's. One of the rifles Richard borrowed, continued Mr Martin, was the Anschutz that had been linked to two of the murders. Although Walter had claimed he borrowed that weapon for months at a time from Ivan, this had been denied by Ivan.

Mr Martin also reminded the jury of the claims Richard had made to a workmate, telling how the police had failed to find all the bodies, including those of the Germans, and how he had said that stabbing a woman was like cutting a loaf of bread. 'Is that not highly suggestive that Richard Milat is the killer?' It was a thought the defence barrister was content to leave with the jury. Mr Martin's job was now over.

All that remained now was for Justice David Hunt to sum up the case and then ask the jury to retire to consider their verdict. The judge was to take seven days to prepare his address to the jury.

On the morning of Thursday 18 July, Justice Hunt emerged from a side door after the usher had, as usual, knocked on it once to alert the court that the judge was coming out.

Justice Hunt was slow and deliberate in his address to the jury, for it was his guidance that would help them decide whether or not to convict Ivan Milat. It soon became clear that the judge had not been impressed with the suggestion by Mr Martin that the accused man had been set up by one of his brothers.

'Why, the Crown says, as far back as January 1990, was there an intention of a Milat family member to put Ivan right in the frame, to set him up as the prime suspect?' the judge asked. 'That is a question which I suggest to you bears some very careful consideration.'

Milat, he said, was entitled to the benefit of any reasonable doubt — the jury did not have to be satisifed that Milat was innocent in order to acquit him. 'I should also warn you that suspicion is not a substitute for proof beyond reasonable doubt.'

On the morning of Friday 19 July a male member of the jury was preparing to leave for the court when his phone rang. A male voice said: 'Look out. If you find my — him — guilty, you're dead.'

The juror reported the incident to a court officer, but kept the threat from his fellow jurors. The judge was informed and the court was closed. After a long discussion between the judge, the prosecution and the defence, it was agreed the trial should continue without the twelfth member. The other jurors were not informed of the reason. But the use of the word 'my' left the judge to comment that the juror believed it could have been one of the Milat brothers who had made the threat

The remaining members of the jury retired to consider their verdict at 2.42 pm on Wednesday 24 July. They had been asked to bring their overnight bags and would be accommodated in a city motel if they had not reached a verdict by the end of the day.

In fact it was not until 10.25 am on Saturday 27 July that the jury walked back and seated themselves on their familiar bench seats. The atmosphere was tense. Most of the male members of the jury were now wearing ties and suits rather than the more casual attire they had worn during the four months that they had listened patiently to the 148 Crown witnesses and six defence witness whose evidence, with the lawyers' and judge's comments, had taken up more than 3500 pages of transcript.

As usual, Ivan Milat, dressed in a charcoal grey suit and a black and white check tie, sat opposite the jurors as they took their places, his eyes watching them for a clue to the verdicts they were about to deliver. Was there a clue in the formal way they were attired?

As Justice Hunt asked if the jury had reached a verdict, the foreman, a bearded man sitting closest to the judge, rose.

'We have,' the foreman replied.

CHAPTER TWENTY-ONE

'Guilty!'

The word rang around the courtroom. And with that answer to the judge's question on how the jury found the prisoner in relation to the first charge, of murdering Deborah Everist, Ivan Milat knew he would never be a free man again.

The foreman repeated the word seven more times, taking in the murders of all the victims and the kidnapping of Paul Onions. Milat remained standing, a hand tightly gripping the woodwork, his rapidly blinking eyes on the foreman as the guilty verdicts echoed around the packed court. But there were other sounds, too — great gasps of relief from the public gallery.

Gill Walters closed her eyes tightly as if uttering a silent prayer of thanks. Mrs Clarke's eyes filled with tears, tears of relief, and put her head on her husband's shoulder. Mrs Everist and Mrs Gibson glanced at the other parents and showed the briefest of smiles, then Mrs Everist began to weep. Her son Timothy put his arm around her. It was over — or at least they had crossed a major hurdle in their grief-stricken lives.

Milat was asked if he had anything to say. 'I am not guilty of it,' he replied, but there was no strength in his voice.

Mr Tedeschi read out Milat's previous convictions: the two offences of breaking and entering, the one of stealing a car, and the three years he had served for being an accessory after the fact of larceny. There was no mention of the rape charge of which he had been acquitted in 1974.

Now it was the turn of Justice David Hunt to deliver his sentence, couched in words that summed up the full horror of the backpacker murders.

The case against the prisoner, he said, was an overwhelming one, and although his legal representatives had displayed a tactical ability of high order and conducted his defence in a skilful and responsible manner, in his own view the jury's verdicts were inevitable. 'I agree entirely with those verdicts. Any other, in my view, would have flown in the face of reality,' he said.

The judge went on to commend the police and the associated government agencies for the extensive and painstaking detection work involved in bringing the case to trial. It had been a massive task and the results were extraordinarily impressive.

Justice Hunt summed up the basic facts of the case, mentioning the discovery of the bodies, which had been covered with branches and leaf litter in a way which would hide them from view but which would nevertheless assist them to decompose rapidly.

'Each of the victims was young. They were between 19 and 22 years old. Each was travelling far from home, the inference being that they would not have been missed for some time if anything happened to them. I am satisfied that each set out along the Hume Highway from near Liverpool in order to hitch-hike to the south. The jury's verdicts mean that the prisoner was involved, either alone or in company, in a criminal enterprise to pick them up there and then to murder them all. In my view, it is inevitable that the prisoner was not alone in that criminal enterprise, but I do not take that fact into account either in aggravation or mitigation when considering what sentences should be imposed.

'By reason of the decomposition of the bodies, the medical evidence does not disclose the actual cause of death for any of the victims. That evidence does, however, indicate the nature of some of the injuries which were inflicted, and any number of those injuries would have qualified as the cause of death. The injuries which were inflicted at the time, whether or not they caused death, were nevertheless so tied up in the commission of these crimes as to be very relevant in determining their objective gravity.'

The judge's voice trembled at times as he delivered his speech. Despite the numerous trials at which he had adjudicated, it was clear that, for all his efforts to ensure emotions did not influence the due process of the law, he was affected by the horror of the case. He was soon to admit that listening to the nature of the injuries had been an ordeal he did not want to repeat.

'I do not propose here to list those injuries individually, or to ascribe those injuries to any one of the victims. I do not wish to cause further distress to the families of the victims, who have had to endure hearing the evidence itself and the description of it which I gave during the course of my summing up. Their understandable distress was evident and it is unnecessary that it should be repeated. In any event, I frankly do not want to go through that ordeal again myself.

'It is sufficient here to record that each of the victims was attacked savagely and cruelly, with force which was unusual and vastly more than was necessary to cause death, and for some form of psychological gratification. Each of two of the victims was shot a number of times in the head. A third was decapitated in circumstances which establish that she would have been alive at the time. The stab wounds to each of three others would have caused paralysis, two of them having had their spinal cords completely severed. The multiple stab wounds to three of the seven victims would have been likely to have penetrated their hearts. There are signs that two of them had been strangled. All but one of them appears to have been sexually interfered with either before or after death.

'These seven young persons were at the threshold of their lives, with everything to look forward to — travel, career, happiness, love, family and even old age.

'Whatever the actual causes of their death may have been in each case, it is clear that they were subjected to behaviour which, for callous indifference to suffering and complete disregard of humanity, is almost beyond belief. They would obviously have been absolutely terrified, and death is unlikely to have been swiftly applied. It is perhaps possible to imagine a worse case, but these murders must unhesitatingly be labelled as falling within the worst class of case.'

His voice falling to almost a whisper at times, the judge said it was not possible to determine — as the Crown had conceded — whether it was Milat himself who had inflicted the particular injuries which caused the death of any particular victim. The fact would have assumed some importance if he had to be sentenced in relation to only one murder. But as he had been shown to have been involved in a criminal enterprise to murder all seven, spanning four different occasions, the prisoner could hardly be heard to say that he did not know the character of the behaviour in which he was allowing himself to become involved on each occasion.

'I am satisfied that he is just as responsible for that behaviour as the person who did inflict the particular injuries which caused the deaths of each of the victims.'

The judge turned to the case of Paul Onions, who he said fitted the same pattern of victim. 'He, too, was a backpacker, young, one who would not have been missed for some time because he was from the United Kingdom and travelling, and he was picked up as a hitch-hiker by the prisoner on the Hume Highway near Liverpool in order to travel south. After establishing that Onions had no friends or family in Australia and was taking his time travelling, the prisoner stopped just short of the turn-off to the Belanglo State Forest and produced a gun and a bag of ropes. When Onions ran away, the prisoner chased and caught him, holding on to his shirt. Onions was fortunately able to escape again. I am satisfied that this was a thwarted attempt to take him into the forest where he, too, was to be murdered, just as the others were.'

Justice Hunt pointed out there were many different purposes to be served in the sentencing process. As both the High Court and the Court of Criminal Appeal had observed, those purposes overlap and the place to be given to each will vary in the different circumstances of different cases. As far as the backpacker murders were concerned, such was their nature that this case was not, in the judge's opinion, one in which there was any 'great utility' in considering the prospects of the prisoner's rehabilitation. Nor was it a case in which the subjective circumstances of the prisoner himself could play any decisive part. The need for the sentence to operate by way of a public deterrence is important, as it always is, in order to ensure that those whose character might incline them to similar behaviour in the future would be reminded powerfully that severe punishment would be imposed should they give in to temptation.

But above all, said Justice Hunt, 'these truly horrible crimes of murder' demanded sentences which operated by way of retribution or — as it was sometimes described — by the taking of vengeance for the injury caused by the prisoner in committing them.

'Not only must the community be satisfied that the criminal is given his just deserts; it is important that those whom the victims have left behind also feel that justice has been done.'

The judge lifted his eyes from his bench and looked for a moment at Milat. Then he told the man he addressed as Ivan Robert Marko Milat that on the third count, in relation to the abduction of Paul Onions, he was sentencing him to a term of penal servitude for six years.

Then came the words which Milat realised would be coming:

'On each of the remaining counts, I sentence you to penal servitude for life, commencing on 22 May 1994 [the day of his arrest and detention], and to be served for the term of your natural life.'

The judge turned to a police officer. 'Take the prisoner out, please.'

Milat removed the earpiece that had helped him hear the evidence and laid it on the bench. Then, without a flicker of emotion on his face and with a team of police and prison officers around him, he turned to his left and walked out of a side door. Police armed with shotguns were waiting in the courtyard to drive him to Sydney's Long Bay Jail.

On the bench, Justice Hunt sighed audibly and his shoulders drooped beneath his scarlet robe. He rose, the court rose with him, and he, too, made his exit from the room where some of the most gruesome evidence in Australian history had been presented.

The parents of the murdered backpackers admitted they were 'relieved but shattered', in the words of Caroline's father, Ian Clarke. They made their way to a room at the top of the court building where they had bravely agreed to face the cameras for a few minutes. They sat in a row, Mrs Patricia Everist, Mrs Peggy Gibson, Mrs Gill Walters, Mr Ray Walters, Mr Clarke and Mrs Jacqueline Clarke. Behind them stood Deborah Everist's brother, Timothy. The mothers were close to tears, biting their lips to hold back the grief that still gripped them.

They were asked how they felt that another killer had still not been arrested. Ray Walters, in a reference to Ivan Milat, replied: 'They have taken out the large part of the cancer. There is still some left, yes.'

Ian Clarke then spoke: 'If it is the case that there is someone else who has not been caught, we have this awful prospect of somebody being on the streets who shouldn't be on the streets. I think there is a clear message for all backpackers: hitch-hiking is not as safe as you think it is.'

The wait for the verdicts had been an emotional time for them all, they admitted, and, in Ian Clarke's words, 'It takes a little while to come up again.' But when they heard the first guilty verdict, they knew that others would follow. It was clear they were torn between relief and deep sadness.

It had been an ordeal for them all, sitting for weeks and months in the court, giving support to those of them who were feeling particularly low at any time, but, as Ray Walters said, it was the last thing they could do for their children.

'We owed it to all our children to be there,' said Ian Clarke. His words were echoed by his wife, Jacqueline. The two of them had visited the forest where their daughter died and paid their respects at the memorial plaque erected in honour of all the murdered backpackers. 'We will not be going back to the forest where Caroline was murdered,' he said. 'We found once was enough.'

They were asked about the police delay in acting on Onions' report about his kidnapping. All the parents said they had no criticism of the police. 'I think with every case you can look back and there is a point where somebody could be caught earlier,' said Ray Walters, who joined the others in praising the police work.

'I know the police were sitting there waiting for a [breakthrough] phone call, apart from all the hard work they were doing, but it is often the case that one phone call is the breakthrough,' said Ian.

Despite their relief at Milat's sentencing, Ray and Gill Walters in particular knew that rough times lay ahead. 'It is going to be flat for all of us,' said Ray. 'We have had a focus while the police have been doing their investigations. When we go back home, that is when the flat period is going to start. It could be a worse period than the last year.'

Fortunately, said Gill, they, like all the families, had many friends who had helped them and given them the courage and confidence to live through what had happened and the enduring pain that was still to come.

The Clarkes planned to shake off the bad times by taking the rest of their family for a holiday once they arrived back in Britain. 'We have got to wipe the slate clean,' said Ian. 'We have a new grand-daughter we have hardly seen. We are not going to give Milat the pleasure of ruining our lives as well as Caroline's. We have got other children that we owe a responsibility to, as well.'

Should parents be worried about children coming to Australia?

'Our kids were desperately unlucky,' said Ian Clarke. 'Ninety-nine point nine per cent of those who come to Australia have a wonderful time and they go home and they never forget it.'

'The problem with the country,' said Ray Walters, 'is that they are so open and friendly, and this is when defences are down. That was the problem with this case.'

Ian expressed the need for children to remain in touch with their parents. 'We found time and again Caroline was ringing from a phone box you could not ring back to, and she'd got 10 cents in her hand, and it was "Hello, mum. Sorry, I can't talk to dad." The message to all parents is: give your children a phone card. It costs, but it's worth it.'

In the wake of the Port Arthur massacre and the gun control debate in Australia, Ian Clarke said that in respect of the backpacker murders they had all noted the 'pretty frightening catalogue' of weapons that had been put together by Milat and his brothers. Emphasising that he was not being critical, he said that no matter how good the gun laws were, they still had to be properly enforced.

While the Clarkes were able to speak of picking up the pieces of their lives and looking forward to spending time with their new grand-daughter, the others still saw major obstacles ahead.

Mrs Gibson was still too upset to speak, but in a written statement she thanked all those people who had helped her and her husband, Ray, through the last six and a half years since their son James went missing. 'The loss of James, the gradual unfolding of how he and the other young people were killed, and being the focus of public attention, have all been very traumatic.' Like the other parents, Peggy Gibson emphasised that the kindness of the men and women of Task Force Air had far exceeded that of duty.

And while kindness and support had helped them all, nothing, they agreed, could really eliminate the grief. 'When you lose a child in these circumstances,' said Ray Walters, 'it is there for ever. I want people to know how much Milat destroys lives like ours.'

'I agree with Ray,' said Mrs Everist. 'It has destroyed our lives as well as those of the children. It has changed my life for ever.'

Gabor Neugebauer's father, Manfred, had sat through the trial and wanted to be there at the end. But he had promised another son he would be back in Germany in time for his birthday, and he had to leave Sydney two days before the verdict.

Before his departure he told of his belief that it would have taken two men to kill his son, who was 186 centimetres (over 6 feet) tall and very strong. Back home when they went to look for firewood, Gabor would cut huge logs and carry whole tree stumps on his shoulders.

Anyone who killed his son, said Manfred, did not deserve to ever be part of human society again.

Those who had been close to Ivan Milat still found words in his support. His 49-year-old brother William said he had always been a 'good bloke', and, just like all his brothers, 'helpful and friendly'. Had the verdicts changed his view of his brother? 'No,' he said, 'I can only take him as I find him.'

Richard Milat, 40, when asked about the suggestion that he should also have been charged, said: 'I've got no fears. I don't reckon they'll arrest me. If they thought it was me, they'd have me now, wouldn't they?'

He even brazened out a television interview, conducted shortly before the verdicts were handed down against his brother. His older brother William, sitting with him for the interview, said they had already been warned Richard could be arrested, but when Richard was asked whether he thought he was 'going inside' he replied: 'I don't think so. No way. 100 per cent positive that I should go inside for murder on any reason. I never killed nobody so why should I go there?'

Should he go to jail as an accomplice to the murders? 'No way. I weren't there. I had nothing to do with it. I never knew anything about it. I still don't. And never will.'

What of the comments he had made about 'more bodies out there'?

'I possibly could have said that. Could be possible. It could be possible people landed on the Moon. I may have said anything.'

Of the comment attributed to him that 'stabbing a woman is like cutting a loaf of bread' he replied: 'I have never cut a woman, so how would I know if it's like cutting a loaf of bread? I've never stabbed a woman, either. I've never stabbed a man, either.'

Elderly Mrs Milat remained convinced of her son Ivan's innocence to the end. Richard, too, was blameless. 'They're both innocent,' she said, leaning on her walking stick on the verandah of the Guildford house that had been a focus of so much of the court proceedings. 'They were living here when those murders were meant to have happened. I did all their ·shing and there was no blood. They're good boys.'

Although she conceded 'her boys' had been in trouble police 'for little things', she said that Ivan, who had ·er boy at school and known to his classmates as professor, was not a violent person. He would ..lk away from an argument at school than get into a

Chalinder Hughes, the woman who had started a relationship with Ivan Milat after meeting him through his sister Shirley at the movies in 1992 when *Basic Instinct* was showing — and who was photographed wearing an identical Benetton top to the one owned by Caroline Clarke — also insisted, in an interview she gave before the verdict, that Milat was an innocent man. He would never strike a woman, she said, let alone rape or murder. 'He has a great respect for women,' she said. 'This I know. Ivan is more likely to walk away than have an argument.'

'I can never remember him carrying a gun,' she said. As for hitch-hikers, she said Milat had told her he didn't like picking them up and had warned her never to hitch-hike.

'We want the world to know,' said William, his wife Carolynne at his side, 'that this affair has hit us all pretty badly. We Milats are not black, two-headed monsters. We are normal family people. Our lives are never going to be the same after this.'

At 8.30 am on Sunday 28 July 1996, the convicted mass murderer was led from Long Bay Jail. He was about to be moved to a 3-metre by 5-metre sandstone cell at the maximum security Maitland Jail in the Hunter Valley north of Sydney, his new and permanent home.

As the prison van raced up the F4 freeway, Milat glanced out through the steel-mesh windows at the eucalypt-covered hills, a landscape similar to that surrounding the Belanglo State Forest.

This time there would be no turning down a side track for murderous intent with helpless victims.

This time it was the savage kidnapper and killer himself who was now under restraint, bound with steel handcuffs, and it was a police guard who was calling the shots, his finger on the trigger of a powerful weapon. For the first time — and the last — Ivan Robert Marko Milat was experiencing what it was like to travel on the highway to nowhere.

THE END